ABOUT THE AUTHOR

A member of the English faculty at Fordham University for over thirty years, Dr. Francis X. Connolly is the author, editor, and coeditor of more than fifteen volumes on various phases of English language and literature, of a novel, GIVE BEAUTY BACK, and of a children's biography of St. Philip Neri. He is a founder of the Catholic Poetry Society, and served as its Chairman of the Board for over a decade. He served for two terms as President of the Catholic Renascence Society. He is currently on the editorial boards of *Thought,* the quarterly review published by Fordham University, of *Spirit,* a magazine of poetry, and of the Catholic Book Club.

Among his awards are the Spirit Medal for Services to Poetry and the Fordham College Alumni Award for distinguished service to the field of Education. Dr. Connolly is codirector of the Fordham Center of Newman Studies. He has written several articles on Newman, and his book about the Cardinal's work will appear in 1964. He is currently preparing a biography entitled NEWMAN: THE MAN AND HIS MISSIONS.

† WISDOM OF THE SAINTS

is a Ridge Press Book
published by Pocket Books, Inc.

Are there paperbound books you want but cannot find at your retail stores?

You can get any title that is in print in these famous series:
POCKET BOOK EDITIONS • CARDINAL EDITIONS • PERMABOOK EDITIONS
THE POCKET LIBRARY • WASHINGTON SQUARE PRESS • ALL SAINTS PRESS
Simply enclose retail price plus 10¢ per book for mailing and
handling costs. Not responsible for orders containing cash.
Please send check or money order to.....Mail Service Dept.
Pocket Books, Inc.
1 West 39th Street
Free catalogue sent on request   New York 18, N. Y.

WISDOM
OF
THE
SAINTS

✝

Francis X. Connolly

 A POCKET BOOK EDITION published by
POCKET BOOKS, INC. • NEW YORK

WISDOM OF THE SAINTS

A *Pocket Book* edition

1st printing.........October, 1963

This original *Pocket Book*** edition is printed from brand-new plates
made from newly set, clear, easy-to-read type.
Pocket Book editions are published by Pocket Books, Inc., and
are printed and distributed in the U.S.A. by Affiliated Publishers,
a division of Pocket Books, Inc., 630 Fifth Avenue, New York 20, N.Y.
*Trademark registered in the United States and other countries.
**Trademark of Pocket Books, Inc., 630 Fifth
Avenue, New York 20, N.Y., in the United States
and other countries.

L

Copyright, ©, 1963 by Francis X. Connolly. All rights reserved.
Published on the same day in Canada by Pocket Books, Inc.
Printed in the U.S.A.

ACKNOWLEDGMENTS

In the introductory material of this book, the Biblical quotations are taken
from the Rembrandt edition of The Holy Bible, imprimatur by Francis Cardinal
Spellman, 1959, unless otherwise noted.

In the selections from the writings of the saints, the Biblical quotations
appear as they do in the sources cited in the following acknowledgments:

St. Cyprian, "On Mortality," from FATHERS OF THE CHURCH, Volume
36. Reprinted by permission of The Catholic University of America Press,
Washington, D.C.

St. Basil, "On Humility," from FATHERS OF THE CHURCH, Volume
9. Reprinted by permission of The Catholic University of America Press,
Washington, D.C.

St. Jerome, "On the Duties of the Clergy," from SELECT LETTERS OF
SAINT JEROME, translated by F. A. Wright, 1933. Reprinted by permission
of the publishers, the Harvard University Press, Cambridge, Mass., and the
Loeb Classical Library.

St. John Chrysostom, "Vanity of Vanities: All Is Vanity" and "Lessons from the Life of Eutropios," from JOHN OF THE GOLDEN MOUTH, translated by Bruno Vandenberghe, O.P. Reprinted by permission of The Catholic University of America Press, Washington, D.C.

St. Augustine, "On the Beatitudes," from FATHERS OF THE CHURCH, Volume 11. Reprinted by permission of The Catholic University of America Press, Washington, D.C.

St. Patrick, "Patrick's Hymn," from THE WORKS OF SAINT PATRICK, translated by Ludwig Bieler. Reprinted by permission of The Newman Press, Westminster, Md., and Longmans, Green & Co., Ltd., London.

St. Benedict of Nursia, "The Rule of St. Benedict," from THE RULE OF ST. BENEDICT, edited and translated by Abbot Justin McCann, O.S.B. Reprinted by permission of The Newman Press, Westminster, Md., and Burns & Oates, Ltd., London.

Canto XXXIII, from Dante's PARADISO (from the DIVINE COMEDY), translated by Laurence Binyon. Reprinted by permission of The Society of Authors, London, and Mrs. Cicely Binyon.

St. Bernard of Clairvaux, "On the Love of God" and "On Charity," from SAINT BERNARD ON THE LOVE OF GOD, translated by Terence Connolly, S.J. Reprinted by permission of Spiritual Book Associates, Inc., New York City.

St. Francis of Assisi, "The Little Flowers of St. Francis," from THE LITTLE FLOWERS OF ST. FRANCIS, translated by Raphael Brown. Reprinted by permission of Doubleday & Co., Inc., New York City.

"Rhapsody to Lady Poverty" and "St. Francis' Peace Prayer," from THE WORDS OF ST. FRANCIS, translated by James Meyer, O.F.M. Reprinted by permission of the Franciscan Herald Press, Chicago.

St. Thomas Aquinas, "The Act of Faith" and "Question: of the Effects of Love," from the book, SELECTED WRITINGS OF ST. THOMAS AQUINAS, selected and edited by Reverend Father M. C. D'Arcy. Reprinted by permission of E. P. Dutton & Co., Inc., New York City (Everyman's Library edition), and J. M. Dent & Sons, Ltd., London.

"The Pange Lingua," from THE MASSES OF HOLY WEEK AND THE EASTER VIGIL, translated by Benedict Avery, O.S.B. Copyrighted and reprinted by permission of The Order of St. Benedict, Inc., Collegeville, Minn.

"The Lauda Sion," from the SAINT ANDREW DAILY MISSAL, translated by Dom Gaspar Lefebvre, O.S.B. Reprinted by permission of The E. M. Lohmann Co., St. Paul, Minn.

St. Thomas Aquinas, "The Teacher," from TRUTH, Volume II, by St. Thomas Aquinas; translated by James McGlynn, S.J., 1953. Reprinted by permission of Henry Regnery Co., Chicago.

St. Catherine of Siena, "Letter to Sister Daniella of Orvieto," from the book, ST. CATHERINE OF SIENA AS SEEN IN HER LETTERS, translated and edited by Vida Scudder. Reprinted by permission of E. P. Dutton & Co., Inc., New York City, and J. M. Dent & Sons, Ltd., London.

"To a Priest Friend," from the SAINTS AND OURSELVES, edited by Philip Caraman, S.J. Reprinted by permission of P. J. Kenedy & Sons, New York City, and Hollis & Carter, Ltd., London.

St. Thomas More, "On the Remembrance of Death," from THE ENGLISH WORKS OF SIR THOMAS MORE, Volume I. Reprinted by permission of Eyre & Spottiswoode (Publishers) Ltd., London, and The Dial Press, Inc., New York City.

St. Ignatius Loyola, "The Spiritual Exercises," from the SPIRITUAL EXERCISES OF ST. IGNATIUS. Reprinted by permission of Catholic Book Publishing Co., New York City.

St. Peter of Alcantara, "On the Miseries of this Life," from the TREATISE ON PRAYER AND MEDITATION, by St. Peter of Alcantara. Reprinted by permission of The Newman Press, Westminster, Md., and Burns & Oates, Ltd., London.

St. Francis Xavier, "Letter LXIX to Father Gaspar Baertz," from THE LIFE AND LETTERS OF SAINT FRANCIS XAVIER, edited by Henry James Coleridge. Reprinted by permission of Burns & Oates, Ltd., London.

St. Teresa of Avila, "The Life of St. Teresa of Jesus," from THE LIFE OF ST. TERESA OF JESUS, written by herself and translated from the Spanish by St. Anselm's Society, London, 1888.

St. John of the Cross, "St. John of the Cross," from THE COMPLETE WORKS OF ST. JOHN OF THE CROSS, edited and translated by E. Allison Peers. Reprinted by permission of The Newman Press, Westminster, Md., and Burns & Oates, Ltd., London.

St. Francis de Sales, "Counsels for Married Persons," from INTRODUCTION TO THE DEVOUT LIFE, translated by Alan Ross. Reprinted by permission of Burns & Oates, Ltd., London.

St. Jane Frances de Chantal, "Instruction XXII," from ST. JANE FRANCES DE CHANTAL. Reprinted by permission of The Newman Press, Westminster, Md.

St. John Eudes, "On Our Obligations to God as Christians" and "On the Choice of a State of Life," from MEDITATIONS ON VARIOUS SUBJECTS, by St. John Eudes. Reprinted by permission of P. J. Kenedy & Sons, New York City.

St. Alphonsus Liguori, "The Way of Salvation and of Perfection," from THE ASCETICAL WORKS, THE WAY OF SALVATION AND OF PERFECTION, Volume 2, edited by Reverend Eugene Grimm. Reprinted by permission of the Redemptorist Fathers, New York City.

St. John Mary Vianney: the Curé D'Ars, "On Envy, a Public Plague," from THE SERMONS OF THE CURÉ OF ARS, translated by Una Morrissy. Copyright 1960, Henry Regnery Co., New York City.

St. Therese of Lisieux: the Little Flower, "The New Commandment; St. Therese, the Little Flower of Jesus," from SAINT THERESE OF LISIEUX, THE LITTLE FLOWER OF JESUS, translated by Reverend Thomas N. Taylor. Reprinted by permission of P. J. Kenedy & Sons, New York City.

TABLE OF CONTENTS

B INTRODUCTION

BEFORE we talk about saintly wisdom we should know just who are saints. The saints are simply holy people, those who keep the Ten Commandments by loving God and their neighbor with their whole heart and soul and mind. In this large sense all holy people are saints. There are millions of saints, many of them at this moment unknown. Many of these unknown saints have never written a line or said anything that anyone thought worth recording. Their wisdom is displayed in the conduct of their lives. They live with God, blessing Him and blessed by Him. These saints are not canonized, that is, they have never been publicly declared saints; nor has a pope commanded the body of the faithful to venerate them by name. These uncanonized saints are honored together with the canonized saints on the feast of All Saints celebrated each year on November 1.

On the other hand, canonized saints are those exceptionally holy people whose outstanding virtues have merited special recognition by the church. Saints with a capital S are the heroes of God who gave up their lives as witnesses to the truth, like Saints Peter and Paul; those who lovingly brought the word to harsh and ungrateful people as missionaries, like St. Boniface and St. Patrick; those who like St. Peter Claver became a slave of slaves, in pure love of God and Man.

These are the canonized saints, that is, they have been publicly declared to be saints by the pope and proposed for veneration to the whole body of the faithful. And since it is these canonized saints whose writings are contained in this book, we ought to know in more detail just what canonization means.

INTRODUCTION

Pope Urban VIII started the formal process of canonization in 1634. This process normally involves a series of steps that culminate in a trial, or cause. The first step begins in the locality where a holy person, usually designated a "servant of God," has lived or worked. There under the bishop's direction, local authorities start what is called "a preliminary inquiry" into the writings, sayings, and actions of the servant of God to determine whether he is indeed heroically virtuous and orthodox in faith. If this inquiry results in a favorable conclusion, the cause or petition is formally presented to the Sacred Congregation of Rites in Rome.

When the Sacred Congregation accepts the cause and decides that it will investigate further, the formal process leading to canonization enters its second phase. The servant of God may now be called Venerable. The third stage is the process of beatification. In this stage the judges review all the evidence presented for and against the Venerable person. Here the emphasis is placed less upon the sanctity of the Venerable, a fact already established, but more upon the desirability of his *public* veneration. Hence, the Congregation weighs all the evidence in writings that favor or oppose public veneration. It examines, with great caution, the evidences for the three or more miracles that canon law requires before a Venerable person may be declared Blessed, or beatified. These miracles, it should be noted, must occur *after* the death of the person proposed for beatification. *After* is the key word here, because these miracles are considered to attest to the desirability of public worship. (A major exception to the canonical requirement of miracles before beatification is made in the case of martyrs, that is, those who freely, patiently, and heroically suffer death from the hands of a persecutor because of their Christian faith.) This third stage ends when the petition for beatification is refused or accepted. If accepted, the pope declares the Venerable person to be Beatified or Blessed. This means that he is regarded as dwelling in the happiness of heaven. The pope publishes his name as Blessed, permits his public veneration in certain places, usually in his native town or in a religious community with which he was associated.

The final stage in the process leads to canonization as a saint. Once again the evidence is reviewed by the Congregation of Rites. The *advocatus Dei,* or advocate of God, presents additional evidence in the form of two new miracles attributable to the intercession of the beatified, miracles that must have occurred after beatification. (Three miracles are required in those exceptional cases where beatification has taken place outside the ordinary processes.) The *advocatus diaboli* (the advocate of the devil) in his turn is solemnly obliged to attack the evidence presented by the advocate of God and, if possible, to adduce evidence contrary to the cause of the Blessed. If the Congregation of Rites approves the cause, the pope then declares the Blessed one a Saint— he commands public veneration in the Saint's honor throughout the universal Church. The Saint is entitled to a special Mass, a special office, or set of official prayers, and a solemn public canonization. This last rite is unusually impressive. Celebrated with great splendor at St. Peter's Cathedral in Rome, it is normally preceded by a nine-day (novena) service at another important church in the city and followed by a great wave of jubilation throughout the Christian world. For Christians, canonization is a foretaste of the joy of the blessed in the Blessed that is promised on the Day of Judgment.

Canonized saints, the saints with a capital S, number about twenty thousand and belong to every race and every generation. They have won a place in the sacred books, the Missal, the Breviary, and the martyrologies. In this book we are concerned with a handful of that twenty thousand, those who, for various reasons, have become widely known, or who may be taken to represent the characteristic mentalities of various bands of Christian brothers.

The famous saints are all strikingly individual. No one could mistake St. Peter for St. Paul, St. Jerome for St. Augustine, St. Ignatius of Loyola for the Little Flower. They differ in temperament, character, race, education. Yet they all possess certain common characteristics. First of all, they were people who knew God. They had certain, absolute faith. They knew that an all-powerful God exists, that He revealed Himself to man in the person of Jesus Christ, who was both divine and human, that He created man in the likeness of Himself—that is, with the power of knowing and choosing—and that He desires for all men an eternally joyful participation in His own life. They believe, in short, that man is the creature of God, belongs to God, and can live with God forever.

These are just a few of the beliefs that they know from the study of God's Revelations, received through scripture and tradition under the guidance of the Holy Spirit.

Moreover, the saints unite to this certain knowledge an immense confidence in God's promises to forgive men their crimes and to preserve them in His friendship. Because they know that the all-powerful and all-loving God desires at all times to give all men the free gift of His own inner life, the saints are a buoyant company, even when they contemplate the worst possibilities of human fate. For them there is always a hereafter, happy beyond telling, where God will reward those who believe and trust Him in spirit and in truth, and there is always the hope that man will win that hereafter of happiness.

Certain knowledge of God and immense confidence in Him are but two of the characteristics the saints share in common. A third characteristic is love. The saints are the supreme lovers of mankind. They have endured the severest tests of love. Where others are selfish, they are selfless. Where others demand, they give. They give up the comforts and pleasures of the body, the allurement of reputation, the gratification of power, the enticement of wealth, the cordialities of domestic life. They even surrender their own wills to that of others by accepting obediently the tasks assigned to them. To this day they lay down their lives for their friends—and by friends they mean the very least of God's children. They give so ardently that they are empty of themselves, yet that emptiness is filled with the presence of God. "I live, no not I, but

Christ lives in me." St. Paul's saying is the universal utterance of the saints.

Small wonder, then, that men, distressed by their faint knowledge of God, paralyzed by their fear of the future, chilled by their impotence to love and to be loved, turn to the saints who are fortified with knowledge, hope, and love. In the fire of the saints men may find light and food and warmth. Moreover, they find a union of friendship that, far from depriving them of personality, enriches, enhances, and fulfills it.

Because the saints are who they are, we seek them out. No doubt, the believer approaches the saint more familiarly and more docilely than the ordinary man of good will. The believer, however weak his faith, thinks of the saint as a particularly favored brother in the family of God. That family, composed of God's adopted children triumphant in heaven, or suffering in purgatory, or struggling through the pilgrimage on earth, shares a common spiritual patrimony earned by the merits of Christ, the Head of the human race, and by the saints. As in all families, one member can intervene for another. Hence, the believer knows that the saint, particularly the one whose name he bears, or who is the patron of his church, or diocese, or region, can and will ask God's help in his behalf. In many Christian homes the saints are invoked a dozen times a day, for patience, for protection, for the finding of lost articles, in short, for the most pressing and the most trivial of human needs.

For the believer the saints are not only brothers. They also are teachers par excellence. They are the scientists in the science of knowing God's mind and will, the artists in the achievement of perfect service of God and man. They know the way to heaven, the way to use the things of earth to get there. They have news of salvation, news forever fresh, for, as each new generation comes to birth, the story of the Life, Death, Resurrection, and Ascension of the God-Man Christ must be retold. They are the voices of God, chosen by Him to listen to His words, to record them, to interpret them, to preach them to all men within the magisterium of the Church. As the liturgy puts it: She (Wisdom) will move him to speak before the assembled people, filling him with the spirit of wisdom and discernment. (Ecclesiasticus 15. 5-6, Ronald Knox translation.)

But if it is not surprising that Christians accept the saints as those who have most closely approximated God's plan for his human creatures, what are we to think of those men of good will who, in increasing numbers, have turned to the wisdom of the saints to appease their hunger for truth and their craving for disinterested friendship? In our grim struggle to retain our freedoms from the grasp of totalitarian power we turn, almost instinctively, to the examples of the saints. St. Joan of Arc, St. Thomas à Becket, St. Thomas More, to mention but a few, are being studied with increasing interest not only by the biographers, but by poets and playwrights. Surely, it is not insignificant that three of the outstanding playwrights of our time—Jean Anouilh, T. S. Eliot, and Christopher Fry— have all written about Becket and have found in his life some illumination of the problems we are facing today.

May it not be said, too, that many men of good will are no longer satisfied with the here and now, earth-bound Utopianism that, in the heyday of scientific euphoria, was offered as a final explanation of man's purpose in life? At the turn of the century, H. G. Wells, the loudest prophet of a new scientific paradise, predicted that men would become gods. Science, he kept repeating, would eradicate disease, wipe out slums, abolish war, remove the necessity of prisons, breed out the inferior human animals, prolong human life almost indefinitely. Scientists, today, are the first to tell us that science does not have all the answers. They go beyond that. They are increasingly aware that science as such has very little to contribute to the solution of those moral and spiritual problems inherent in our advanced technology, especially in our horrifying capacity for mutual destruction. To what wisdom, then, are we to turn? Some have embraced the bitter, stale cynicism of the existentialists, some the sweet, stale, optimism of the peace-of-mind cult—those well-meaning tranquilizers who would have us often change the face of reality. These extremes of cynicism and optimism are half truths. But, as Stephen Leacock once said, "A half-truth, like a half-brick, is always more forcible as an argument than a whole one; it carries further." These half-truths do indeed carry further, judging by the many who have accepted them.

Yet some will always turn to the wisdom of the saints, a wisdom that is as bitter as that of the existentialists but never despairing, as uplifting as that of the optimists but never unreal, a wisdom that is concerned with all aspects of human life, both here and hereafter. This kind of wisdom, full of dazzling perspectives and minute interrelationships, will always offend the immature. It is never quick with ready answers; it never promises easy solutions. It is full of hard sayings; it never flatters. It reserves its praise for God; it counts no man happy until he has died worthily, and, even then, it repeats that God alone is holy. It makes no compromises with the subtleties of truth.

One reason for this is that the saints are voicing the great mysteries, and the essence of a mystery is that it is a truth, the word of God, that cannot be fully understood. The central mysteries of the Christian religion cannot be as simple as $2 + 2 = 4$, although that intellectual fact is mysterious too. They are, in fact, puzzling to human reason. Christ is one in substance with the Father and the Holy Spirit, yet all three members of the Holy Trinity possess distinct personalities. Three Persons in One God. Christ is truly God and truly man. Mary, Christ's human mother, is at once a virgin and a mother. These mysteries are profoundly above, beyond, and below the superficial clarities that may be extracted from observation and inference. So, too, the fact of man's dual nature as a creature of flesh and spirit, Adam's double role of sinner and saint, Calvary's aspect of sorrow and joy—these are paradoxes that must be carefully adjusted. Yet, while the saints cannot fully disclose these mysteries according to the standards of human reason, they do clarify them. The mission of clarification, a mission that demands theological learning, rhetorical tact, the grace of teaching—this mission results in the wisdom of the saints.

It does not surprise, then, that the wisdom of the saints

does not make light reading. "It would be a serious mistake," writes Richard Cardinal Cushing about spiritual reading in general, "to think that this kind of reading can be made superficially attractive. If for no other reason, spiritual reading cannot appeal to our lighter emotions and our less cultivated tastes because it is concerned essentially with our deeper and more permanent interests. As we must discipline ourselves to introduce the rule of reason into our natural lives and to avoid the excessive self-indulgence which blinds us to our divinely appointed destiny, so we must discipline ourselves to seek out and to meditate upon the books which will instruct and inspire us in the deeper intellectual and effective activity. . . ."

Thus, the saints cannot make their wisdom superficially attractive because they can never reduce mystery to the neat and comprehensible categories devised by human reasoning. At the same time, they do employ all the resources of human reason to explain what can be explained. For them, human reason is one of the best of God's gifts, a light by which man can see, not only the truths of the natural order, but also the reasonableness of accepting divine mysteries on the word of a Perfect Being. Not all the saints are intellectuals in the present use of that term. Some were simple men whose school was the heart. But all are, without exception, respectful of human reason. And most of those who excelled in teaching were, from the earliest days of Christianity, skilled in the learning of their day. St. John the Evangelist and St. Paul used Judaic biblical scholarship, Greek philosophy, and rhetoric to make evident the truths of God's revelation. Later on, St. John Chrysostom, St. Jerome, St. Augustine, and St. Thomas Aquinas assimilated the best that their ages offered to make men see. And so it is down to the present.

The readers of this book will, no doubt, find that the saints are repeating, in one fashion or another, the wisdom of the Gospels. They will note how habitually each counsel, each argument, each meditation, springs from the teachings of Christ recorded in the New Testament. Hence, they may say to themselves, "But it was all there, all the time." It was, and is, there. The essence of the wisdom of the saints is the wisdom of Christ. The saints are other Christs, united to Him as members of His mystical Body, and they have in a sense no message of their own.

What is new or original is the application of the truths of Christ's revelation to special occasions, purposes, and audiences. The saints translate, or interpret the Christian message, "Be ye perfect as my Heavenly Father is perfect," in the particular context and tone of a given time, language, and occasion. Sometimes, addressing hardened sinners, they do not hesitate to utter a pessimistic prophecy in the harshest tones of pain and suffering. Nor do they avoid a forthright appeal to salutary fear, in the absence of more worthy motives. At other times, treating of human weakness, they speak optimistically of God's compassion, of Christ's kindness to the adulterous Samaritan woman, of the woman taken in sin, of Dismas, the good thief, who hung on a neighboring cross. At times they write with the scrupulous precision of theologians addressing men of learning; at other times in a spontaneous, lyrical fashion, as befitting a *jongleur de Dieu*, a minstrel of God, celebrating the innocent revels of Feast and Holyday, as if salvation were already achieved. Sometimes their starting point, the occasion of their discourse, is a great historical event, the presence of plague, the invasion of barbarians, the death of an emperor, for many of the saints lived in the midst of history as bishops, popes, even kings. Sometimes they transcend history and speak as if the only existing realities were God and the soul.

Hence, the wisdom of the saints will come to the reader with different accents, compelling him to listen or to read with varying degrees of sensibility and with a more or less developed historical imagination. But this exercise in sensibility and imagination, however exacting, has its special rewards. It compels us to shed our routine judgments and prejudices, to take less for granted, to dig out the permanent realities that lie beneath the superficial differences of time and place. As a result, all readers of good will, all those who are seeking truth and are open to it, may discover in these selections sources of strength. They may develop in themselves resources that, in

INTRODUCTION

this perilous time, are infinitely more assuring than bigger and better bombs and bank accounts.

A word on the selections themselves. It need hardly be said that no book, much less one of this size, can perfectly represent the writings of the saints. Here we can only hope to give some of the main threads in the weave of wisdom, stressing the principal message of faith, hope, and love, and the principal means by which each soul, according to his particular state in life, can achieve that degree of perfection which will merit him eternal life. We have not attempted to be up-to-date, that is, to draw our selections chiefly from recent saints whose writings are closer to the modern idiom, or exclusively from topics that are of immediate contemporary concern. In presenting the wisdom of the saints we do not have to be timely because, as your reading will discover, that wisdom is timeless.

ST. LUKE

(d. 74)

S T. Luke, author of the Third Gospel and *The Acts of the Apostles* in the New Testament, shares with Saints Matthew, Mark, and John the honor of being an evangelist, one who announces the good news of Christ's birth, death, resurrection, and ascension. He was born at Antioch, in Syria. At the time of his birth this Greek capital ranked with Rome and Alexandria as a cultural, administrative, and commercial center of the Roman Empire. We know few details of St. Luke's early life. But we do know, especially from the testimony of his own writing, that he received an excellent education in letters, philosophy, and medical science and that he became a Christian in the very early days of the church. In the Christian community at Antioch he learned by heart the testimony of the many witnesses of Christ's life.

An early disciple and companion of St. Paul, St. Luke began to accompany the apostle on his missionary journeys at Troas, in Asia Minor, in 51 A.D. With Paul, who called him "the most beloved physician" and "his fellow-laborer," he traveled to Macedonia and to the other cities of Greece, preaching the Gospel and helping to found Christian communities. When Paul was imprisoned in Caesarea for two years, Luke was his constant visitor. When Paul was sent to Rome, Luke went with him. During St. Paul's two years' confinement in Rome, St. Luke again was his faithful companion and assistant. It was in Rome, in 63, the year St. Paul was set free, that St. Luke wrote *The Acts of the Apostles*, a brief history of the early days of the church, written to correct the many false rumors that had sprung up, particularly concerning the mission of St. Paul.

During St. Paul's last imprisonment, St. Luke remained by

1

his side. After St. Paul's death, his work was carried on by St. Luke in Greece. St. Luke's Gospel was composed sometime before the year 70. He died in Thebes, in Boeotia, in 74.

In addition to his skills as a physician and a writer, St. Luke is traditionally credited with eminence as a painter and sculptor. Among his several paintings of the mysteries of Christ's life, that of the Virgin in the Borghese Chapel of the Basilica of St. Mary Major in Rome is the most famous.

St. Luke's Gospel, from which the selection below is taken, is regarded as the most literary of the Four Gospels. Among its many distinctive features is its rendering of the parables. In the parable of the Good Samaritan that follows, note particularly the remarkable compression of the story, the lucidity of each phrase, the inevitability of the lesson it contains. The lesson, of course, is love.

THE GOSPEL
ACCORDING TO ST. LUKE

CHAPTER 10, VERSES 25-37

And behold, a certain lawyer got up to test Him, saying, "Master, what must I do to gain eternal life?" But He said to him, "What is written in the Law? How dost thou read?" He answered and said, "Thou shalt love the Lord thy God with thy whole heart, and with thy whole soul, and with thy whole strength, and with thy whole mind; and thy neighbor as thyself." And He said to him, "Thou hast answered rightly; do this and thou shalt live." But he, wishing to justify himself, said to Jesus, "And who is my neighbor?" Jesus answered, "A certain man was going down from Jerusalem to Jericho, and he fell in with robbers, who after both stripping him and beating him went their way, leaving him half-dead. But, as it happened, a certain priest was going down the same way; and when he saw him, he passed by. And likewise a Levite also, when he was near the place and saw him, passed by. But a certain Samaritan as he journeyed came upon him, and seeing him, was moved with compassion. And he went up to him and bound up his wounds, pouring on oil and wine. And setting him on his own beast, he brought him to an inn and took care of him. And the next day he took out two denarii and gave them to the innkeeper and said, "Take care of him; and whatever more thou spendest, I, on my way back, will repay thee." "Which of these three, in thy opinion, proved himself neighbor to him who fell among the robbers?" And he said, "He who took pity on him." And Jesus said to him, "Go and do thou also in like manner."

ST. JOHN
THE EVANGELIST
(d. circa 101)

JOHN, later called the Evangelist, son of Zebedee and Salome, brother of St. James the Greater, is the writer of the Fourth Gospel. No human figure of the New Testament stands out more vividly than John. We meet him as a young man of about twenty-five years, a fisherman of Galilee, and a disciple of St. John the Baptist, when Christ called him and St. James to join St. Peter and St. Andrew as His first disciples. With Saints Peter and James he witnessed the Transfiguration of Christ on Mount Thabor. At the Last Supper, he "whom Jesus loved" reclined next to his Savior, rested his head upon the Master's breast and learned from Him that Judas would be the betrayer. That night he accompanied Jesus to the Garden of Gethsemane and witnessed the Master's agony and His arrest by the henchmen of the High Priest. Throughout the trial, the suffering, and the crucifixion, John was never absent from Christ's side.

Standing beneath the cross, he observed every moment of pain, then the death, and the final thrust of the centurion's spear, and the gush of blood and water from Christ's side. He heard Christ commend His mother to his care and himself to Mary's. It was he who placed the broken Body in Mary's lap. When, on Easter Sunday, Mary Magdalene and the other women returned in confusion from the empty tomb, it was John who, outrunning St. Peter, was first to the tomb. A few days later, fishing in Lake Tiberias, he saw the risen Christ, called to St. Peter, and both were joyfully reunited with their Master. After the Ascension, John joined Peter in preaching at the Temple of Jerusalem and in miraculously healing the crippled. Between prison and scourgings, John, together with Peter, preached in Samaria and the neighboring country.

As guardian of Mary, St. John remained in Asia Minor, governing the new churches, chiefly from his residence in Ephesus. In 95, during the great persecution under the Emperor Domitian, St. John was arrested and sent to Rome, where he suffered the pains, if not the death, of martyrdom, and was then exiled to the island of Patmos, where he experienced the visions that are recorded in the Apocalypse. In 97 he returned to Ephesus to resume the guidance of the Asian churches. Shortly thereafter, alarmed by the misinterpretations of heretics who denied the divinity of Christ, he composed the Fourth Gospel.

As St. John grew older and became unable to preach, his sermons were shortened to one line: "My dear children, love one another." When he was asked why he said the same thing over and over again, he answered, "Because it is the precept of the Lord, and if you comply with it you do enough." The same message is contained in the first epistle that is represented below.

THE FIRST EPISTLE
OF ST. JOHN THE APOSTLE

CHAPTER 2, VERSES 1-29

My dear children, these things I write to you in order that you may not sin. But if anyone sins, we have an advocate with the Father, Jesus Christ the just; and He is a propitiation for our sins, not for ours only but also for those of the whole world.

And by this we can be sure that we know Him, if we keep His commandments. He who says that he knows Him, and does not keep His commandments, is a liar and the truth is not in him. But he who keeps His word, in Him the love of God is truly perfected; and by this we know that we are in Him. He who says that he abides in him, ought himself to walk just as He walked.

Beloved, no new commandment am I writing to you, but an old commandment which you had from the beginning. The

5

old commandment is the word which you have heard. Again, a new commandment I am writing to you, and this is true both in Him and in you. Because the darkness has passed away and the true light is now shining. He who says that he is in the light, and hates his brother, is in the darkness still. He who loves his brother abides in the light, and for him there is no stumbling. But he who hates his brother is in the darkness, and walks in the darkness, and he does not know whither he goes; because the darkness has blinded his eyes.

I am writing to you, dear children, because your sins are forgiven you for His Name's sake. I am writing to you, fathers, because you know Him who is from the beginning. I am writing to you, young men, because you have conquered the evil one. I am writing to you, little ones, because you know the Father. I am writing to you, fathers, because you know Him who is from the beginning. I am writing to you, young men, because you are strong and the word of God abides in you, and you have conquered the evil one. Do not love the world, or the things that are in the world. If anyone loves the world, the love of the Father is not in him; because all that is in the world is the lust of the flesh, and the lust of the eyes, and the pride of life; which is not from the Father, but from the world. And the world with its lust is passing away, but he who does the will of God abides forever.

Dear children, it is the last hour; and as you have heard that Antichrist is coming, so now many antichrists have arisen; whence we know that it is the last hour. They have gone forth from us, but they were not of us. For if they had been of us, they would surely have continued with us; but they were to be made manifest, that not one of them is of us. But you have an anointing from the Holy One and you know all things. I have not written to you as to those who do not know the truth, but as to those who know it, and because no lie is of the truth. Who is the liar but he who denies that Jesus is the Christ? He is the Antichrist who denies the Father and the Son. No one who disowns the Son has the Father. He who confesses the Son has the Father also. As for you, let that which you have heard from the beginning abide in you. If that abides in you which you have heard from the beginning, you also will abide in the Son and in the Father. And this is the promise that He has given us, the life everlasting. These things I have written to you concerning those who lead you astray. And as for you, let the anointing which you have received from Him, dwell in you, and you have no need that anyone teach you. But as His anointing teaches you concerning all things, and is true and is no lie, even as it has taught you, abide in Him.

And now, dear children, abide in Him, so that when He appears we may have confidence, and may not shrink ashamed from Him at His coming. If you know that He is just, know that everyone also who does what is just has been born of Him.

CHAPTER 3, VERSES 1-24

Behold what manner of love the Father has bestowed upon us, that we should be called children of God; and such we are. This is why the world does not know us, because it did not know Him. Beloved, now we are the children of God, and it has not yet appeared what we shall be. We know that, when He appears, we shall be like to Him, for we shall see Him just as He is. And everyone who has this hope in Him makes himself holy, just as He also is holy. Everyone who commits sin commits iniquity also; and sin is iniquity. And you know that He appeared to take our sins away, and sin is not in Him. No one who abides in Him commits sin; and no one who sins has seen Him, or has known Him.

Dear children, let no one lead you astray. He who does what is just is just, even as He is just. He who commits sin is of the devil, because the devil sins from the beginning. To this end the Son of God appeared, that He might destroy the works of the devil. Whoever is born of God does not commit sin, because His seed abides in him and he cannot sin, because he is born of God. In this the children of God and the children of the devil are made known. Whoever is not just is not of God, nor is he just who does not love his brother. For this is the message that you have heard from the beginning, that we should love one another; not like Cain, who was of the evil one, and killed his brother. And wherefore did he kill him? Because his own works were wicked, but his brother's just. Do not be surprised, brethren, if the world hates you. We know that we have passed from death to life, because we love the brethren. He who does not love abides in death. Everyone who hates his brother is a murderer. And you know that no murderer has eternal life abiding in him.

In this we have come to know His love, that He laid down His life for us; and we likewise ought to lay down our life for the brethren. He who has the goods of this world and sees his brother in need and closes his heart to him, how does the love of God abide in him? My dear children, let us not love in word, neither with the tongue, but in deed and in truth.

In this we know that we are of the truth, and in His sight we set our hearts at rest. Because if our heart blames us, God is greater than our heart and knows all things. Beloved, if our heart does not condemn us, we have confidence toward God; and whatever we ask, we shall receive from Him, because we keep His commandments and do those things that are pleasing in His sight. And this is His commandment, that we should believe in the name of His Son Jesus Christ, and love one another, even as He gave us commandments. And he who keeps His commandments abides in God, and God in him. And in this we know that He abides in us, by the Spirit whom He has given us.

CHAPTER 4, VERSES 1-21

Beloved, do not believe every spirit, but test the spirits to see whether they are of God; because many false prophets have gone forth into the world. By this is the spirit of God known: every spirit that confesses that Jesus Christ has come in the flesh, is of God. And every spirit that severs Jesus, is not of God, but is of Antichrist, of whom you have heard that he is coming, and now is already in the world.

You are of God, dear children, and have overcome him, because greater is He who is in you than he who is in the world.

They are of the world; therefore of the world they speak and the world listens to them. We are of God. He who knows God listens to us; he who is not of God does not listen to us. By this we know the spirit of truth and the spirit of error.

Beloved, let us love one another, for love is from God. And everyone who loves is born of God, and knows God. He who does not love does not know God; for God is love. In this has the love of God been shown in our case, that God has sent His only-begotten Son into the world that we may live through Him. In this is the love, not that we have God, but that He has first loved us, and sent His Son as a propitiation for our sins. Beloved, if God has so loved us, we also ought to love one another.

No one has ever seen God. If we love one another, God abides in us and His love is perfected in us. In this we know that we abide in Him and He in us, because He has given us of His Spirit. And we have seen, and do testify, that the Father has sent His Son to be Savior of the world. Whoever confesses that Jesus is the Son of God, God abides in Him and he in God. And we have come to know, and have believed, the love that God has in our behalf. God is love, and he who abides in love abides in God, and God in him.

In this is love perfected with us, that we may have confidence in the Day of Judgment; because as He is, even so are we also in this world. There is no fear in love; but perfect love casts out fear, because fear brings punishment. And he who fears is not perfected in love. Let us therefore love, because God first loved us. If anyone says, "I love God," and hates his brother, he is a liar. For how can he who does not love his brother, whom he sees, love God, whom he does not see? And this commandment we have from Him, that he who loves God should love his brother also.

CHAPTER 5, VERSES 1-21

Everyone who believes that Jesus is the Christ is born of God. And everyone who loves Him who begot, loves also the one begotten of Him. In this we know that we love the children of God, when we love God and do His commandments. For this is the love of God, that we keep His commandments; and His commandments are not burdensome. Because all that is born of God overcomes the world; and this is the victory that overcomes the world, our faith. Who is there that overcomes the world if not he who believes that Jesus is the Son of God?

This is He who came in water and in blood, Jesus Christ; not in the water only, but in the water and in the blood. And it is the Spirit that bears witness that Christ is the truth. For there are three that bear witness [in heaven: the Father, the Word, and the Holy Spirit; and these three are one. And there are three that bear witness on earth]: the Spirit, and the water, and the blood; and these three are one. If we receive the testimony of men, the testimony of God is greater; for this is the testimony of God which is greater, that He has borne witness concerning His Son. He who believes in the Son of God has the testimony of God in himself. He who does not believe the Son, makes Him a liar; because he does not believe the witness that God has borne concerning His Son.

And this is the testimony, that God has given us eternal life; and this life is in His Son. He who has the Son has the life. He who has not the Son has not the life.

These things I am writing to you that you may know that you have eternal life—you who believe in the Name of the Son of God.

And the confidence that we have toward Him in this, that if we ask anything according to His will, He hears us. And we know that He hears us whatever we ask; we know that the requests we make of Him are granted. He who knows his brother is committing a sin that is not unto death, shall ask, and shall give life to him who does not commit a sin unto death. There is sin unto death; I do not mean that anyone should ask as to that. All lawlessness is sin, and there is a sin unto death.

We know that no one who is born of God commits sin; but the Begotten of God preserves him and the evil one does not touch him. We know that we are of God, and the whole world is in the power of the evil one. And we know that the Son of

God has come and has given us understanding, that we may know the true God and may be in His true Son. He is the true God and eternal life.

Dear children, guard yourselves from the idols.   Amen.

ST. PETER

(d. circa 65)

SIMON, son of Jona, brother of St. Andrew, was a Galilean fisherman of the town of Bethsaida on Lake Genesareth. Ardent, industrious, deeply religious, he was a follower of St. John the Baptist and yearned for the Messiah, whose early coming St. John had promised. As soon as he met Christ he recognized Him as the Messiah and received his new name, Cephas, or Peter, the Rock. Henceforth he is the most prominent of the apostles, singled out as the leader to whom Christ gave the keys of the Kingdom of Heaven, always listed first in the group. He was one of the witnesses of the Transfiguration and of the Agony in the Garden. Despite the special confidence Christ showed him, and his own devotion to the Master, Peter denied knowing Jesus three times the night preceding the execution. His repentance, however, followed immediately upon the denial and continued, tradition tell us, the rest of his life. After the Resurrection he was again specifically commissioned by Christ to "Feed My lamb, feed My sheep"—that is, to take command of His church.

The Acts of the Apostles tells how Peter's inspired preaching after the Ascension and the Descent of the Holy Spirit on the first Whit Sunday won thousands of converts and earned him persecution and imprisonment, and later deliverance from prison by an angel. After the persecution Peter visited and preached in the neighboring parts of Palestine. He then founded the church at Antioch, where the followers of Christ first received the name of Christians. Proceeding to Rome, the capital of the Empire, he presided over the infant church for about twenty-five years. His residence in Rome was interrupted, however, by many missionary journeys, by occasional banishments, and by his attendance at the Council of Jerusalem in 51.

St. Peter himself did not write an account of Christ's life, but St. Mark, the author of the Second Gospel, his constant disciple and companion, may be said to have based his rendition of Christ's life on St. Peter's teachings and conversations. St. Peter wrote his epistles in Rome. The first, addressed to the converted Jews of his homeland, has long been admired for its majesty and vigor of style, its admirable compression, and its tone of humble authority.

St. Peter died as a martyr, with St. Paul, during the terror under the Emperor Nero. According to tradition he was crucified head down, by his own request, since he felt unworthy to be put to death in the same manner as his Master. First buried with St. Paul in the catacombs outside the city, his body was later interred at the foot of Vatican Hill, just under the present site of St. Peter's Cathedral.

Together with St. Paul, St. Peter from the earliest time inspired the greatest affection as well as awe. He is represented as a short, curly-haired, energetic man, full of compassion for the weaknesses of his fellow men.

St. Peter's tomb became the first shrine of Christendom. Thence, from all over the world, came pilgrims to venerate him whom St. John Chrysostom called "the mouth of all the apostles, the leader of that choir, the head of that family, the president of the whole world, the foundation of the Church, the burning lover of Christ."

THE FIRST EPISTLE
OF ST. PETER THE APOSTLE

CHAPTER 3, VERSES 8-22

Finally, be all like-minded, compassionate, lovers of the brethren, merciful, humble; not rendering evil for evil, or abuse for abuse, but contrariwise, blessing; for unto this were you called that you might inherit a blessing. For, "He who would love life, and see good days, let him refrain his tongue from evil, and his lips that they speak no deceit. Let him turn away from evil and do good, let him seek after peace and pursue it. For

13

the eyes of the Lord are upon the just, and His ears unto their prayers; but the face of the Lord is against those who do evil."

And who is there to harm you, if you are zealous for what is good? But even if you suffer anything for justice's sake, blessed are you. So have no fear of their fear and do not be troubled. But hallow the Lord Christ in your hearts. Be ready always with an answer to everyone who asks a reason for the hope that is in you. Yet do so with gentleness and fear, having a good conscience, so that wherein they speak in disparagement of you they who revile your good behavior in Christ may be put to shame. For it is better, if the will of God should so will, that you suffer for doing good than for doing evil. Because Christ also died once for sins, the Just for the unjust, that he might bring us to God. Put to death indeed in the flesh, He was brought to life in the spirit, in which also He went and preached to those spirits that were in prison. These in times past had been disobedient when the patience of God waited in the days of Noe while the ark was building. In that ark a few, that is, eight souls were saved through water. Its counterpart, Baptism, now saves you also (not the putting off of the filth of the flesh, but the inquiry of a good conscience after God), through the resurrection of Jesus Christ; who is at the right hand of God, swallowing up death that we might be made heirs of eternal life; for He went into heaven, Angels, Powers and Virtues being made subject to Him.

ST. PAUL

(circa 5—

circa 65)

I N what the Greek historian Xenophon called "the great and happy city of Tarsus," the capital of Cilicia in Asia Minor, there was born in 5 A.D. to a Jewish family, of the tribe of Benjamin, a son whom they named Saul. Because this family was well to do, and had obtained the important privilege of Roman citizenship, they also gave their son the Roman name Paul. They belonged to a very strict sect among the Jewish community, called "the people apart," or the Pharisees, as opposed to the Sadducees, who had assimilated liberal Greek and Roman ways, and the Essenes, who were extremely rigorous monks living in desert monasteries. In Tarsus, Paul received an education typical among Pharisees. He heard the Bible read in Hebrew and then expounded in the vernacular Aramaic and Greek. When he was about fifteen, he was sent to Jerusalem, the religious center of Judaism, to study rabbinical law under Gamaliel, a lawyer whom St. Luke identifies in Acts 5:33 as one "who was held in esteem by all the people."

After five years' study, Paul returned to Tarsus to learn a trade—in his case tentmaking—in accordance with Jewish custom. Hence he was in Tarsus during the public life, death, and Resurrection of Christ. Like all religious Jews, he was aware of the claims that Christ was the Messiah and of the numerous accounts of His miracles. Paul resisted the claims chiefly because, "as a fierce champion of the traditions handed down by my forefathers," he regarded them as subversions of Jewish law put forward by ignorant Galileans. He plunged into the fight against the followers of Christ and

15

witnessed the stoning of St. Stephen, the first martyr. Soon he became the greatest scourge of the Christians in Palestine.

How Paul suddenly was converted while on the way to persecute the Christians at Damascus, after the Resurrection of Jesus, is the most crucial story in the early church. Let Paul tell it in his words, as he did to King Agrippa, at Caesarea, in 59 A.D. (Acts 26, verses 12-18 in Ronald Knox translation.)

"I was making my way to Damascus, with powers delegated to me by the chief priests, when, journeying at mid-day, I saw, my lord king, a light from heaven surpassing the brightness of the sun, which shone about me and my companions. We all fell to the ground, and I heard a voice which said to me, in Hebrew, 'Saul, Saul, why dost thou persecute Me? This is a thankless task of thine, kicking against the goad.' 'Who are You, Lord?' I asked. And the Lord said, 'I am Jesus, Whom Saul persecutes. Rise up and stand on thy feet; I have shewn Myself to thee that I may single thee out to serve Me, as the witness of this vision thou hast had, and other visions thou will have of Me. I will be thy deliverer from the hands of thy people, and of the Gentiles, to whom I am now sending thee. Thou shalt open their eyes and turn them from darkness to light, from the power of Satan to God, so that they may receive, through faith in Me, remission of their sins and an inheritance among the saints.' "

Paul was never to forget that shattering experience on the road to Damascus. He became a Christian, began preaching at Damascus, retired to Arabia to pray and meditate, returned to Damascus, whence he was expelled by the Jews. This time he went to Jerusalem where he met St. Peter and St. James, and then returned to Tarsus for five years.

His active apostolic career may be said to have begun at Antioch in 43, where he began, with Saints Barnabas and John Mark, a missionary journey to Cyprus, Pisidia, and Lycaonia. After meeting with the apostles in Jerusalem in 49, he undertook, this time with Silas as his companion, a second mission through Lycaonia, Pisidia, Galatia, Macedonia, Athens, and Corinth. Titus was his assistant on a third journey (53-56), which encompassed Galatia and Phrygia and involved a long stay at Ephesus.

On these missionary travels Paul preached first to the Jews in the synagogues, and, when rejected, to the Gentiles. His epistles were written to the churches he founded, almost always in response to some particular situation that developed in his absence. Thus his letter to the Corinthians was aimed to distinguish genuine Christian love, which the new converts sometimes confused with the ecstacies of pagan mysticism. His letter to the Galatians insists that true salvation comes from Christ, not from adherence to an external law, such as the Jewish law of circumcision. His letter to the Ephesians stresses the spiritual union of Christ with His church in opposition to those who were attempting to lead them "astray with empty words."

Eventually, Paul was denounced to the authorities, imprisoned for two years at Caesarea, sent to Rome, released, and finally imprisoned again and beheaded in Rome near the Ostian Way. Paul's incredible missionary journeys, his constant sufferings, his absolute dedication to the God Who lived within him and in Whom he lived—all these are communicated through his words. For Paul, more than others, was aware of the unity of Christ and His members, of "Christ incorporating the entire company of believers into Himself to form the new man. Vivified by one and the same sap, inspired by the identical spirit, a single living being takes form and grows to the perfect stature whose dimensions are the secret of God. God, who created the world in the beginning, has taken it into His creative hands a second time. The first time, it was to give things their being; the second time it is to endow things with His own. And this work of love comes from the Father, through the Son, in the Holy Spirit. A secularized humanity in a world empty of the spirit was no part of God's plan. He wants to see man in Christ."

It was this vision of Paul, derived from the vision of God Himself, that inspires the wisdom of the saints.

THE FIRST EPISTLE
OF ST. PAUL
TO THE CORINTHIANS

CHAPTER 13

And I point out to you a yet more excellent way. If I should speak with the tongues of men and of angels, but do not have charity, I have become as sounding brass or a tinkling cymbal. And if I have prophecy and know all mysteries and all knowledge, and if I have all mysteries and all knowledge, and if I have all faith so as to remove mountains, yet do not have charity, I am nothing. And if I distribute all my goods to feed the poor, and if I deliver my body to be burned, yet do not have charity, it profits me nothing.

Charity is patient, is kind; charity does not envy, is not pretentious, is not puffed up, is not ambitious, is not self-seeking, is not provoked; thinks no evil, does not rejoice over wickedness, but rejoices with the truth; bears with all things, believes all things, hopes all things, endures all things.

Charity never fails, whereas prophecies will disappear, and tongues will cease, and knowledge will be destroyed. For we know in part and we prophesy in part; but when that which is perfect has come, that which is imperfect will be done away with. When I was a child, I spoke as a child, I felt as a child, I thought as a child. Now that I have become a man, I have put away the things of a child. We see now through a mirror in an obscure manner, but then face to face. Now I know in part, but then I shall know even as I have been known. So there abide faith, hope and charity, these three; but the greatest of these is charity.

THE EPISTLE
OF ST. PAUL
TO THE
GALATIANS

CHAPTER 5

Stand fast, and do not be caught again under the yoke of slavery. Behold, I, Paul, tell you that if you be circumcised, Christ will be of no advantage to you. And I testify again to every man who has himself circumcised, that he is bound to observe the whole Law. You who would be justified in the Law are estranged from Christ; you have fallen away from grace. For we in the Spirit wait for the hope of justice in virtue of faith. For in Christ Jesus neither circumcision is of any avail, nor uncircumcision, but faith which works through charity.

You were running well; who hindered you from obeying the truth? This persuasion is not from him who calls you. A little leaven ferments the whole mass. I have confidence in you in the Lord, that you will not think otherwise; but he who disturbs you will bear the penalty, whoever he may be. But I, brethren, if I still preach circumcision, why am I still persecuted? Then is the stumbling-block of the cross removed! Would that those who are unsettling you would mutilate themselves!

For you have been called to liberty, brethren; only do not use liberty as an occasion for sensuality, but by charity serve one another. For the whole Law is fulfilled in one word: Thou shalt love thy neighbor as thyself. But if you bite and devour one another, take heed or you will be consumed by one another.

But I say: Walk in the Spirit, and you will not fulfill the lusts of the flesh. For the flesh lusts against the spirit, and the spirit against the flesh; for these are opposed to each other, so that you do not do what you would. But if you are led by the Spirit, you are not under the Law. Now the works of the flesh are manifest; which are immorality, uncleanness, licentiousness, idolatry, witchcrafts, enmities, contentions, jealousies, anger, quarrels, factions, parties, envies, murders, drunkenness, carousings, and suchlike. And concerning these I warn you, as I have warned you, that they who do such things will not attain the Kingdom of God. But the fruit of the Spirit is: charity, joy, peace, patience, kindness, goodness, faith, modesty, continency. Against such things there is no law. And they who belong to Christ have crucified their flesh with its passions and desires. If we live by the Spirit, by the Spirit let us also walk. Let us not become desirous of vainglory, provoking one another, envying one another.

THE EPISTLE
OF ST. PAUL
TO THE
EPHESIANS

CHAPTER 5

Be you, therefore, imitators of God, as very dear children and walk in love, as Christ also loved us and delivered Himself up for us an offering and a sacrifice to God to ascend in fragrant odor. But immorality and every uncleanness or covetousness, let it not even be named among you, as becomes saints; or obscenity or foolish talk or scurrility, which are out of place; but rather thanksgiving. For know this and understand, that no fornicator, or unclean person, or covetous one (for that is idolatry) has any inheritance in the kingdom of Christ and God. Let no one lead you astray with empty words; for because of these things the wrath of God comes upon the children of disobedience. Do not, then, become partakers with them. For you were once darkness, but now you are light in the Lord. Walk, then, as children of light (for the fruit of the light is in all goodness and justice and truth), testing what is well pleasing to God; and have no fellowship with the unfruitful works of darkness, but rather expose them. For of the things that are done by them in secret it is shameful even to speak; but all the things that are exposed are made manifest by the light: for all that is made manifest is light. Thus it says, "Awake, sleeper, and arise from among the dead, and Christ will enlighten thee." See to it therefore, brethren, that you walk with care: not as unwise but as wise, making the most of your time, because the days are evil. Therefore do not become foolish, but understand what the will of the Lord is. And do not be drunk with wine, for in that is debauchery; but be filled with the Spirit, speaking to one another in psalms and hymns and spiritual songs, singing and making melody in your hearts to the Lord, giving thanks always for all things in the Name of our Lord Jesus Christ to God the Father.

Be subject to one another in the fear of Christ. Let wives be subject to their husbands as to the Lord; because a husband is head of the wife, just as Christ is head of the church, being Himself Savior of the body. But just as the church is subject to Christ, so also let wives be to their husbands in all things.

Husbands, love your wives, just as Christ also loved the church, and delivered Himself up for her, that He might sanctify her, cleansing her in the bath of water by means of the word; in order that He might present to himself the church in all her glory, not having spot or wrinkle or any such thing, but that she might be holy and without blemish. Even thus ought husbands also to love their wives as their own bodies. He who loves his own wife, loves himself. For no one ever hated his own flesh; on the contrary he nourishes and cherishes it, as Christ also does the church (because we are members of His Body, made from His Flesh and from His Bones). "For this cause a man shall leave his father and mother, and cleave to his wife; and the two shall become one flesh." This is a great mystery—I mean in reference to Christ and to the church. However, let each one of you also love his wife just as he loves himself; and let the wife respect her husband.

ST. JAMES

(d. 62)

ST. James was surnamed the Less, thus distinguishing him from his fellow disciple, St. James the Great. Probably James was so called because he was younger and shorter than James the Great, but certainly not because he was any less important in the early history of the church. The exact date James was born to Alpheus and Mary of Cleophas is unknown. However, his mother, Mary of Cleophas, is believed to have been a close relative of Mary, the Mother of Christ, for she is referred to (John 19:25) as a "sister" of Mary, according to the Jewish custom of calling close relatives "brethren." For this same reason St. James is called a "brother" of the Lord (Galatians 1:19).

James is mentioned in all four lists of the twelve apostles, is clearly identified as the first Bishop of Jerusalem, and is known to have taken an active part in the Council of Jerusalem in 51. Apparently he remained in Jerusalem afterward, ministering to the converted Jews until he was stoned and clubbed to death in 62 in an outburst of hostility which came shortly before the final Jewish revolt against the Romans.

The chief importance of St. James' epistle is in its echoing of the teaching of Christ. It is a supplement, therefore, to the written Gospels, an example of the many spoken Gospels that preceded the circulation of the versions by the four Evangelists, Matthew, Mark, Luke, and John. Moreover, it is particularly concerned with the theme of wisdom. Addressed to the Jews, possibly to show how the doctrine of Christ fulfilled the moral laws set forth in the Wisdom books of the Old Testament, its key word is *Wisdom*. Not simply the intelligence of the philosopher, or the developed conscience of the naturally good man, or even an external conformity to the laws of

Moses. The wisdom with which James is concerned derives from divine inspiration and support. It proceeds from an internal, humble obedience as well as from an outward conformity. It is a quality of mind and heart alike, a doing of the truth that is, in short, a supernatural morality, a life lived according to the will of God.

Hence St. James' epistle may well be taken as a bridge between the old law and the new, a special stress on the unity of Revelation. Compare this epistle with the thoughts set forth in the selection from Wisdom 7:7-30 below:

Therefore I prayed, and prudence was given me;
  I pleaded, and the spirit of Wisdom came to me.

I preferred her to scepter and throne, and deemed riches
  nothing in comparison with her.

Nor did I liken any priceless gem to her;
  because all gold, in view of her, is a little sand,
  and before her, silver is to be accounted mire.

Beyond health and comeliness I loved her,
  and I chose to have her rather than the light,
  because the splendor of her never yields to sleep.

Yet all good things together came to me in her company,
  and countless riches at her hands;

And I rejoiced in them all, because Wisdom is their leader,
  though I had not known that she is the mother of these.

Simply I learned about her, and ungrudgingly do I share—
  her riches I do not hide away;

For to men she is an unfailing treasure;
  those who gain this treasure win the friendship of God,
  to whom the gifts they have from discipline commend them.

ST. JAMES

Now God grant I speak suitably
   and value these endowments at their worth:
   for he is the guide of Wisdom and the director of the wise.

For both we and our words are in his hand,
   as well as all prudence and knowledge of crafts.

For he gave me sound knowledge of existing things,
   that I might know the organization of the universe and
   the force of its elements,

The beginning and the end and the midpoint of times,
   the changes in the sun's course and the variations of
   the seasons.

Cycles of years, positions of the stars,
   natures of animals, tempers of beasts,

Powers of the winds and thoughts of men,
   uses of plants and virtues of roots—

Such things as are secret I learned, and such as are plain;
   for Wisdom, the artificer of all, taught me.
For in her is a spirit intelligent, holy, unique,
Manifold, subtle, agile, clear, unstained, certain,
Not baneful, loving the good, keen, unhampered,
   beneficent, kindly,

Firm, secure, tranquil, all-powerful, all-seeing,
And pervading all spirits, though they be intelligent,
   pure and very subtle.

For wisdom is mobile beyond all motion,
   and she penetrates and pervades all things by
 reason of her purity.

For she is an aura of the might of God
and a pure effusion of the glory of the Almighty;
therefore nought that is sullied enters into her.

For she is the refulgence of eternal light,
the spotless mirror of the power of God,
the image of his goodness.

And she, who is one, can do all things,
and renews everything while herself perduring;
and passing into holy souls from age to age,
she produces friends of God and prophets.

For there is nought God loves, be it not one who
dwells with Wisdom.

For she is fairer than the sun
and surpasses every constellation of the stars.
Compared to light, she takes precedence,
for that, indeed, night supplants,
but wickedness prevails not over Wisdom.

THE EPISTLE OF
ST. JAMES THE APOSTLE

CHAPTER 1, VERSES 1-27

James, the servant of God and of our Lord Jesus Christ,
to the twelve tribes that are in the Dispersion: greeting.

Esteem it all joy, my brethren, when you fall into various
trials, knowing that the trying of your faith begets patience.
And let patience have its perfect work, that you may be
perfect and entire, lacking nothing.

But if any of you is wanting in wisdom, let him ask it of
God, Who gives abundantly to all men, and does not reproach; and it will be given to him. But let him ask with
faith, without hesitation. For he who hesitates is like a wave

of the sea, driven and carried about by the wind. Therefore, let not such a one think that he will receive anything from the Lord, being a double-minded man, unstable in all his ways.

But let the brother of lowly condition glory in his high estate, and the rich man in his low condition; for he will pass away like the flower of the grass. For the sun rises with a burning heat and parches the grass, and its flower falls and the beauty of its appearance perishes. So too will the rich man wither in his ways.

Blessed is the man who endures temptation; for when he has been tried, he will receive the crown of life which God has promised to those who love Him.

Let no man say when he is tempted, that he is tempted by God; for God is no tempter to evil, and He Himself tempts no one. But everyone is tempted by being drawn away and enticed by his own passion. Then when passion has conceived, it brings forth sin; but when sin has matured, it begets death. Therefore, my beloved brethren, do not err.

Every good gift and every perfect gift is from above, coming down from the Father of Lights, with Whom there is no change, nor shadow of alteration. Of His own will He has begotten us by the word of truth, that we might be, as it were, the first-fruits of His creatures.

You know this, my beloved brethren. But let every man be swift to hear, slow to speak, and slow to wrath. For the wrath of man does not work the justice of God. Therefore, casting aside all uncleanness and abundance of malice, with meekness receive the ingrafted word, which is able to save your souls. But be doers of the word, and not hearers only, deceiving yourselves. For if anyone is a hearer of the word, and not a doer, he is like a man looking at his natural face in a mirror; for he looks at himself and goes away, and presently he forgets what kind of man he is. But he who has looked carefully into the perfect law of liberty and has remained in it, not becoming a forgetful hearer but a doer of the work, shall be blessed in his deed. And if anyone thinks himself to be religous, not restraining his tongue but deceiving his own heart, that man's religion is vain. Religion pure and undefiled before God the Father is this: to give aid to orphans and widows in their tribulation, and to keep oneself unspotted from this world.

ST. CYPRIAN
OF CARTHAGE
(190—258)

CYPRIAN was born in Carthage about 190, of noble Roman parents. His education, according to the manner of the time, was in rhetoric, the classics, philosophy, and the law. For the first fifty years of his life he remained a pagan. But like most of his fellow lawyers he was keenly aware of Christianity, if only because of the controversies brought to light by writers such as Clement of Alexandria, Origen, and Tertullian. In 248 he met a holy priest named Caecilius, through whom he was converted. It was no ordinary conversion. Suddenly, completely, he relates, "the water of regeneration washed me, the light from on high shone upon me and . . . certainly replaced the doubt in my soul." Within a year of his conversion Cyprian was ordained a priest and, shortly thereafter, just before the persecution under the Emperor Decius, he was chosen by enthusiastic popular acclaim to be Bishop of Carthage.

Cyprian's episcopate came at a most perilous time. Christians had enjoyed a long period of peace, during which time many of them had acquired property and held high office, even those that were associated with the pagan priesthood. Hence, when Decius the Emperor required all citizens under pain of death to offer incense to himself as emperor, thus acknowledging his divinity, some Christians apostatized, some equivocated, and some were martyred. Cyprian fled into hiding.

After the Decian persecution, a rigorist element, led by some of the followers of Tertullian, demanded extreme penances of the lapsed Christians, while others advocated a second baptism. On the other hand, the laxist element, headed by Novatus of Carthage, attempted to set up a "human church" that condoned compromise and diluted penances. Cyprian, supporting Pope Cornelius, adopted a middle course in which penance was tempered by mercy—a position subsequently upheld by the Council of Carthage. As a result of the controversies and the schisms and heresies that were fomented during this period, Cyprian wrote his great masterpiece, *The Unity of the Church*, in which he argued that "One cannot have God for one's Father without the Church as one's Mother."

His sermons were so effective and he preached with such compelling logic, learning, and charm that he changed completely the spiritual tone of the Christian community, not only in Carthage, but throughout North Africa where he was accepted as leader of the church. There was uncertainty at the time of the Decian persecution; there was resolution, in 257, when the Emperor Valerius attempted once again to compel Christians to worship the pagan gods. No one event demonstrates this more effectively than Cyprian's own death. In 258, two officers attached to the staff of Galerius Maximus, the proconsul, arrested him in his exile at Curuba and brought him to Carthage.

Embarrassed to deal harshly with a man of senatorial rank, Galerius began: "You know that the divine emperor has ordered you to sacrifice to the gods." "Yes," replied Cyprian, "I know that. But I will not do it." "Be careful, I beg you. Think a little. Regard your own safety." Cyprian cut through the proconsul's official politeness. "Do what you must," he said. "In a case as clear as this I need not deliberate." Regretfully, wearily, Galerius shrugged his shoulders. He wrote on the tablet:

"We order that Thascius Cyprianus be put to death by the sword."

"Thanks be to God," said Cyprian.

As Cyprian walked serenely to the place of execution, he murmured his prayers. His people followed. Not one of the pagans mocked him. He saluted his executioner and directed his deacons to give the man twenty-five pieces of gold for his trouble. Cyprian then removed his outer garments, and bowed down to receive the sword.

Such was Cyprian, whose example was even more eloquent than his words. He was prepared for death, as he had prepared others in homilies like the one reproduced below.

ST. CYPRIAN
ON MORTALITY

Nay, rather, if the Christian recognizes and understands under what condition, under what law he has believed, he will know that he must labor more in the world than others, as he must carry on a greater struggle against the assault of the devil. Divine Scripture teaches and forewarns, saying: "Son, when thus comest to the service of God, stand in justice, and in fear, and prepare thyself for temptation" [Ecclesiastes 2:1], and again: . . . "in thy sorrow endure, and in thy humiliation keep patience, for gold and silver are tried in the fire" [Ecclesiastes 2:4-5].

Thus Job, after the losses of his property, after the deaths of his children, and after being grievously tormented also by ulcers and worms, was not vanquished but was tried, who, showing the patience of his devout mind in the very midst of his afflictions and sufferings says: "Naked came I out of my mother's womb, and naked also shall I go under the earth; the Lord gave, and the Lord hath taken away, as it seemeth best to the Lord so is it done: blessed be the Name of the Lord" [Job 1:21]. And when his wife also urged him in impatience at the severity of his suffering to utter something against God in complaining and hateful language, he answered and said: "Thou hast spoken like one of the foolish women: if we have received good things at the hand of God shall we not endure the evil? In all these things which befell him Job sinned not by his lips in the sight of the Lord" [Job 2:10]. And, therefore, the Lord God bears witness to him, saying: "Hast thou noticed my servant Job? There is no one like him in the earth, a man without complaint, truthful and serving God" [Job 1:8]. And Tobias, after his splendid works, after the many glorious commendations of his mercy, having suffered blindness of the eyes, fearing and blessing God in his adversity, by that very affliction of his body increased in praise. And him also his wife tried to corrupt, saying: "Where are your acts of clemency? Behold what are you suffering!" [Tobias 2:14]. But he, steadfast and firm in his fear of God and armed for all endurance of suffering by the faith of his religion, did not yield in his affliction to the temptations of his weak wife, but deserved more of God through his greater patience. And afterwards the angel Raphael praises him and says: "It is honorable to reveal and confess the works of God. For when Sarra and I prayed I offered the memory of your prayer before the splendor of God: and because you buried the dead, likewise, and because you did not hesitate to rise and leave your dinner and you went and buried the dead, I was sent even to tempt you. And again, God sent me to cure you and Sarra your daughter-in-law: for I am Raphael one of the seven holy angels who stand and serve before the splendor of God" [Tobias 12:11-15].

This endurance the just have always had; this discipline the apostles maintained from the law of the Lord, not to murmur in adversity, but to accept bravely and patiently whatever happens in the world, since the Jewish people always offended in this, that they murmured very frequently against God, as the Lord God testifies in Numbers, saying: "Let their murmuring cease from me and they shall not die" [Numbers 17:25]. We must not murmur in adversity, beloved brethren, but must patiently and gravely bear with whatever happens, since it is written: "A contrite and humble heart God does not despise" [Psalms 50: 19]. In Deuteronomy also the Holy Spirit through Moses admonishes us, saying: "The Lord God shall afflict thee and cast famine on thee and shall examine in thy heart if thou hast kept his precepts well or not" [Deuteronomy 8:2], and again: "The Lord your God tempts you to know if you love the Lord your God with your whole heart and with your whole mind" [Deuteronomy 13:3].

Thus Abraham pleased God because, in order to please God, he neither feared to lose his son nor refused to commit parricide. You cannot lose your son by the law and the chance of mortality, what would you do if you were ordered to kill your son? The fear of God and faith ought to make you ready for all things. Though it should be the loss of private property, though it should be the constant and violent affliction of the members by wasting diseases, though it should be the mournful and sorrowful tearing away from wife, from children, from departing dear ones, let not such things be stumbling blocks for you, but battles; nor let them weaken or crush the faith of the Christian, but rather let them reveal his valor in the contest, since every injury arising from present evils should be made light of through confidence in the blessings to come. Unless a battle has gone before there cannot be a victory; when a victory has been won in the conflict of battle, then a crown also is given to the victors. The pilot is recognized in the storm, in the battle-line the soldier is tested. Light is the boast when there is no danger; conflict in adversity is the trial of truth. The tree which is firmly held up by a deep root is not shaken by onrushing winds, and the ship which has been framed with strong joints is beaten by the waves but is not staved in; and when the threshing floor treads out the harvest the strong hard grain scorns the winds; the empty straw is whirled and carried away by the breeze.

Thus also the Apostle Paul, after shipwrecks, after scourgings, after many grievous tortures of the flesh and body, says that he was not harassed but was corrected by adversity, in order that while he was the more heavily afflicted he might the more truly be tried. There was given to me, he says, a sting of my flesh, an angel of Satan, to buffet me lest I be exalted. For which thing thrice I besought the Lord, that it might depart from me. And He said to me: "My grace is sufficient for thee: for power is made perfect in infirmity" [2 Corinthians 12:7-9]. When, therefore, some infirmity and weakness and desolation attacks us, then is our power made perfect, then our faith is crowned, if though tempted it has stood firm, as it is written: "The furnace trieth the potter's vessels, and the trial of affliction just men" [Ecclesiastes 27:5]. This finally is the difference between us and the others who do not know God, that they complain and murmur in adversity, while adversity does not turn us from the truth of virtue and faith, but proves us in suffering. . . .

We should consider, beloved brethren, and we should reflect constantly that we have renounced the world and as strangers and foreigners we sojourn here for a time. Let us embrace the day which assigns each of us to his dwelling, which on our being rescued from here and released from the snares of the world, restores us to paradise and the kingdom. What man, after having been abroad, would not hasten to return to his native land? Who, when hurrying to sail to his family, would not more eagerly long for a favorable wind that he might more quickly embrace his dear ones? We account paradise our country, we have already begun to look upon the patriarchs as our parents. Why do we not hasten and run, so that we can see our country, so that we can greet our parents? A great number of our dear ones there await us, parents, brothers, children; a dense and copious throng longs for us, already secure in their safety but still anxious for our salvation. How great a joy it is both for them and for us in common to come into their sight and embrace! What pleasure there in the heavenly kingdom without fear of death, and with an eternity of life the highest possible and everlasting happiness; there the glorious choir of apostles, there the throng of exultant prophets, there the innumerable multitude of martyrs wearing crowns on account of the glory and victory of their struggle and passion, triumphant virgins who have subdued the concupiscence of the flesh and body by the strength of their continency, the merciful enjoying their reward who have performed works of justice by giving food and alms to the poor, who in observing the precepts of the Lord have transferred their earthly patrimony to the treasuries of heaven. To these, beloved brethren, let us hasten with eager longing! Let us pray that it may befall us speedily to be with them, speedily to come to Christ. May God see this our purpose. May Christ look upon this resolution of our mind and faith, Who will give more ample rewards of His charity to those whose longings for Him have been greater.

ST. BASIL
THE GREAT
(329—379)

BASIL was born in Caesarea, the metropolis of Cappadocia, of a family distinguished alike for its piety, culture, and heroic lineage. Grandson of a martyr and St. Macrina the Elder, son of St. Basil the Elder and of St. Emmelia, brother of St. Gregory of Nyssa, St. Peter Sebaste, and St. Macrina the Younger, he was destined to equal them in greatness as a scholar, monk, bishop, and human being.

His early ambition was directed toward scholarship. He showed brilliant promise at Caesarea and later at Constantinople, where he was a pupil of the celebrated pagan rhetorician, Libanios, with whom he maintained a lifelong friendship. Far from rejecting secular culture as useless, he pursued it still more eagerly at Athens where, with his great friend St. Gregory Nazianzen, he achieved a fame that spread throughout Greece. Both Basil and Gregory were importuned to remain at Athens. Gregory yielded for a while, but Basil went home to Caesarea.

There he founded a school of rhetoric, pleaded cases at the bar, and continued his study of philosophy. To him this was not just the technical thinking of the philosophers, but all the good things they said about justice and truth. Philosophy was eternal wisdom, the pursuit of the good life. Yet, for a time, Basil must have hesitated in that pursuit, for his brother St. Gregory remarked that he was puffed up beyond measure with his own importance and that his sister St. Macrina speedily took him in hand and directed him toward the glories of eternity.

At all events, Basil soon abandoned his worldly career and

decided to become a monk. In 357 he visited the monasteries and hermitages in Syria, Mesopotamia, and Egypt. Returning home, he founded a monastery in Pontus, near one already established by his sister Macrina. Here he worked out a plan for community life that became the foundation of eastern and western monasticism. He stressed the alternation of study, work, and prayer and, above all, the virtues of humility, patience, and charity. Clearly, Basil had found the way of life that suited him. But the needs of the church were so great that he was persuaded to accept ordination as a priest in 362, and consecration as Bishop of Caesarea in 370.

As a bishop he was equally famous for his theological teachings and his institution of social services. His theology, embodied in treatises and sermons, was especially illuminating in its explanations of the role of the Holy Spirit and in opposing the then-powerful heresies of the Arians and the Manichaeans. But Basil was an outstanding man of action, too. We must love our neighbor, he kept repeating, and "Man's neighbor is man." He organized elaborate institutions to house widows and orphans, to take care of the sick (he himself waited on the lepers), and to protect the homeless. These Basileiads, or cities of the poor, often were more important than the towns in which they were located. Some civil governors were worried because they quickly became the centers of social life. To one protesting governor Basil wrote:

"Who is wronged by the shelters we have built for strangers, for travelers, for those with illnesses needing treatment, or by the necessary aids we have provided for them—nurses, doctors, pack animals and men to lead them?" All those things are improvements which, he adds shrewdly, "give glory to the Governor, on whom the credit naturally falls."

St. Basil's stress on the importance of humility, the subject of the homily reproduced below, did not minimize the importance of courage. St. Gregory of Nazianzen reports this conversation between Basil and the Prefect Modestus, the representative of the Emperor Valens.

"You, Basil, what do you mean by opposing so great a

Prince and not yielding to him as others do? You have refused to worship as the Emperor does."

"I have a Sovereign whose will is otherwise. I can worship no creature."

"What do you take me for?"

"For a thing of nought while you give me such orders."

"Have you no fear of my power?"

"Fear what?"

"Confiscation, exile, tortures, death."

"Think of something else. What is confiscation if one has nothing to lose? Home is everywhere for God's pilgrim. . . . Tortures cannot hurt a body so frail that one stroke would bring death . . ."

"No one ever before spoke to me like this."

"Perhaps you have never met a bishop."

ON HUMILITY

Bear in mind that true proverb: "God resisteth the proud but to the humble He giveth grace" [I Peter 5:5, James 4:6]. Keep as your familiar that word of the Lord: "Everyone that humbleth himself shall be exalted and he that exalteth himself shall be humbled" [Luke 14:11]. Be not an unjust judge of yourself and do not weigh your case favorably to yourself. If you appear to have something in your favor, do not, counting this to your credit and readily forgetting your mistakes, boast of your good deeds of today and grant yourself pardon for what you had done badly yesterday and in the past. Whenever the present arouses pride in you, recall the past to mind and you will check the foolish swelling of conceit. If you see your neighbor committing sin, take care not to dwell exclusively on his sin, but think of the many things he had done and continues to do rightly. Many times, by examining the whole and not taking the part only into account, you will find that he is better than you. God does not examine man according to the part, for He says: "I come to gather together their words and thoughts" [Isaias 66:18]. Furthermore, when He rebuked Josaphat for a sin committed in an unguarded moment, He mentioned also the good he had done, saying: "But good works are found in thee" [II Paralipomenon 19:3].

Such reminders as these regarding self-exaltation we should keep reciting constantly to ourselves, demeaning ourselves that we may be exalted, in imitation of the Lord who descended from heaven to utter lowliness and who was, in turn, raised to the height which befitted Him. In everything which concerns the Lord we find lessons in humility. As an infant, He was straightway laid in a cave, and not upon a couch but in a manger. In the house of a carpenter and of a mother who was poor, He was subject to His mother and her spouse. He was taught and He paid heed to what He needed not to be told. He asked questions, but even in the asking He won admiration for His wisdom. He submitted to John—the Lord received baptism at the hands of His servant. He did not make use of the marvelous power which He possessed to resist any of those who attacked Him, but, as if yielding to superior force, He allowed temporal authority to exercise the power proper to it. He was brought before the high priest as though a criminal and then led to the governor. He bore calumnies in silence and submitted to His sentence, although He could have refuted the false witnesses. He was spat upon by slaves and the vilest menials. He delivered Himself up to death, the most shameful death known to men. Thus, from His birth to the end of His life, He experienced all the exigencies which befall mankind and, after displaying humility to such a degree, He manifested His glory, associating with Himself in glory those who had shared His disgrace. Of this number, the blessed disciples are first, who, poor and destitute, passed through this world, not adorned with the knowledge of rhetoric, not accompanied by a throng of followers, but unattended, as wanderers and solitaries, traveling on land and sea, scourged, stoned, hunted, and, finally, slain. These are divine teachings inherited from our fathers. Let us follow them, so that out of our abasement may spring up eternal happiness, that true and perfect gift of Christ.

But how shall we, casting off the deadly weight of pride, descend to saving humility? If such an aim governed our conduct under all circumstances, we should not overlook the least detail on the ground that we would suffer no harm therefrom. The soul comes to take on a resemblance to its preoccupations and it is stamped and molded to the form of its activities. Let your aspect, your garb, your manner of walking and sitting, your diet, bed, house and its furnishings reflect a customary thrift. Your manner of speaking and singing, your conversation with your neighbor, also, should aim at modesty rather than pretentiousness. Do not strive, I beg you, for artificial embellishment in speech, for cloying sweetness in song, or for a sonorous and high-flown style in conversation. In all your actions, be free from pomposity. Be obliging to your friends, gentle toward your slaves, forbearing with the forward, benign to the lowly, a source of comfort to the afflicted, a friend to the distressed, a condemner of no one. Be pleasant in your address, genial in your response, courteous, accessible to all. Speak not in your own praise, nor contrive that others do so. Do not listen to indecent talk, and conceal insofar as you can your own superior gifts. On the other hand, where sin is concerned, be your own accuser [Proverbs 18: 17], and do not wait for others to make the accusation. Thus, you will be like a just man who accuses himself in the first speech made in court, or like Job who was not deterred by the crowd of people in the city from declaring his personal guilt before all [Job 31:34]. Be not rash in rebuking, nor quick to do so. Do not make accusation while your passions are aroused (for such action savors of willfulness), nor condemn anyone in matters of slight consequence as if you yourself were perfectly just. Receive those who have fallen away and give them spiritual instruction, "considering thyself also lest thou be tempted," as the Apostle advises [Galatians 6:1]. Take as much care not to be glorified among men as others do to obtain this glory, as you remember the words of Christ, that one forfeits a reward from God by voluntarily seeking renown from men or doing good to be seen by men. "They have received their reward," He says [Matthew 6:2]. Do not cheat yourself by desiring to be seen by men, for God is the great Witness. Strive for glory with God, for His is a glorious recompense. Suppose you have been deemed worthy of the episcopate and men throng about you and hold you in esteem. Come down to the level of your subordinates, "not as lording it over the clergy" [I Peter 5:3], and do not behave as worldly potentates do. The Lord bade him who wishes to be first to be the servant of all [Mark 10:44]. To sum up, strive after humility as becomes a lover of this virtue. Love it and it will glorify you. Thus you will travel to good purpose the road leading to that true glory which is to be found with the angels and with God. Christ will acknowledge you as His own disciple before the angels [Luke 12:8] and He will glorify you if you imitate His humility, for He says: "Learn of me because I am meek and humble of heart and you shall find rest to your souls" [Matthew 11:29]. To Him be glory and empire for ever and ever. Amen.

ST. JEROME
(340—420)

AS if to raise up champions to preserve the faith during the approaching collapse of the Roman Empire, Providence supplied the church with some of its greatest fathers. Basil, Gregory of Nazianzen, Ambrose, and Augustine were all born of the same generation. Eusebius Hieronymus—in English, Jerome—was born the same decade as Chrysostom. Like him, he came from a well-to-do family, with estates in Stridon, near Aquileia, not far from Trieste. Again like Chrysostom, Jerome was brilliantly endowed and, at the age of twelve, his parents sent him to Rome for his education. Jerome probably had the great Donatus, whose *Ars Grammatica* was used from the Fourth through the Sixteenth Century as a text for Latin composition, and the best rhetoricians, among them Victorinus, of whom St. Augustine wrote in his *Confessions*.

For eight years Jerome pursued his studies in Rome, where he mastered the Greek and Roman classics, enjoyed the pleasures of the great city, and began collecting a library that was to follow him in his travels and solace him in his travails. Although he was baptized before he left Rome and was affected by the tradition of the martyrs, Jerome was, at this stage, more the brilliant and argumentative scholar than he was the Christian saint.

When, in accordance with Roman law, he left the city, Jerome traveled throughout Gaul. In Trèves, the administrative center of the province, he came upon ascetics and solitaries who had been disciples of St. Athanasius, the exiled Bishop of Alexandria. There he experienced the same fervent desire for the monastic life that had inspired the saints in the East. He went home and joined a group of ascetics near Aquileia. With his brother and sister, his friends Bonosus, Niceas, Rufinus, and Evagrios, Jerome formed a company of idealists who prayed, studied, and worked together. "It was," he reminisced later, "a chore of the blessed."

Evagrios took Jerome to Antioch, housed him in his villa, and introduced him to the flourishing cultural life of the great eastern capital. Jerome plunged with scholarly cupidity into new sources of learning. Then came the celebrated dream that whetted his almost blunted intention to pursue the monastic life. In that dream he stood before the great Judge, who said to him: "You are a Ciceronian, not a Christian. Where your treasure is there is your heart." He awoke, convinced that he must abandon his study of the classics and go to the desert. There, in a cave, he lived a life of great physical austerity. But he did not, nor could he, abandon his scholarly activity. He brought books from Antioch and copyists to transcribe manuscripts and began to study the texts of the Scripture in Greek and Hebrew.

In 382 he returned to Rome by way of Antioch and Constantinople. Soon Pope Damasus, bent on the reform of a segment of the Christian faith which had compromised with the pagans, made Jerome—already a severe critic of clerical laxity and laic worldliness—his assistant and secretary. Jerome plunged fervently into a task that was as gratifying to his natural instincts as it was to his supernatural virtues. In his letters and treatises he satirized with unusual literary skill the pampered aristocrats and their curled and perfumed parasites among the clergy. Fiercely he held up his own ideals of virginity and asceticism. This provoked savage counterattacks against him—and against Damasus. "Men who used to kiss my hands," Jerome said, "were secretly biting me with viper's teeth."

But neither Jerome nor Damasus were mere objectors. Their prime aim was to restore the vigor of the Apostolic Church. Hence Damasus directed Jerome to prepare an accurate, up-to-date Latin version of the New Testament for the

Roman public. In this task Jerome's twin loves, the word of God and literary scholarship, harmonized completely. In a very short time this first great Christian humanist had produced the Latin New Testament. Moreover, Jerome had formed what were in effect the first convents in Rome. A group of pious women—Marcella and her friends Furia, Fabiola, and Asella, St. Paula and her three remarkable daughters Blesilla, Paulina, and Eustochium—admiring Jerome's scholarship and piety, asked him to instruct them in the study of Scripture and in the love of God. Soon their houses were centers of Christian learning and the headquarters of active charity among the poor. These women and some men (although Jerome complained satirically about the absence of devoted men) mastered Greek and studied Hebrew, helped Jerome in his research, copied his manuscripts, and earned from this somewhat misogynous scholar the supreme accolade: He admitted that he could learn from them.

After Damasus' death in 384, Jerome, more than ever in pursuit of the monastic ideal, left Rome for the Holy Land. St. Paula and Eustochium joined him in Bethlehem where they formed three monasteries, two for women and one for men. Jerome consented to be ordained a priest by the Bishop of Antioch on condition that he remain a monk. For thirty-six years, until his death in 420, Jerome remained there, amid many viscissitudes, to complete his translations of the Old Testament, his commentaries, his letters, his sometimes bitter polemics against heretics, schismatics, old friends, new enemies, and sometimes, sad to relate, his fellow saints. The Empire tumbled down around him. Alaric sacked Rome and the Huns poured into the East. Jerome wept at the loss of a civilization that, for all its decadence, represented the finest achievement of human effort. He wept, and he continued to write, sustained by this twin vocation of monasticism and scholarship.

The letter to Nepotian (Letter LIII, in the collected works, written in 394 A.D.) reveals many of St. Jerome's predominant traits: his rhetorical training, his fondness for the classics, his attraction to the ascetic life, his concern for virginity, his devotion to Holy Scripture. Nepotian was the nephew of Heliodorus, Bishop of Attinum, a lifelong friend of Jerome.

ON THE DUTIES OF
THE CLERGY

You ask me, my dearest Nepotian, in your letters from across the sea, and you ask me often, to set out for you in a brief digest some rules of life, showing how one who has renounced service in the world's army to become a monk or a clergyman may keep to the straight path of Christ and not be led astray into the haunts of vice. When I was a young man, scarcely more than a boy, and was trying to curb the first tides of youthful wantonness by the hardships of the desert, I wrote a letter of exhortation to your reverend uncle Heliodorus, to show him the feelings of the friend he had deserted by the tears and remonstrances with which it was filled. In that production I indulged my youthful fancy, and being still fired with enthusiasm for the teaching of the rhetoricians, I decked out some parts of it with the flowery language of the schools. Today, however, my hair is grey, my forehead furrowed and dewlaps, like those of an ox, hang from my chin. As the poet says: "The cold blood round my heart now hinders me" [Virgil, Georgics, II, 484]; and in another passage: "Age carries all things, e'en the mind, away" [Virgil, Bucolics, IX, 51]; and a little later: "Those songs are all forgotten, and his voice has left poor Moeris" [Bucolics, IX, 53].

. . . Listen to one who is your brother in orders and your father in years, one who can guide you from faith's cradle to perfect manhood, and by setting forth precepts of life step by step may instruct others in instructing you. I know that from your uncle, the reverend Heliodorus who is now one of Christ's bishops, you have already learned and are still daily learning all that is holy and that you have the rule of his life as an example of virtue set before you. Take then this letter of mine for what it is worth and join my precepts to his, so that the one may train you in a monk's duties, the other may teach you to be a perfect clergyman.

A clergyman then, who is a servant in Christ's Church, should first know the meaning of his name; and when he has that accurately defined, he should then strive to be what he is called. For since the Greek *cleros* means "lot" or "portion," the clergy are so named, either because they are the Lord's portion, or else because the Lord is theirs. Now he who himself is the Lord's portion, or has the Lord for his portion, must so bear himself as to possess the Lord and be possessed by Him. He who possesses the Lord and says with the prophet: "The Lord is my portion" [Psalms 73:26], can have nothing outside the Lord; for if he has anything except the Lord, the Lord will not be his portion. For example, if he has gold and silver, land and inlaid furniture, with portions such as these the Lord will not deign to be his portion. If I am the Lord's portion and in the line of His inheritance, I receive no portion among the other tribes, but like the Priest and the Levite I live on tithes, and serving the altar am supported by the altar offerings. Having food and raiment I shall be satisfied with them, and naked shall follow the naked cross. So I beseech you and "again and yet again my words repeat" [Virgil, *Aeneid*, III, 436], do not think that clerical orders are but a variety of your old military service; that is, do not look for worldly gain when you are fighting in Christ's army, lest, having more than when you first became a clergyman, you hear it said of you: "Their portions shall not profit them" [Jeremiah 12:13]. Let poor men and strangers be acquainted with your modest table, and with them Christ shall be your guest. Avoid, as you would the plague, a clergyman who is also a man of business, one who has risen from poverty to wealth, from obscurity to a high position. "Evil communications corrupt good manners" [I Corinthians 15:33]. You despise gold; the other loves it. You trample money underfoot; he pursues it. You delight in silence, peacefulness, solitude; he prefers talking and effrontery, the markets and the streets and the apothecaries' shops. When your ways are so diverse, what unity of heart can there be between you?

A woman's foot should seldom or never cross the threshold of your humble lodging. To all maidens and to all Christ's virgins show the same disregard or the same affection. Do not remain under the same roof with them; do not trust your chastity in the past. You cannot be a man more saintly than David, or more wise than Solomon. Remember always that a woman drove the tiller of Paradise from the garden that had been given him. If you are ill let one of the brethren attend you, or else your sister or your mother or some woman of universally approved faith. If there are no persons marked out by ties of kinship, or reputation for chastity, the Church maintains many elderly women who by their services can both help you and benefit themselves, so that even your sickness may bear fruit in almsgiving. I know of some whose bodily recovery coincided with spiritual sickness. There is danger for you in the ministrations of one whose face you are continually watching. If in the course of your clerical duties you have to visit a widow or a virgin, never enter the house alone, and let your associates be men whose fellowship brings no disgrace. If a reader or acolyte or psalmsinger comes with you, let their character, not their dress, be their adornment; let them not wave their hair with curling tongs but let their outward looks be a guarantee of their chastity. Never sit alone and without witnesses with a woman in a quiet place. If there is anything intimate she wants to say, she has a nurse or some elderly virgin at home, some widow or married woman. She cannot be so cut off from human society as to have no one but yourself to whom she can trust her secret. Beware of men's suspicious thoughts, and if a tale can be invented with some probability avoid giving the scandalmonger his opportunity. Frequent gifts of handkerchiefs and ties, pressing a woman's dress to your lips, tasting her food beforehand, writing her fond and flattering *billets-doux*, of all this a holy love knows nothing. "My honey, my light, my darling"—lover's nonsense like this, and all such wanton playfulness and ridiculous courtesy, makes us blush when we hear it on the stage, and seems detestable even on the lips of worldlings. How much more loathsome is it then in the case of monks and clergymen who adorn the priesthood with their vows and their vows with the priesthood! I say this not because I fear such errors in you or in any holy man, but because in every order, in every rank and sex, both good and bad people are to be found, and to condemn the bad is to praise the good.

I am ashamed to say it, but priests who serve idols, actors, charioteers, and harlots can all inherit property: clergymen and monks alone are by law debarred, a law passed not by persecutors but by Christian emperors [By Valentinian, 368 A.D.—Ed.]. I do not complain of the enactment, but it grieves me to think that we deserved it. A cautery is a good thing, but how is it I have a wound that needs a cautery? The law's precaution is stern and prudent; yet even so greed is not checked. By a fiction of trusteeship we elude its provisions, and, as though imperial enactments were of more importance than Christ's commands, we fear the laws and despise the Gospels. If there must be an heir, let the church inherit from the children who are her flock, the church who bore, reared and fed them. Why do we thrust ourselves in between mother and children? It is the glory of a bishop to provide means for the poor, but it is a disgrace for any priest to think of wealth for himself. Though I was born in a humble home beneath the roof of a country cottage and once could scarcely get enough millet and coarse bread to satisfy the howlings of my stomach, yet now I turn up my nose at wheaten flour and honey cakes, I know the various kinds of fish and their different names, I can tell for certain on what coast an oyster has been picked [Juvenal 4:140], I can distinguish by the taste from what province a bird comes, and it is the rarity of a dish and, in the last stage, the money that is wasted on it that gives me pleasure.

I have been told that in some cases disgraceful court is paid to old men and women who have no children. These servile flatterers fetch the basin, sit by the bed, and catch in their own hands ordure and spittle. They tremble at the doctor's appearance, and with quivering lips inquire if his patient is better. If for a little while the old fellow plucks up some strength, they are at their wits' end, and while they pretend to be glad their greedy soul suffers torments within. For they are afraid that they may have wasted their attentions, and they compare an old man with a good hold on life to Methuselah. How great would be their reward with the Lord, if they did not hope for immediate profit. With what labor do they seek an empty inheritance! At less trouble they could have bought for themselves the pearl of Christ.

Read God's Book continually: nay, never let the sacred volume be out of your hand. Learn, so that you may teach. Hold fast to the words of faith, according to sound doctrine, so that you may be able thereby to exhort and refute the gainsayers. "Continue thou in the things that thou hast learned and hast been assured of, knowing of whom thou hast learned them" [II Timothy 3:14]; and "Be ready always to give an answer to every man that asketh you a reason of the hope and faith that are in you" [I Peter 3:15]. Your deeds must not belie your words, lest, when you are speaking in church, some one may say to himself :"Why do you not practice what you preach?" A teacher fond of good living may fill his own stomach and then discourse on the benefits of fasting; even a robber can possibly accuse others of greed; but in a priest of Christ mind and mouth should be in harmony.

Be obedient to your bishop, and respect him as your spiritual father. Sons love, slaves fear. "If I be a father," says the Scripture, "where is mine honor? and if I am a master, where is my fear?" [Malachi 1:6]. In your case one and the same man has many titles to your respect: he is monk, bishop, uncle. But even bishops should realize they are priests, not lords; they should give to clergymen the honor that is their due, so that the clergy may offer them the respect proper to bishops. The orator Domitius spoke to the point when he said: "Why should I treat you as leader of the Senate, when you do not treat me as a senator?" [Cicero, *De Oratore* 3:1]. We should recognize that a bishop and his presbyters are like Aaron and his sons. There is but one Lord and one Temple; there should be also but one ministry. Let us always remember the charge which the Apostle Peter gives to priests: "Feed the flock of God which is among you, taking the oversight thereof not by constraint but willingly as God would have you; not for filthy lucre but of a ready mind; neither as being lords over God's heritage but being examples to the flock, and that gladly, that when the chief shepherd shall appear ye may receive a crown of glory that fadeth not away" [I Peter 5:2]. It is a very bad custom in some churches for presbyters to be silent and to refrain from speech in the presence of bishops, on the ground that these latter would either be jealous of them or think it unbecoming to be listeners. The Apostle Paul says: "If anything be revealed to another that sitteth by, let the first hold his peace. For ye may all prophesy one by one that all may learn and all may be comforted; and the spirits of the prophets are subject to the prophets. For God is not the author of confusion but of peace" [I Corinthians 14:30]. A wise son is a glory to his father; and a bishop should rejoice in his own good judgment, when he chooses such to be priests of Christ. . . .

Avoid somber garments as much as bright ones. Showiness and slovenliness are alike to be shunned: the one savors of vanity, the other of boastfulness. To walk abroad without a linen vest is not praiseworthy: the good thing is not to have money to buy one. In any case it is absurd and scandalous to boast of having neither napkin nor handkerchief, while all the time your purse is well filled. There are some who give a trifle to the poor that they may themselves receive a larger sum, under the cloak of almsgiving seeking their own personal gain. Such conduct should be called almshunting rather than almsgiving. Thus it is that birds, beasts, and fishes are caught. A small piece of bait is put on the hook; and lo! they draw up a fine lady's purse. The bishop, to whose care the church is entrusted, knows whom he should appoint as almoner to the poor. It is better for me not to have anything to give than to be shameless in begging. It is a kind of arrogance also to wish to seem more generous than he who is

Christ's bishop. "We cannot all do all things" [Virgil, *Bucolics*, 8:63]. In the Church one man is the eye, another the tongue, another the hand, another the foot, another the ear, the belly, and so on. Read Paul's epistle to the Corinthians, and see how one body is made up of different members. A rough simple brother should not think himself saintly just because he knows nothing; he who is well educated and eloquent must not imagine that holiness consists in a ready tongue. Of the two imperfections a holy clumsiness is much better than a sinful eloquence. . . .

Avoid entertaining the worldly at your table, especially those who are swollen with office. You are the priest of a crucified Lord, one who lived in poverty and on the bread of strangers, and it is a shameful thing for a consul's attendants and bodyguard to keep watch before your door, and for a provincial judge to have a better luncheon with you than he would get in his palace. If you urge that you do this in order that you may plead for the unhappy and the oppressed, a worldly judge pays more regard to a self-denying cleric than to a rich one, he respects your sanctity more than your wealth. Or if he is the sort of man who only listens to clergymen over the wine bowl, I will gladly forgo any benefit from him, and will address my prayer to Christ who is more able to help than any judge. For it is better to trust in the Lord than to put your confidence in men; it is better to fix your hopes in the Lord than to expect anything from princes [Psalms 118:9].

Never smell of wine, lest the philosopher's words be said of you: "This is not a kiss but a wine sip." Priests who reek of wine are condemned by the apostle and forbidden by the old law. Those who serve the altar must not drink either wine or shechar, the law says [cf. Leviticus 10:9 and Luke 1:15]; the word shechar in Hebrew means any intoxicating drink, whether it is made from barley, or from fruit juice, or from honey boiled down into a rough sweet liquor, or from pressed dates, or from the thick syrup strained from a decoction of corn. Anything that intoxicates and disturbs the mind's balance you must avoid as you avoid wine. I do not say that we should condemn a thing that God made, since indeed Our Lord was called a winebibber [Matthew 11:19], and Timothy was allowed wine in moderation because of his weak stomach [I Timothy 5:23]; but I claim that those who drink wine should have some reason of age or health or some peculiarity of constitution. If even without wine I am all aglow, if I feel the fire of youth and am inflamed by hot blood, if I am of a strong and lusty habit of body, then I will readily forgo the wine cup, in which I may well suspect that poison lurks. The Greeks have a pretty proverb which perhaps in our language loses some of its force: "A fat paunch never breeds fine thoughts."

Impose upon yourself such fasting as you are able to bear. Let your fasts be pure, chaste, simple, moderate, and free from superstition. What good is it to abstain from oil and then to seek after food that is troublesome to prepare and difficult to get, dried figs, pepper, nuts, dates, wheaten flour, honey, pistachios? All the resources of the garden are laid under contribution to avoid eating ordinary bread. I have heard that some people outrage nature, and neither drink water nor eat bread, but imbibe fancy decoctions of pounded herbs and beet juice, using a shell to drink from, in place of a cup. Shame on us! We do not blush at such silliness and we feel no disgust at such superstition. Moreover, by such fancifulness we seek a reputation for abstinence. The strictest fast is bread and water: but as that brings no glory with it and bread and water are our usual food, it is reckoned not a fast but an ordinary and common matter.

Beware of angling for compliments, lest you lose God's favor in exchange for the people's praise. "If I yet pleased men," says the apostle, "I should not be the servant of Christ" [Galatians 1:10]. He ceased to please men and became Christ's servant. Through good and bad report on right hand and on left Christ's soldier marches; he is not elated by praise nor crushed by abuse; he is not puffed up by riches nor depressed by poverty; he despises joy and sorrow alike. The sun will not burn him by day nor the moon by night [Psalms 121:6]. Do not pray at the corners of a square, lest the breeze of popular favor interrupt the straight course of your prayers. Do not broaden your fringes and wear phylacteries for show, or wrap yourself in despite of conscience in Pharisaic ostentation [Matthew 6:5 and 23:5]. It is better to carry all this in the heart, rather than on the body, to have God's approval rather than to please the eyes of men. Would you know what kind of ornaments the Lord requires? Have prudence, justice, temperance, fortitude. Let these be your four cardinal points, let them be your four-in-hand to carry you, Christ's charioteer, at full speed to your goal. No necklace can be more precious than these, no jewels can make a brighter galaxy. On every side they form a decoration, a girdle, a defense; they are both an ornament and a protection; their jewels are turned into shields. . . .

ST. JOHN CHRYSOSTOM
(347—407)

ECUNDUS, the *Magister Militum,* or field marshal of the Imperial Army in Syria, lived only a short time after his wife, Anthusa, gave birth to his second child, who was named John. He left his twenty-year-old widow a large fortune and a great name. Anthusa quickly resolved not to remarry, but to devote her life to her children and to good works. Although a strict Christian in the half-pagan city of Antioch, she was as attentive to the intellectual education of John as she was to his moral formation.

John attended the best schools and later, at the university, he studied under the celebrated Libanios, now living in his native city after a notable career in Constantinople and Athens, and the philosopher Andragathios. The former helped him to master the classic poets, historians, and orators, the latter the philosophers, particularly Plato, who remained his favorite throughout his life. Libanios particularly admired John. Asked whom he wished to succeed him as head of the school, he said, "John, if the Christians had not stolen him." Libanios' reference may have been to the fact that, in 367, his brilliant pupil had entered the class of catechumens and was baptized in 370.

For John, as for other devout Christians of the Fourth Century, baptism meant not just formal enrollment as a Christian, but a life of severe penance, complete denial of worldly ambition, and often dedication to the monastic life. Hence, shortly after his mother's death, he gave away his wealth and spent six years as a monk and a hermit in the region of Antioch. But, as in the case of St. Basil, the local bishops needed this scholarly recluse as a priest and a preacher. He was ordained a priest in 386. Shortly thereafter

53

he began to earn the name Chrysostom—the mouth of gold. He spoke so eloquently that his audiences frequently burst into applause. In 387, when a mob wrecked the statues of the Emperor Theodosius and the Emperor threatened to raze the beautiful city, John's sermons allayed both the rebellion of the people and the royal wrath.

So great was the fame of his preaching, the soundness of his doctrine, and the power of his example that he was sought after throughout the Empire. It was inevitable that he would become a bishop. Where, when, and how this took place is an extraordinary story closely linked with the career of an amazing man, Eutropios. Eutropios was a castoff child of low birth. As a boy slave he had been castrated and sold to a general, who in turn gave him to his daughter as a wedding present. She used him as a personal servant until he displeased her and she threw him out to starve in the streets. Picked up by a merciful officer of the court he was given a menial job in the imperial household of Theodosius. Inch by inch he rose to become chief imperial chamberlain. When Theodosius died he was succeeded by his son Arcadius (and his wife Eudoxia). The weakling Emperor and the calculating Empress agreed to make Eutropios a consul, a title held in greatest honor and normally reserved for the nobility. Eutropios was well in control of the Empire when the Bishop of Constantinople died. Immediately Eutropios was besieged by candidates for the office. Knowing that he charged a fixed price for all appointments (he had a chart for that purpose publicly displayed in his office), some offered bribes. But the serious Christians begged the Emperor for a worthy bishop. Eutropios, for a reason he soon regretted, suggested John.

As soon as he was consecrated, John set about reforming the capital city. He sold the goods of his predecessor, gave the money to the poor, founded hospitals and asylums, spoke out against the corruption of the court. Moreover, he persisted in extending the right of sanctuary to all who sought refuge in the churches, even to the many enemies or victims of Eutropios himself. Soon Eutropios induced the Emperor to rescind the law granting the right of sanctuary.

Eutropios, who caused tablets to be erected naming himself as third founder of the Empire, had reached the dizzy height of all dictators—absolute power—when the ground began to tremble. Eudoxia, the Empress, grew jealous of his power. Tribigild, marshal of the Gothic troops, mutinied, and Gaïnas, ordered by Eutropios to quell the mutiny, joined the rebellion. She persuaded Arcadius to depose Eutropios. This he did, granting the eunuch only his life. Hunted by the mobs of his enemies, the wretched Eutropios sought sanctuary in the very church whose right of sanctuary he had nullified.

The mob pursued him to the church. Chrysostom mounted the pulpit; the curtains before the main altar parted to reveal Eutropios crouching beside the altar. John began his famous sermon on "Vanity of Vanities: All Is Vanity." At the end, the audience that had come thirsting for blood departed weeping for pity. But Chrysostom saved Eutropios only for a time. He was sent to exile in Cyprus, later to be recalled, tried, and put to death. John himself was to suffer from Eudoxia's envy. Shortly thereafter he was accused of calling the Empress a Jezebel and of "encouraging the multitude to revolt." He was exiled to Cucusus and died at Comana, as a result of a journey deliberately made difficult. By the time he died, his speeches and writings had already made him great among the doctors of the church.

VANITY OF VANITIES:
ALL IS VANITY

THE INSTABILITY OF EARTHLY POSSESSIONS

Never more than now can one exclaim: "Vanity of vanities: all is vanity" [Ecclesiastes 1:2].

Where now is the brilliant splendor of the Consul? Where are the gleaming torches? Where the thundering applause, the dances, banquets and feastings? Where the wreaths and garlands? The festivities of the city with their flattering ovations at shows and circus? A wind has arisen and blown the leaves to the ground to show us the once magnificent tree in all its nakedness, shaken and trembling to its very roots. So violent has been the gale that it has managed to uproot that tree, roots and all. Where are now the pretended friends? Where the splendid banquets, and luxurious repasts? The row of noisy guests? The daily drinking-parties, and the refinery of your cookery; the slaves of your highness, who spoke and acted at your beck and call? All that is as night and dream. At dawn it has disappeared. Spring-blossoms they were, withered with the close of spring. Shadows they were which have slipped by like smoke which has evaporated; bubbles which have burst; a mere cobweb rent asunder.

Wherefore do we repeat the saying of the Divine Spirit: "Vanity of vanities and all is vanity." That sentence should be written on our walls and in our streets, upon doors and entrances, and we should ponder over it continually. Since deception, falsity and the whole masquerade of earthly things seem to have an appearance of truth for the generality of people, we should incite our neighbors, daily and at every meal and meeting, to remember and to remind others: "Vanity of vanities, all is vanity."

Have I not always told you: Riches are a volatile thing: a slave fleeing from its master. But my warning displeased you. Fortune is an ungrateful servant, but you would not believe me. And see now, experience itself has taught you what it is: not only a deserter, an ungrateful creature, but a murderer. Did I not tell you—but those warnings excited your anger still more—that I loved you more than all your flatterers? Did I not say to you that wounds caused by the hand of a friend are preferable to the flattering caress of an enemy? Had you but accepted the former, you would not now be complaining of killing kindnesses. My wounds were to effect a cure, whilst their flatteries prepared an incurable evil. Call upon them now, your stewards, your satellites, who cleared the way for your passage and praised you everywhere. They are gone. They renounced your friendship, and liberated themselves from your tyranny.

But we others proceed in a different manner. We do not abandon you in your distress; we comfort him who is afflicted. We save and protect him. And the same Church that you fought against, opens her arms to receive you. While the famous shows, the cause of your repeated attacks on us, have treacherously sent you to death.

We never ceased asking you: Why do you act thus? What harm has the Church done to you? By persecuting her you are only bringing yourself to the verge of the precipice. But all warnings were in vain. Moreover those who most benefited from your generosities were the first to whet their swords against you. The Church, though she has suffered scandalously from your injustice, now hastens to protect you from the ambushes which strew your path.

LESSONS FROM THE LIFE OF EUTROPIOS

Far be it from me to insult a fallen victim by my speech. I speak in order to warn those still standing, in order that they may not fall. No, I am not here to re-open wounds but to prevent others. Not to cast the drowned into the flood but to show those who are slumbering in the lap of luxury how to avoid the dangers of fortune. How so? By pointing to the instability of human creatures, as is seen in that striking example. He did not mistrust the world and is expiating for it now. He would not believe in either his own experience or the advice of another. You at least who think so much of fortune, profit by this lesson; for nothing is more fragile, more transitory than human possessions. Let he who will find an adequate name for the description of such a vacillating creature, he will still be far from the truth. Vain smoke, grass, dream, spring-blossoms or whatever else you call it, there is no use seeking further because it is more fragile, more unreal than nothingness.

But richness is not only nothingness. It also means beetling height. Eutropios is a proof. Who reached higher than that man? Did he not rule the world by riches? Did he not reach the summit of greatness? Inspire respect and fear? And now . . . his misery exceeds that of any prisoner: he deserves more pity than his slaves; he is more needy than a beggar dying from starvation. In terror he sees swords threatening him; chasms opening under his feet; executioners appearing on the place of execution. All that in place of his former pleasures, the memory of which cannot soothe his sufferings. Poor man, full daylight is as midnight to him. Blinded is he as if behind thick walls. How terrifying such a situation, and how incapable we feel of describing it accurately with all the horror of such an agony.

What, I ask you, can be added to that which I have said above, which will show him in his true light? Yesterday the soldiers invaded the sanctuary to seize him brutally at the altar where he was hiding. His face was then like that of a dead man, and his whole body seemed inanimate. He stood there gnashing his teeth as even now. He is shivering and trembling, he can hardly breathe; he weeps.

THE SALVATION OF EUTROPIOS

Once more, I say, despite all that, I do not intend to reproach him, nor do I wish to mock him in his misfortune. On the contrary, I wish to soften your hearts, incite you to mercy, and prove to you that the punishment he has received suffices. Many of you are so inhuman that you blame us, as if we had committed a crime in admitting Eutropios to our sanctuary. It is to calm these revengeful sentiments that I have drawn this picture of his misery. What, dear audience, is the reason for your discontent?

That an enemy and a persecutor of the Church be now seeking refuge within her? But in this we have further reason for praising the Lord, who has permitted the great fall of this enemy of the Church in order to proclaim more loudly her might and meekness. Her might, since the aggressor himself, consequent on his attack directed against her, has succumbed miserably. Her meekness, since she has protected the enemy under her shield, taken him under her wings, placed him in utter security, and with no rancor for past injustice, has opened her arms to him with infinite generosity. This is indeed more admirable than any monument set up in token of victory. This confounds the pagans, intimidates the Jews, and throws into full light the beauty of the Church. She respects her enemy and now that the matter is deprived of everything, that all repel and persecute him; she alone like a tender mother, shelters him under her mantle. She protects him from the Emperor's wrath and does not give him up to the people's hatred or the threats of his bloodthirsty enemies. This is the finest adornment of the altar.

A fine adornment, I hear you say—an evil doer, a miser, a plunderer clinging to the altar. Cease that talk. Do you forget that a public sinner, a prostitute, touched and embraced the feet of Jesus? Such an act was not a cause of reproach for the Lord Jesus but one of wonder and praise. The impure did not infect the chaste; but he, the all pure and holy, raised the prostitute to chastity by his contact. And so beware of all feelings of vengeance. Remember we are the disciples of Him Who, on the cross, said: "Forgive them, for they know not what they do."

You maintain that the man through his evil laws and decrees suppressed the right of asylum. What does that matter since events have proved he acted wrongly? He is in any case the first now to repudiate that unjust law by his presence here, and to proclaim this warning by his silence: "Do not act as I have done if you do not wish to suffer like me." His misfortune in this way is a lesson to us. From the altar a brilliant light shines and reflects the truth that through its imposing power he has captured the lion in chains.

Although the throne, purple and diadems are the symbols of Majesty, a greater symbol is there when at the feet of royalty lie barbarians, their hands tied behind their backs, their heads bent low. That this man has taught you all this without opening his mouth, is seen by your haste to come here and the crowded audience. What a brilliant show displays itself before my eyes. What a rush of people, as numerous as to a feast. Virgins have left their rooms, wives their homes, men the street, all to come and witness human misery to see the fragility of earthly things, and the rending of the world's mask which, no later than yesterday, bewitched you by its show. The spell now broken, its face has become like the wrinkled features of an old woman. Disgrace has blown away all the make-up.

What has not been done on this day of misfortune? What power has not been manifested?

Of a man happy and respected throughout the world, it has made an outcast of society. Approach, rich of this world here is something to be learnt. See how he who mastered the world has been thrown from power; fear contracts his limbs; he is more frightened than a hare or frog. Fear alone fixes him to the spot.

Tremble, O rich, at such a spectacle, calm your passion quell your pride and learn the truth of this Bible saying: "All flesh is like grass and human vanity like a field-flower: the grass withers, the flower fades. Our earthly days are but idle smoke" [Isaias 40:6-7, Psalms 36:2, 101-4].

Enter, poor and needy; look upon this spectacle and murmur no longer against your lot. Learn to accept with gratitude what poverty offers you: a safe shelter, a haven free from storm; a secure fortress. Were you given your choice, you should choose your present state in preference to the temporary though fatal possession of wealth. Do you realize now how the misfortune of this single man has become a blessing for rich and poor; high and low, nobleman and slave Do you see now how everyone here receives a true remedy for his ills and returns home healed?

GOD'S PARDON AND THE EMPEROR'S MERCY

Have I succeeded in touching your hearts, calming your anger, subduing your inhuman feelings, moving you to mercy? I certainly hope so. I can read it in your faces; your tears prevent my doubting it. And now since your strong hearts have softened as clay, let us once more continue to work together. Let the fruits of mercy ripen, the ears of corn wave; let us implore the Emperor, or rather pray that God himself may melt his anger, and by softening his heart, obtain his favor and liberty.

No sooner had Eutropios taken refuge in the temple than a remarkable change took place. When the Emperor was informed of Eutropios' flight there, he endeavored to calm his soldiers who, with loud shouts of indignation, clamored for his death. He addressed them lengthily, inviting them not to consider the crimes of the accused as his good deeds. He personally would be condescending toward him. As for his evil acts they were to be forgiven in consideration of human weakness. The people nevertheless would not listen. They insisted upon vengeance on account of the offense committed against His Majesty. The soldiers clamored all the more loudly, stamping their feet and brandishing their swords. The Emperor could not restrain the tears which fell from his kind eyes. This alone succeeded in influencing the people's compassion for obtaining the right of asylum for the victim clutching to the altar.

Therefore are we bound to follow that noble example. Since the Emperor has forgiven everything; since he has pardoned the insults, what shame would be yours to pursue your bitter rancor. Would you after such behavior, dare to approach the sacred Mysteries? Could you join in the prescribed prayer: "Forgive us our trespasses as we forgive them that trespass against us," if you do not pardon others? He may have grieved you much, done you great injustice. I do not deny that, but I say just this: It is not the time for severity but for kindness; not for judgment but for mercy; not for dispute but for mutual agreement; not for condemnation but for compassion and forgiveness.

Let us bury all hatred and bitterness. Let us rather beg for mercy and God's goodness upon the offender, and that he will save him from the death threatening him so that he may have time for repentance. Let us all together beseech the Emperor to respect both Church and altar, and before the Holy Table to grant us the life of this man. The Emperor will be grateful to us for acting in this manner. The Lord will not wait for his approbation before praising us but will reward us generously for our goodness toward his creature. For if he hates and proves the cruel and heartless, he is merciful and full of love toward the good. And if that merciful man be just as well, God will reserve him a bright crown. If he is a sinner, God will pardon him and recompense him for that mercy shown to his fellow-men. For has He not said: "I will have mercy and not sacrifice" (Osea 4:6)? Everywhere in Holy Scripture, we see the Lord granting mercy and forgiving sin.

When we ourselves show mercy as at the present moment, we render ourselves worthy of God's grace; we make reparation for our faults and glorify his Church. Our kind-hearted Emperor will praise us and the people acclaim us. To the uttermost parts of the earth our charity will be published and all the nations will extol it.

Let us therefore humbly implore the favor of the Emperor to grant this request. Let us beg and pray that the prisoner, the refugee, the supplicant be delivered. By so doing we shall obtain the glory that is to come through the grace of our Lord Jesus Christ to whom be honor, glory and power, now and for evermore.

Amen.

ST. AUGUSTINE
(354—430)

A N African of the Africans is a phrase used to describe Augustine because his passionate temperament, intellectual ardor, and love of polemics are so representative of the rich tempestuous life of Roman Christianity in North Africa. For North Africa, Carthage in particular, was the center of Latin Christianity down to the Fourth Century. Before Augustine there were Tertullian, Cyprian, Lactantius —names that rank with Origen, Basil, and Athanasius in the East.

Born in Tagaste, son of Patricius, a well-born Roman, and St. Monica, he was brought up as a Christian, although like many of his time he postponed his baptism. He went to the school of rhetoric in Carthage where he immediately won the highest distinctions. There, too, he became greatly interested in philosophy and, as a result of reading Cicero's *Hortensius,* he aspired to become a true lover of wisdom. He turned to the Scriptures and found them excessively simple. He read too the books of the Manichees, whose fashionable doctrine permitted their followers to rationalize their lustful desires and activities. At eighteen, Augustine returned to Tagaste where he taught rhetoric and, to his mother's intense chagrin, took a concubine who bore him a son, Adeodatus, whom he deeply loved. Ambitious for a greater success than the provinces could afford him, he went to Rome, where he taught from about 376 to 384.

His Manichaean associates then procured for him a professorship of rhetoric in Milan—at that time the seat of the Empire and the see of the great St. Ambrose. Here St. Monica joined him and rejoiced to find that, although he was not yet a Catholic, he had grown to despise the doctrines of the Manichees. This change was largely the result of prolonged study of Plato's theories. Monica now urged him to validate his marriage and advance his career. "I was all hot for honors, money, marriage," he wrote of these times. But he was "hot" too for wisdom and he was listening to the sermons of St. Ambrose with growing alarm. For here was a lawyer, a philosopher, a man of highest rank, who gave a singularly coherent account of the Scriptures and presented God as the true source of all wisdom. Augustine sought Ambrose out but could elicit from him no personal attention. "When he saw me," Augustine wrote, "he often broke out in praise of Monica . . ." who had never ceased to pray for her brilliant and passionate son.

The story of his conversion is told in one of the world's great books, St. Augustine's *Confessions*, an autobiography that reveals the depths of the human soul perhaps more completely than any book yet written. Soon after his baptism in April, 387, Augustine returned to Tagaste where he lived the monastic life with a group of friends. But this peaceful and joyous life of prayer and learning was soon interrupted. The Bishop of Hippo insisted on ordaining him a priest in 391 and in 395 on consecrating him as coadjutor bishop; "I was caught and made a priest, and once that step had been taken I was made a bishop." When his friends congratulated him, he reminded them that he had made a shipwreck of himself and that the God who made him had remade him. One reason for his writing the *Confessions* was to avoid vainglory.

St. Augustine's career as a bishop had two facets. First he was the teacher of his flock. Here we see him seated in his church expounding a text of the Bible, as in the homily that is reproduced below. For the church at large he sometimes wrote systematic treatises on important subjects such as *On the Trinity* and *On the Works of Monks*. For the most part, however, Augustine conceived his mission to be not only the salvation of his own flock, but also the conversion of heretics and pagans. Had he not once been one of them? So, he appeared frequently in great public debates with his old adversaries, the Manichaeans, and the Donatists, and later the Pelagians. At times he spoke to large throngs, once as many as sixty times, with immense skill and great effect. Although a passionate orator, he had none of Jerome's instincts for invective. Heresies, he felt, were the products of thinking men and he offered his thoughts in rebuttal. Besides these debates Augustine wrote many treatises, one hundred and nineteen in all, together with many letters.

St. Augustine's greatest work, *The City of God,* began as an answer to an objection raised by the pagans. After the sack of Rome by the Goths in 410 and the subsequent eruptions by other barbarian hordes, the pagans began to ascribe the fall of the Empire to the Christians. Christianity, the rumor went, had sapped the strength of the Empire by its doctrine of meekness and nonbelligerence; moreover, the old gods had avenged themselves upon those who had overthrown them. Augustine refuted these charges by retorting that Rome was made great not by the gods, but first by her old republican virtues and then by her Christian subjects, and that the cause of her present defeat was her unbridled luxury and her failure to accept Christianity. Then he went on to draw a distinction between two cities founded on two kinds of love: the City of God, founded on the love of God and of truth, and the City of Earth, founded on the love of self and of pleasure. "Tell me what a people loves and I shall tell you what it is." A massive book, as encyclopedic in its information as it is subtle in its reasoning, *The City of God* set forth for ages to come a Christian philosophy of history, an explanation of how one can be in this world yet not of it.

Augustine's last years witnessed the increasing collapse of the Empire. As if to demonstrate his theories of history, the invasion of North Africa occurred at least partly through the corruption of Boniface, the imperial commander. Boniface invited the Vandals, already entrenched in Spain, to support him in a rebellion. Once across the Straits of Gibraltar these savage Arians ravaged the country. Their main fury was against the church. In 430, they laid siege to Hippo where Augustine was fatally ill. He refused to flee. "When the people remain and the ministers flee and the ministration is suspended, what is that but the guilty flight of hirelings, who care not for the sheep?" His last days were spent reading the penitential psalms which he had written out and placed against the wall of his cell. As he read them, he wept.

ON THE BEATITUDES

Blessed are the poor in spirit, for theirs is the kingdom of heaven.

Blessed are the meek, for they shall possess the earth.

Blessed are they who mourn, for they shall be comforted.

Blessed are they who hunger and thirst for justice, for they shall be satisfied.

Blessed are the merciful, for they shall obtain mercy.

Blessed are the clean of heart, for they shall see God.

Blessed are the peacemakers, for they shall be called children of God.

Blessed are they who suffer persecution for justice' sake, for theirs is the kingdom of heaven.

[St. Matthew (5:3-10)]

Dearly beloved, you have joined with us in listening to the reading of the Holy Gospel. May the Lord assist us while we address you on the portion that has been read, in order that our words may be appropriate to your needs and may bear spiritual fruit in your daily lives. Everyone who hears the word of God ought to bear in mind that his life ought to be conformed to what he hears. Therefore, let him not disregard that word in his conduct while he seeks to praise it with his lips. If the word of God is sweet to hear, how much sweeter must it be to do? I, indeed, may be likened to those who sow the seed; you are the fields in which the word of God is sown. May the seed perish not; may the harvest be plentiful. You have joined with us in listening to the words which Christ our Lord spoke to His disciples when they had drawn near to Him: "And opening his mouth He taught them, saying: 'Blessed are the poor in spirit, for theirs in the kingdom of heaven,'" and so forth. Thus the one true Master, saying those things which we have briefly summarized for you, taught His disciples as they were drawing close to Him. [At this point, Augustine had undoubtedly summarized all the Beatitudes, but either then or later a scribe substituted the expression, "and so forth."—Ed.] You have now drawn close to us, in order that we, with the help of that same Master, may address you and teach you. And, while we are expounding the truths which so great a Master has pronounced, what could be more helpful for us than to do what He has told us? Therefore, be poor in spirit, so that the kingdom of heaven may be yours.

Why should you be afraid to be poor? Consider the riches of the kingdom of heaven. Yes, men fear poverty. But they ought to have a greater fear of iniquity. For, when poverty will have passed away, then will come the great happiness of the righteous, because they will then be free from all anxiety. In this present life, fear is all the more increased and covetousness is all the more unloosed according as there is an increase of those things which are called riches, for those things are not true riches. Were I to ask you, you could mention many a rich man. But, could you name one of them who is free from anxiety? The rich man is in a frenzy to increase his riches, and he is in trepidation lest he lose them. How could such a servant be free? A slave, indeed, is the servant of any mistress. Can the servant of avarice then be free? Hence: "Blessed are the poor in spirit."

What does it mean to be poor in spirit? The poor in spirit need not be poor in worldly possessions, but they must be moderate in their desires. The man who is poor in spirit is a humble man. God gives ear to the sighs of the humble, and does not despise their petitions. So, when the Lord delivered his Discourse, [the Sermon on the Mount], He based its very beginning on humility, which means poverty. You could find a godly man who has an abundance of worldly wealth, but such a man is not puffed up with pride. You could also find a man so poverty-stricken that he has neither ownership nor possession of any worldly goods. There is no more assurance for the latter than for the former. The one is poor in spirit, because he is humble; the other is poor, indeed, but not poor in spirit. Thus it is that, when Christ the Lord said: "Blessed are the poor," He added the clause, "in spirit." Therefore, I urge all of you who are poor and have heard those words not to seek to become rich.

Hear the words that were spoken, not by me, but by the Apostle. Hear what he has said: "And godliness with contentment is indeed great gain. For we brought nothing into this world, and certainly we can take nothing out. Having food and clothing, with that let us be content. For those who seek to become rich fall into temptation and snare." He did not say: Those who *are* rich. He said: Those who *seek to become* rich. So he said: "Those who seek to become rich fall into temptation and a snare and into many vain and harmful desires, which plunge men into destruction and perdition. For covetousness is the root of all evils; and some, pursuing it, have strayed from the faith and have involved themselves in many troubles" [I Timothy 6:6-10]. The name of riches is, as it were, sweet-sounding to the ear. But, "Many vain and harmful desires"—does that sound sweet? "Destruction and perdition"—does that sound sweet? To be "involved in many troubles"—does that sound sweet? Be not so misled by one false good that you will thereby cling to so many real evils. The holy Apostle was not addressing the rich when he used those words; he was addressing the poor, lest they should seek to become what they were not. So, let us see what words he used in his charge to those whom he found rich. We have told you what you ought to be told, and you who are poor have heard us. Now, if any one of you is rich, then listen to the selfsame holy Apostle.

Among the other admonitions which he gave in writing to his disciple Timothy, he included the following: "Charge the rich of this world." (The word of God had found them rich, for, if it had found them poor, he would have used the words we have already quoted.) Hence, he says: "Charge the rich of this world not to be proud and not to trust in the uncertainty of riches, but to trust in the living God, who provides all things in abundance for our enjoyment. Let them be rich in good works, let them give freely, let them share with others, let them provide for themselves a good foundation against the time to come, in order that they may lay hold on the true life" [I Timothy 6:17-19]. Let us now devote a little time to the consideration of those few words. First of all, he says: "Charge the rich not to be proud." For riches, more than anything else, engender pride. Of course, if the rich man is not proud, he has already spurned his riches and has fixed his hopes in God. On the other hand, if he is proud, he does not possess his riches; he is possessed by them. Such a man may be compared with the Devil. What, indeed, does he have, since he has not God?

The Apostle also admonished the rich "not to trust in the uncertainty of riches." A man's regard for his riches ought to be so moderated that he will bear in mind that what he has can perish. Let him lay hold, therefore, on that which he cannot lose. So, when the Apostle had told the rich "not to trust in the uncertainty of riches," he then told them "to trust in the living God." Yes, riches can be lost; and may they be lost in such a way that you will not be lost with them. The Psalm addresses the rich man, and mocks him if he puts his trust in riches. It says: "Although man walks according to the image of God" [The exact words of Psalm 38:7 are "But man passes as an image."—Ed.]. (Man has indeed been created to the image of God. Let him therefore acknowledge himself to be what he has been created. Let him lose what he himself has made, and let him remain what God has made him.) So the Psalm says: "Although man walks in the image of God, yet shall he be disquieted in vain." How shall he be disquieted in vain? "He is storing up treasures, and he knows not for whom he has gathered them." The living notice this with regard to the dead. They see that in many cases the children do not possess the property of their deceased parents, but that they either squander their inheritance by dissipation or lose it through chicanery. Worse still, others are contending for a man's possessions while the man himself is dying. In fact, many are murdered for the sake of their riches. All that they possessed in this life, they have left behind. And with what dejection of spirit have they made their exit hence to stand before Him whose commands from heaven they had not obeyed? As for you, therefore, let your true riches be God Himself, "who provides all things in abundance for our enjoyment." . . . .

"Blessed are the meek, for by inheritance they shall possess the land." The meek are those who do not resist the will of God. How do they practice meekness? When things are going well with them, they give praise to God; when things are going badly, they do not blaspheme Him. For their good works, they give glory to God; for their sins, they blame themselves. They shall inherit the land. What land shall they inherit, but the land of which the Psalmist says: "Thou art my hope, my portion in the land of the living"? [Psalms 141:6].

"Blessed are they who mourn, for they shall be comforted." My brethren, mourning is a sorrowful thing, for it is the sob of one who is sorry. Does anyone mourn, except for one who is dead? But, every sinner ought to mourn for himself, since there is nothing else so dead as a man in sin. Yet, how marvelous! If he mourns for himself, he comes to life again. Let him mourn through repentance, and he shall be comforted through forgiveness.

"Blessed are they who hunger and thirst for justice, for they shall be satisfied." This means that in this land of ours they are hungry for justice. Elsewhere, where no one will sin, they shall have such a fullness of justice as the holy angels enjoy. But, while we are hungry and thirsty for justice here, let us continue to say to God: "Thy will be done on earth, as it is in heaven" [Matthew 6:10].

"Blessed are the merciful, for they shall obtain mercy." Having said: "Blessed are they who hunger and thirst for justice, for they shall be satisfied," it was most timely for Him to add: "Blessed are the merciful, for God will show mercy to them." You are hungry and thirsty for justice, and, being hungry and thirsty, you are God's beggar. Now, while you stand as a beggar before the door of God, another man stands as a beggar before your door. Howsoever you deal with your beggar, in that same way will God deal with His.

"Blessed are the pure of heart, for they shall see God." If

any man has put into practice all that has been already said (in expounding the beatitudes already discussed), his heart is now being purified. Such a man has a pure heart, for he is not displaying a false friendship while harboring enmity in his heart. Where the eye of God beholds, there the hand of God bestows a crown. In your heart, let there be neither approval nor praise for anything which delights you there. If evil concupiscence occasions a pleasant sensation, let no consent be given; if it flames into passion, let God be implored against it that the heart may be inwardly aroused and cleansed, for it is within the heart that petition is made to God Himself. Be sure to make the chamber clean if you wish to invite God to enter it, and clean it from within, in order that God may vouchsafe to hear you. At times, the tongue is silent while the soul is sighing, for within the chamber of the heart supplication is being made to God. Let there be nothing in it to offend the eyes of God, nothing to displease Him. If you are earnestly striving to make your heart pure, call upon Him who will not disdain to make it a clean abode for Himself, and who will deign to abide with you. Can it be that you are afraid to provide hospitality within your home for such a mighty potentate? Are you perturbed about it? Are you like certain stolid or stingy men who are wont to be afraid that they will be constrained to furnish the hospitality of their homes to some important personages who may be passing by? Of course, there is nothing greater than God. But be not perturbed about the narrowness of your chamber, for He will enlarge its capacity. You have nothing good enough to set before Him? Receive Him, and He will provide the feast for you. Yes—and what is still more pleasant for your ears to hear—He will give you Himself to eat. He will be your nourishment, for He has said: "I am the bread that has come down from heaven" [John 6:41]. Such bread as this will always refresh and never fail. Hence: "Blessed are the pure of heart, for they shall see God."

"Blessed are the peacemakers, for they shall be called the children of God." Who are the peacemakers? They are those who make peace. Do you see two persons at odds with each other? Try to restore peace between them. To one of them, speak well of the other; to the latter, speak well of the former. After the manner of an angry man, one of them may have told you something bad about the other. Do not reveal it. Bury within your bosom any disparaging remarks you have heard from the man in anger. Let harmony be the constant aim of your advice. If you would be a peacemaker between two of your friends who are at odds, begin by making peace with yourself. You must first have peace within yourself, whereas you may now be striving and contending with yourself every day.

Take the case of the man who said: "The flesh lusts against the spirit, and the spirit against the flesh; for these are opposed to each other, so that you do not do what you would" [Galatians 5:17]. These are the words of the same holy Apostle who also says: "For according to the inner man, I am delighted with the law of God; but I see another law in my members, warring against the law of my mind and making me prisoner to the law of sin that is in my members" [Romans 7:22-23]. Did not this man have strife within himself? Now, if there is a daily strife within a man, and if it is occasioned by a constant praiseworthy effort to prevent his lower appetite from gaining ascendancy over his higher faculty, to prevent lust from overcoming the mind, to prevent concupiscence from prevailing over wisdom, then there is a righteous peace which you ought to attain within yourself. This kind of peace consists in keeping all your lower desires in subjection to that higher faculty which is within you and in which the image of God is. This faculty is called mind; it is also called intelligence. In this faculty, faith is enlivened, hope is strengthened, and charity is inflamed.

Now, do you wish to have your mind prepared and ready to control your carnal desires? Then, let the mind itself be obedient to a higher power. In that way, it will control your lower desires, and you will have peace with yourself—the peace which is genuine, well-established, and orderly in the highest degree. What is the orderly arrangement of this peace? There is no arrangement more orderly; the mind obeys God and commands the flesh. Of course, the flesh still has its infirmities, but this was not the case in paradise. It is through sin that the flesh has been reduced to this condition; because of sin, it makes the bond (of union with the soul) an occasion of discord against us. In order to bring our flesh into harmony with our soul, One who is without sin has come and has deigned to give us "the pledge of the Spirit" [II Corinthians 5:5]. "For whoever are led by the Spirit of God, they are the children of God" [Romans 8:14]. "Blessed are the peacemakers, for they shall be called the children of God." As yet we are not free from all this warfare, which saps our strength because of our weakness. For as long as we do not consent to our carnal desires, we are, as it were, engaged in battle against them. But there will be no contention whatever when death will have been swallowed up in victory. Hear how it is that there will be no contention then. This is what the Apostle says: "For this corruptible body must put on incorruption, and this mortal body must put on immortality. But when this mortal body puts on immortality, then shall come to pass the word that is written, 'Death is swallowed up in victory'" [I Corinthians 15:53-55]. The war is over; it is concluded in peace. Listen to the shout of the victors: "O death, where is thy contention? O death, where is thy sting?" The meaning of that cry of the victors is this: No enemy of any kind will be left; there will be no strife within, and no attack from without. Hence, "Blessed are the peacemakers, for they shall be called the children of God."

"Blessed are they who suffer persecution for justice's sake." The added clause, "for justice's sake," marks the difference between the martyr and the thief. Even the thief suffers persecution, but he suffers it for his evil deeds; he is not seeking to gain a crown, he is suffering a just penalty. It is the cause for which he suffers, and not the punishment inflicted, that makes a man a martyr.

First, he must willingly embrace the cause; then he can tranquilly suffer the punishment. There were three crosses in the same place when Christ endured His passion. Hanging on the middle cross, He had a thief hanging beside Him on the right-hand side and another on the left. If you consider merely the sufferings they were undergoing, you will find no cases more alike. Yet, one of the thieves gained paradise through the cross, for Christ, acting as judge while hanging on the middle cross, condemned the proud thief and came to the aid of the thief who was humble. The cross of Christ became Christ's tribunal. Since He had this power while under judgment, what will be His power when He comes to render judgment? To the thief who had confessed his sins, Christ said: "Amen I say to thee, this day thou shalt be with me in paradise" [Luke 23:43]. That thief was his own accuser. But of what did he accuse himself when he said: "Lord, remember me when thou comest into thy kingdom?" This is what he meant: I acknowledge the evil I have done; so, let me be crucified until Thou comest (into Thy kingdom). Then, because everyone that humbles himself shall be exalted [Matthew 23:12], Christ at once pronounced the sentence and granted forgiveness. He said: "This day thou shalt be with me in paradise."

But was not the Lord wholly buried in the tomb that day? At any rate, His body was to be in the tomb. Yes, and his soul was to be in hell—not that He was to be confined in hell, but that He was to release those who were confined there. Now, since His soul was to be in hell that very day and since His body was to be in the tomb, how could Christ say: "This day thou shalt be with me in paradise"? In the person of Christ is there nothing more than body and soul? Does it escape you that, "In the beginning was the Word, and the Word was with God, and the Word was God"? [John 1:1]. Does it escape you that Christ is "the power of God and the wisdom of God"? [I Corinthians 1:24]. And where is it that the wisdom of God is not? Of that wisdom, is it not written: "She reaches from end to end mightily, and orders all things sweetly"? [Wisdom 8:1]. Therefore, the Lord was speaking of the person of the Word when He said: "This day thou shalt be with me in paradise." That is to say: With regard to My soul, I descend into hell, but as regards My divinity, I depart not from paradise.

Dearly beloved, to the best of my ability I have expounded

all the beatitudes enunciated by Christ; yet I see that you are eager to hear more. Our love toward you has induced us to speak at length. Perhaps we could say more, but it is better that you should carefully ponder and profitably digest what has been said.

ST. PATRICK

(385—461)

"I am Patrick, a sinner," goes the opening sentence of St. Patrick's *Confession*, "most unlearned, the least of all the faithful, and utterly despised by many." His father was Calpurnius, a deacon, himself the son of Potitus, a priest; his mother was Concessa. Both were Romanized Celts, landowners, of good family, and of some local importance in Bannauem Taburnia in the southwest corner of the then Roman province of Britannia, where, probably, their son Magonus Sucatus Patricius was born around 385 A.D. Although Patrick's parents were Christian and his father of ecclesiastical status, neither his general upbringing nor his education were more than superficially religious. In his brief *Confession*, Patrick states that, "We turned away from God, and did not keep His Commandments and did not obey our priests, who used to remind us of our salvation." Frequently, too, he bewailed his inattention to his studies, a neglect that resulted in a lifelong rusticity of speech and writing.

When Patrick was sixteen a company of Irish raiders landed near his home, captured him, and sold him as a slave to a chieftain or Druid named Miliuc Maccu Boin, who lived near Slemish, in the present county of Antrim. There Patrick was a sheepherder. In enforced solitude he began to pray, to weep for his sins, and by voluntary resignation to the trials of his slavery to earn the rewards of faith and fortitude. In the woods and on the mountains he fasted and prayed constantly. One night six years after his capture he heard in his sleep: "It is well that you fast, soon you will go to your own country. See, your ship is ready." In confidence he left his master, walked two hundred miles to the shore where he found a ship preparing to take a cargo of Irish hounds to Gaul. From Gaul he returned to his old home, where again he was directed by a voice in a dream. The voice was that of a whole people. "We pray thee, holy youth, to come and again walk among us as before."

To prepare himself for his mission to Ireland Patrick went to Gaul where he resided in Auxerre under the patronage of St. Germanus. For fourteen years Patrick repaired his lack of learning while he lived the monastic life of work and prayer. Then, yielding to the requests of small groups of Christians in the southeast of Ireland, Pope Celestine decided to send bishops to the still predominantly pagan country. His first choice was Palladius, who died after establishing a few churches in Leinster. Then Patrick was consecrated bishop, probably about 431. Immediately he began the work of setting up sees in Ireland on a quasi-monastic pattern, reforming the clergy, and preaching to the pagans. "All Ireland believed him," wrote one commentator, "and he baptized almost all of it." With three assistant bishops from Gaul, he established his principal see at Tara, afterwards founded hundreds of monasteries composed chiefly of sons and daughters of chieftains, and hundreds of churches.

If we do not have accurate details about St. Patrick's conversion of Ireland, we do know in general what he left after him. Among a group of tribes which were not only divided but mutually hostile, he spread a single orthodox faith, a hierarchy of abbot-bishops, a reverence of learning, a social unity that respected native customs while it introduced the Roman culture. He modified the laws and customs and demonstrated a personal example of great sweetness mingled with singular audacity, an appetite for asceticism mellowed by lyric mysticism, and a tradition of missionary zeal that in succeeding centuries helped in the conversion of Scotland, England, and, after that, numerous areas of the European continent. In the dark ages of Europe the flame that St. Patrick lit on the hill of Slane in defiance of the barbarians helped to keep alive not only religion, but human culture as well. When he died, on March 17, 461, at Saul, in Ulster, after thirty years of ministry, he left Ireland perhaps the most Christian country in the

West. He was buried at Downpatrick, which remained a great center of pilgrimage until the English razed it in 1539.

A charming legend about St. Patrick has it that, at the beginning of his mission, he retired to the mountain called Croagh Patrick where, in imitation of Christ, he prayed and fasted forty days and forty nights. As he was groaning over his past sins and overwhelmed by the task that confronted him, God decided to lighten his burden by revealing to Patrick the good that he would accomplish. So He said to the souls of the saints yet unborn: "Go up, O ye saints, to the mountain that is higher than all the other mountains of the West, and bless the folk of Ireland." Then, taking the form of birds, the souls of the saints flew up to the holy mountain and so great was their number that they darkened the sky.

St. Patrick left us few writings. His *Confessions*, written in his old age, expresses his gratitude to God, a justification of his rule over the church in Ireland, and sorrow for his sins. His *Letter to the Soldiers of Coroticus* is a fierce denunciation of native Britons who had slaughtered a band of Patrick's Irish converts. There are fragments of letters and sayings and the *Lorica*, or *Breastplate*, whose text, dating from the Eighth or Ninth Century, conserves an oral version that goes back to Patrick. Certainly its vigor, its doctrinal emphasis, and its simplicity all accord very well with what we know of Patrick.

PATRICK'S HYMN

Patrick made this hymn. It was made in the time of Loegaire, son of Niall. [Loegaire, or Laogaire, was "high king" of all Ireland from 428 to 462, according to the Irish annals.] The cause of its composition, however, was to protect him and his monks against deadly enemies that lay in wait for the clerics. And this is a breast-plate of faith for the protection of body and soul against devils and men and vices. When anyone shall repeat it every day with diligent intentness on God, devils shall not dare to face him, it shall be a protection to him against every poison and envy, it shall be a defense to him against sudden death, it shall be a breast-plate to his soul after his death. Patrick sang this hymn when ambuscades were laid against his coming by Loegaire, that he might not go to Tara [in County Meath; residence of the "high kings"] to sow the faith. And then it appeared before those lying in ambush that they (Patrick and his monks) were wild deer, with a fawn (Benén) [Benén, or St. Benignus, one of Patrick's earliest disciples, joined the saint while still a boy and so is said to have appeared to the assassins as a fawn] following them. And its name is "Deer's Cry."

I arise today
    through a mighty strength, the invocation of the Trinity,
    through belief in the Threeness,
    through confession of the Oneness
    toward the Creator.

I arise today
    through the strength of Christ with His Baptism,
    through the strength of His Resurrection with His Ascension,
    through the strength of His descent for the Judgment of Doom.

I arise today
    through the strength of the love of Cherubim,
    in obedience of Angels,
    in the service of the Archangels,
    in hope of resurrection to meet with reward,
    in prayers of Patriarchs,
    in predictions of Prophets,
    in preachings of Apostles,
    in faiths of Confessors,
    in innocence of Holy Virgins,
    in deeds of righteous men.

I arise today
    through the strength of Heaven:
    light of Sun,

brilliance of Moon,
splendor of Fire,
speed of Lightning,
swiftness of Wind,
depth of Sea,
stability of Earth,
firmness of Rock.

I arise today
   through God's strength to pilot me:
God's might to uphold me,
God's wisdom to guide me,
God's eye to look before me,
God's ear to hear me,
God's word to speak for me,
God's hand to guard me,
God's way to lie before me,
God's shield to protect me,
God's host to secure me—
   against snares of devils,
   against temptations of vices,
   against inclinations of nature,
   against everyone who shall wish me ill,
   afar and anear,
   alone and in a crowd.

I summon today all these powers between me (and these
    evils)—
   against every cruel and merciless power that may op-
    pose my body and my soul,
   against incantations of false prophets,
   against black laws of heathenry,
   against false laws of heretics,
   against craft of idolatry,
   against spells of women and smiths [smiths were be-
    lieved to possess magical powers.—Ed.] and wizards,
   against every knowledge that endangers man's body and
    soul.

Christ to protect me today
    against poison, against burning,
    against drowning, against wounding,
    so that there may come abundance of reward.
Christ with me, Christ before me, Christ behind me,
Christ in me, Christ beneath me, Christ above me,
Christ on my right, Christ on my left,
Christ where I lie, Christ where I sit, Christ where I arise,
Christ in the heart of every man who thinks of me,
Christ in the mouth of every man who speaks of me,
Christ in every eye that sees me,
Christ in every ear that hears me.

I arise today
    through a mighty strength, the invocation of the Trinity,
    through belief in the Threeness,
    through confession of the Oneness
    toward the Creator.

Salvation is of the Lord.
Salvation is of the Lord.
Salvation is of Christ
May Thy salvation, O Lord, be ever with us.

ST. BENEDICT
OF NURSIA
(480—543)

ONE of the often-told tales of medieval literature is that of the last meeting of St. Benedict and his sister St. Scholastica. They dwelt near each other, in the mountains of central Italy, Benedict as abbot of the great monastery of Monte Cassino, Scholastica as abbess of a convent five miles to the south at Plombariola. They met once a year at a house between the monastery and the convent where they prayed together and exchanged their reflections on their spiritual life. At this last meeting Scholastica, aware of her coming death, desired to prolong the conversation, but Benedict was unwilling to pass the night outside the monastery for that would transgress the rule. Scholastica, in tears, prayed God to turn aside her brother's resolution. Almost immediately there broke out a violent mountain storm that prevented Benedict's return.

Benedict said to his sister: "God forgive you. What have you done?"

"I asked you a favor, and you refused it; I have asked Almighty God and He has granted it."

They spent the night in discourse about holy death. Three days later St. Scholastica died and Benedict, standing in contemplation on Monte Cassino, saw her soul rise to heaven in the shape of a dove.

The story was cherished because it seemed to signify the paradox of monastic life: its repression of self-indulgence and its indulgent expression of the ineluctably human core, the rigors of the code and the supervening charity of Divine Compassion; above all, the triumph of prayer over the resistance not only of evil but, as here, of good will itself. It was a kind of celestial joke that reassured those who may have been intimidated by monastic austerity that, at bottom, the essence of man's relation to God is that of the love and understanding of a child for a loving and understanding father. Scholastica triumphed, as St. Gregory the Great said, because hers was the greater love.

Yet it is misleading to suggest that St. Benedict was less alert than his sister to the necessary mutual love of God and man. His rule, a portion of which is reproduced below, is a flourishing tree in which asceticism, like the pruning fork, is not an end in itself but a means of cutting away the dead branches and the choking vines that, allowed to grow, would leave no room for love. For Benedict knew, by direct experience, that love of God was a virtue and virtue a strength that was acquired only through vigorous spiritual exercise.

Born in Nursia, in 480, of good family, he had little knowledge of the vices of the world until he went to Rome at about the age of fifteen to pursue his higher studies. Rome, still suffering from the systematic pillage of Gaieseric, King of the Vandals, was even more licentious than it had been in the times of Jerome and Augustine. Benedict fled from Rome, pursued by his old nurse Cyrilla, bent on offering her sincere but unwanted services. He evaded her and continued traveling until he met a monk, Romanus, who instructed him, brought him to a cave near Subiaco, and for three years furnished him with a share of his own meager meals. He might have remained a solitary hermit had not a pious priest been inspired to seek him out. Soon, too, wandering shepherds discovered him and the fame of his sanctity spread throughout the countryside. Sought out by the monks of Vicovara to replace their abbot, he refused to abide with them when he found their life irregular and their motives unpurified. He returned to Subiaco where he established his twelve monasteries. And thence, in 529, he went to Monte Cassino where he established another monastery. In a lifetime of continuous dedication to work, prayer, and study, St. Benedict fashioned a rule of life that in a most remarkable way promoted both authority and freedom, religion and culture, stability and growth.

In the centuries that followed immediately, Benedictine

ST. BENEDICT OF NURSIA

Monasticism expanded rapidly and became the chief instrument of reforming the church, of evangelizing the still-pagan countries of England and Germany, and of preserving in a barbarous age the culture of antiquity. The spiritual family of St. Benedict was to give the church twenty-four popes, two hundred cardinals, five thousand saints, and some fifteen thousand writers and scholars.

THE RULE
OF ST. BENEDICT

An abbot who is worthy to rule a monastery should always remember what he is called and realize in his actions the name of a superior. For he is believed to be representative of Christ in the monastery, and for that reason is called by a name of his, according to the words of the Apostle: "Ye have received the spirit of the adoption of sons, whereby we cry Abba, Father." Therefore the abbot ought not to teach, or ordain, or command anything which is against the law of the Lord; on the contrary, his commands and teaching should be infused into the minds of his disciples like the leaven of divine justice. Let the abbot remember always that at the dread Judgment of God there will be an examination of both these matters, of his teaching and of the obedience of his disciples. And let the abbot realize that the shepherd will have to answer for any lack of profit which the Father of the family may discover in his sheep. On the other hand, if the shepherd has spent all diligence on an unruly and disobedient flock and devoted his utmost care to the amending of its vicious ways, then he will be acquitted at the Judgment and may say to the Lord with the prophet: "I have not hid thy justice within my heart: I have declared thy truth and thy salvation; but they have despised and rejected me." And so at the last, for these sheep disobedient to his care, let death itself bring its penalty.

Therefore, when anyone has received the name of abbot, he ought to rule his disciples with a twofold teaching, displaying all goodness and holiness by deeds and by words, but by deeds rather than by words. To intelligent disciples let him expound the Lord's commandments in words; but to those of harder hearts and ruder minds let him show forth the divine precepts by his example. And whatever he has taught his disciples to be contrary to God's law, let him show by his example that it is not to be done, lest while preaching to others he should himself become a castaway, and lest God should some day say to him in his sin: "Why dost thou repeat my commandments by rote, and boast of my covenant with thee? For thou hast hated to amend thy life and hast cast my words behind thee." And again: "Thou sawest the speck of dust in thy brother's eye and didst not see the beam in thy own."

Let him not make any distinction of persons in the monastery. Let him not love one more than another, unless he find him better in good works and obedience. Let not a freeborn monk be put before one that was a slave, unless there be some other reasonable ground for it. But if the abbot, for just reason, think fit so to do, let him fix anyone's order as he will; otherwise let them keep their due places; because, whether slaves or freemen, we are all one in Christ, and have to serve alike in the army of the same Lord. "For there is no respect of persons with God." In this regard only are we distinguished in his sight, if we be found better than others in good works and humility. Therefore let the abbot show an equal love to all, and let the same discipline be imposed on all in accordance with their deserts.

For the abbot in his teaching ought always to observe the rule of the Apostle, wherein he says: "Reprove, persuade, rebuke." He must adapt himself to circumstances, now using severity and now persuasion, displaying the rigor of a master or the loving-kindness of a father. That is to say, that he must sternly rebuke the undisciplined and restless; but the obedient, meek, and patient, these he should exhort to advance in virtue. As for the negligent and rebellious, we warn him to reprimand and punish them. And let him not shut his eyes to the faults of offenders; but as soon as they begin to appear, let him as he can, cut them out by the roots, mindful of the fate of Heli, the priest of Silo. Those of gentle disposition and good understanding should be punished, for the first and second time, by verbal admonition; but bold, hard, proud, and disobedient characters should be checked at the very beginning of their ill-doing by the rod and corporal punishment, according to the text: The fool is not corrected with words; and again: "Beat thy son with the rod and thou shalt deliver his soul from death. . . ."

In all things, therefore, let all follow the Rule as master, nor let anyone rashly depart from it. Let no one in the monastery follow the will of his own heart; nor let anyone presume to contend impudently with his abbot, or to contend with him at all when outside the monastery. Should he presume to do so, let him, undergo the discipline of the Rule. The abbot himself, however, should do all things in the fear of God and observance of the Rule, knowing that he will certainly have to render an account of all his judgments to God, the most just Judge. But if the business to be done in the interests of the monastery be of lesser importance, let him use the advice of the seniors only. It is written: "Do all things with counsel, and thy deeds shall not bring thee repentance."

In the first place, to love the Lord God with all one's heart, all one's soul, and all one's strength.

Then, one's neighbor as oneself.

Then not to kill.

Not to commit adultery.

Not to steal.

Not to covet.

Not to bear false witness.

To honor all men.

Not to do to another what one would not have done to oneself.

To deny oneself, in order to follow Christ.

To chastise the body.

Not to seek soft living.

To love fasting.

To relieve the poor.

To clothe the naked.

To visit the sick.

To bury the dead.

To help the afflicted.

To console the sorrowing.

To avoid worldly conduct.

To prefer nothing to the love of Christ.

Not to yield to anger.

Not to nurse a grudge.

Not to hold guile in one's heart.

Not to make a feigned peace.

Not to forsake charity.

Not to swear, lest perchance one forswear oneself.

To utter truth from heart and mouth.

Not to render evil for evil.

To do no wrong to anyone, and to bear patiently wrongs done to oneself.

To love one's enemies.

Not to render cursing for cursing, but rather blessing.

To bear persecution for justice' sake.

Not to be proud.

Not a winebibber.

Not a glutton.

Not somnolent.

Not slothful.

Not a grumbler.

Not a detractor.

To put one's hope in God.

To attribute to God, and not to self, whatever good one sees in oneself.

But to recognize always that the evil is one's own doing, and to impute it to oneself.

To fear the Day of Judgment.

To dread hell.

To desire eternal life with all spiritual longing.

To keep death daily before one's eyes.

To keep constant guard over the actions of one's life.

To know for certain that God sees one everywhere.

When evil thoughts come into one's heart, to dash them at once on the rock of Christ and to manifest them to one's spiritual father.

To keep one's mouth from evil and depraved talk.

Not to love much speaking.

Not to speak vain words or such as move to laughter.

Not to love much or violent laughter.

To listen gladly to holy reading.

To apply oneself frequently to prayer.

Daily in one's prayer, with tears and sighs, to confess one's past sins to God.

To amend those sins for the future.

Not to fulfill the desires of the flesh.

To hate one's own will.

To obey in all things the commands of the abbot, even though he himself (which God forbid) should act otherwise: remembering the Lord's precept: "What they say, do ye; but what they do, do ye not."

Not to wish to be called holy before one is holy; but first to be holy, that one may more truly be called so.

To fulfill God's commandments daily in one's deeds.

To love chastity.

To hate no man.

Not to be jealous.

Not to give way to envy.

Not to love contention.

To shun vainglory.

To reverence the old.

To love the young.

To pray for one's enemies in the love of Christ.

To make peace with one's adversary before sundown.

And never to despair of God's mercy.

Behold these are the tools of the spiritual craft. If we employ them unceasingly day and night, and on the Day of Judgment render account of them, then we shall receive from the Lord in return that reward which he himself has promised: "Eye hath not seen nor ear heard, what God hath prepared for those that love him." Now the workshop, wherein we shall diligently execute all these tasks, is the enclosure of the monastery and stability in the community.

ST. BERNARD
OF CLAIRVAUX
(1090–1153)

THAT St. Bernard was one of the greatest figures
in the Twelfth Century we have no less an authority than
Dante, whose standards of holiness were exceptionally severe.
St. Bernard dominates the last three cantos of *The Divine
Comedy*. He first appears in *Paradiso*, Canto XXXI, line 60,
to take the place of Beatrice who has conducted Dante into
heaven. Thus Bernard becomes Dante's chief guide as befits
one who "even in this world's woe by contemplation tasted
of that peace, . . . that impassioned bliss of love." It is Bernard, the great mystic of the Middle Ages who bids Dante
to contemplate the beauty of the Virgin before he is vouchsafed a vision of the Divine Trinity. In Canto XXXII, St.
Bernard explains the mysteries of revelation and urges Dante
to join him in the prayer to the Virgin that opens Canto
XXXIII, the conclusion and the climax of one of the world's
great poems:

> Maiden and Mother, daughter of thine own Son,
>   Beyond all creatures lowly and lifted high,
>   Of the Eternal Design the cornerstone!
> Thou art she who did man's substance glorify
>   So that its own Maker did not eschew
>   Even to be made of its mortality.
> Within thy womb the Love was kindled new
>   By generation of those whose warmth supreme
>   This flower to bloom in peace eternal grew.
> Here thou to us art the full noonday beam
>   Of love revealed: below, to mortal sight,
>   Hope, that forever springs in living stream.

Lady, thou art so great and hast such might
  That whoso crave grace, nor to thee repair,
  Their longing even without wing seeketh flight.
Thy charity doth not only him up-bear
  Who prays, but in thy bounty's large excess
  Thou oftentimes dost even forerun the prayer.
In thee is pity, in thee is tenderness,
  In thee magnificence, in thee the sum
  Of all that in creation most can bless.
Now he that from the deepest pit hath come
  Of the universe, and seen, each after each,
  The spirits as they live and have their home,
He of thy grace so much power doth beseech
  That he be enabled to uplift even higher
  His eyes, and to the Final Goodness reach.
And I who never burned with more desire
  For my own vision than for his, persist
  In prayer to thee—my prayers go forth in choir,
May they not fail!—that thou disperse all mist
  Of his mortality with prayers of thine,
  Till joy be his of that supreme acquist.
Also I implore thee, Queen who can'st incline
  All to thy will, let his affections stand
  Whole and pure after vision so divine.
The throbbings of the heart do thou command!
  See, Beatrice with how many of the blest,
  To second this my prayer, lays hand to hand.

St. Bernard's role in *The Divine Comedy* is warranted by
history as well as by Dante's sense of dramatic propriety.
For Bernard was the supreme lover of God and his Virgin
Mother, and he gave voice to that love in language so personal, so persuasive, so heart-stirring that he earned for himself the title of "Mellifluous Doctor."

Born in the castle of Fontaines, near Dijon, son of Tesculin,
one of the great lords of Burgundy, and of Alice, daughter
of the Seigneur of Monbard, he was brought up by his pious

mother who had consecrated him to the service of God. Instead of the usual military education of the medieval nobility, Bernard received his training from the canons of the church at Chatillon sur Seine. There he remained until he was nineteen, when he returned to Fontaines. But shortly afterward, accompanied by his four brothers and thirty noblemen, he applied to the then Abbot of Citeaux, St. Stephen Harding, for acceptance into the austere, reforming order of the Cistercians.

So great was his progress that in 1115 he was sent to found a new monastery at Clairvaux, near Langres in Champagne. There his fasts and vigils were so intense that he became ill. After his recovery he began a public career forced upon him by the growth of his order, by the demands of his turbulent era, and by his fame as a preacher, a worker of miracles, and a mediator of disputes. As the Cistercian reform developed, thousands of Christians petitioned for entrance into the monasteries. Since from Clairvaux alone there derived sixty-eight abbeys, Bernard the Abbot had to travel constantly. He was active, too, in winning acceptance of the rightfully elected Pope Innocent II in 1130. Invited to the council of loyal French bishops, he quickly became their spokesman in the difficult task of persuading King Henry I of England and the Emperor Lothair to recognize the rights of the lawful pope. Pope Innocent kept him by his side in his travels during which he reconciled city after city to His Holiness' rule and kept thrusting aside invitations to become bishop or archbishop. His mediation was extended even to the political world, for he brought peace among rebels and the emperor, and the emperor and his chief rivals. Nor did he neglect the conversion of sinners, for his diplomatic missions gave him numerous opportunities to touch the hearts of many proud feudal lords. He averted pogroms of the Jews and mitigated the oppression of peasants.

Just as he was concerned for the unity of the visible church and the Empire, so too was he jealous of the purity of its doctrine. When Abelard and his disciples, particularly Arnold of Brescia, proposed certain errors, he first admonished them privately and then publicly attacked their heretical views, securing thereby the condemnation of their doctrines. Himself an indefatigable writer and preacher (he wrote some thirteen treatises, about 330 sermons, and over 500 letters), he set forth the doctrines of mystical theology with great learning, clarity, and poetic fervor.

When his spiritual son, Bernard of Pisa, the Cistercian Abbot of Tre Fontane in Rome, became Pope Eugenius III in 1145, Bernard's influence became even greater. He quickly wrote to Eugenius five essays on the duties and responsibilities of his high office and enlisted the support of the Cardinals in his behalf. In 1147 the pope commissioned him to preach the Second Crusade, which he did all over France and in the chief cities of Germany. In the same year he accompanied the Papal Legate on a mission to convert Albigensian heretics in Languedoc and Aquitaine, where he performed several notable public miracles. On one occasion he blessed bread and gave it to the people, promising them that the sick among them, upon eating it, would be cured. The Bishop of Chartres, who was standing nearby, added the caution, "That is, if they taste with a right faith, they shall be cured." "I say not so," added Bernard, "but assuredly they that taste shall be cured that you may know by this that we are sent by authority derived from God, and preach His truth."

Next to St. Benedict, St. Bernard is the chief founder of western monasticism as well as a Doctor of the Universal Church. His influence is keenly felt in the thriving Trappist monasteries in the United States. He died at his Abbey in 1153 after having foretold his own death.

ON THE LOVE OF GOD

Love is a natural affection, one of four. They are well-known; there is no need of mentioning them by name. It would therefore be just that what is natural should serve its own Author before all others. Hence the first commandment is called the greatest: "Thou shalt love The Lord thy God," etc. [Matthew

22:37]. But since nature is rather weak and feeble, it is impelled, by the necessity to preserve itself, to serve itself first. It is carnal love by which before all other things man loves himself for his own sake. For as yet he is aware only of himself. As it is written: "first . . . that which is natural [animale]; afterwards that which is spiritual" [I Corinthians 15:46]. Nor is it imposed by any command, but implanted in nature; for who "ever hated his own flesh" [Ephesians 5:29]. But truly if this love, as is its wont, begins to be too precipitate or too lavish and is not at all satisfied with the riverbed of necessity, overflowing rather widely it will be seen to invade the fields of pleasure. At once its overflowing is held in check by the commandment that opposes itself to it: "Thou shalt love thy neighbor as thyself" [Matthew 22:39]. It happens, very justly indeed, that the sharer in nature should not be excluded from a part in grace as well, especially in that grace which is inborn in nature itself. If a man finds it a burden, I do not say to relieve his brother in matters of necessity but to administer to his pleasures, let him restrain his own unless he wishes to be a transgressor. Let him be as indulgent as he likes to himself, so long as he is mindful to show the same degree of indulgence to his neighbor. The bridle of temperance is put upon you, O man, out of the law of life and discipline lest you should go after your concupiscences and perish; lest in the goods of nature you become a slave to your soul's enemy, that is, to lust. How much more justly and honorably do you give such things to your fellow-sharer, that is, your neighbor rather than to your enemy! And if indeed, according to the advice of the wise man, you turn away from your own pleasures [cf. Ecclesiastes 28:30], and according to the teaching of the Apostle, content with food and raiment [cf. I Timothy 6:8], you find it no burden to withhold your love for a little while "from carnal desires which war against the soul" [I Peter 2:11]; surely, I think, what you take away from your soul's enemy you will find no burden to bestow upon the sharer of your nature. Your love will then be both temperate and just if what is taken from your own pleasures is not denied to your brother's needs.

Thus carnal love is made neighborly when it is extended to the common good.

But if, while you are sharing what you have with your neighbor, even the necessities of life should, perchance, be lacking to you, what will you do? What indeed, unless with all confidence you should "ask of *Him* Who giveth to all men abundantly, and upbraideth not" [James 1:5]; "Who openest thy hand, and fillest with blessing every living creature" [Psalms 144:16]? There is no doubt, surely, that He who is not absent in the midst of plenty will gladly be present in the time of need. He says, at length: "seek ye first the kingdom of God and His justice, and all these things shall be added to you" [Luke 12:31]. He promises that He will of His own accord give whatever is necessary to him who restricts himself in superfluities and loves his neighbor. This surely, is to seek first the kingdom of God and to implore help against the tyranny of sin, that you prefer to bear the yoke of modesty and restraint rather than endure that sin should reign in your mortal body. But this, too, is part of the righteousness in question, not to possess the gift of nature independently of him whose common nature you share.

Nevertheless, in order that to love one's neighbor may be a matter of perfect justice, it is imperative that it be referred to God as its cause. Otherwise how can he love his neighbor without alloy who does not love him in God? He surely cannot love in God who does not love God. God must be loved first, in order that one's neighbor, too, may be loved in God. God, therefore, Who makes all else that is good, makes Himself to be loved. And He does it as follows. He Who fashioned nature, it is He Who shields it from harm as well. For it was so fashioned that it should have as a necessary Protector, Him whom it had as Maker, in order that what could not have come into being save through Him, should not be able to subsist at all without Him. And lest the creature might not know this about itself and consequently (which God forbid) in its pride arrogate to itself the benefits it had received from its Creator, the same Maker, in His high and salutary counsel wills that man should be harassed with troubles; so that when man has failed and God has come to his assistance, while man is being delivered by God, God, as is fitting, may be honored by man. For this is what He says: "call upon Me in the day of trouble: I will deliver thee, and thou shalt glorify Me" [Psalms 49:15]. Thus it comes to pass in this wise that animal and carnal man, who knew how to love no one except himself, may begin even for his own sake to love God too, because in Him beyond a shadow of doubt, as he has often learned from experience, he can do all things—those, to be sure, which it is good to be able to do—and without Him he can do nothing.

And so now he loves God, but still for his own sake, not for Himself. It is, however, a sort of prudence to know what you are able to do by yourself, what with God's help, and to preserve yourself guiltless for Him who keeps you unharmed. But if tribulation assails you again and again, and on this account there occurs an oft-repeated turning towards God; and as often, there follows deliverance obtained from God, is it not true that even though the breast were of steel or the heart of stone in one so many times rescued, it must of necessity be softened at the grace of the Rescuer so that man might love God not merely for his own sake but for God Himself.

From the occasion that arises from frequent needs it is necessary that man should frequently, in repeated petition, go to God Who in such petition is tasted, and it is by tasting that it is proved how sweet is the Lord [cf. Psalms 33:9]. Thus it happens that when once His sweetness has been tasted, it draws us to the pure love of God more than our need impels. Just as in the case of the Samaritans who said, speaking to the woman who had announced that the Lord was come: "We now believe, not for thy saying: for we ourselves have heard Him, and know that this is indeed the Savior of the world" [John 4:42], similarly I say, we too, following their example, speaking to our flesh may justly say: We now love God, not for your necessity; for we ourselves have tasted and know how sweet is the Lord. For it is true that a need of the flesh is a sort of speech, and the benefits which it knows from experience it proclaims in transports of joy. And so for one who feels thus, it will not now be hard to fulfill the commandment in regard to loving his neighbor. For he truly loves God and in this way also loves the things which are God's. He loves purely and it is no burden for the pure to be obedient to a command; rather, *purifying* his heart, as it is written, *in* the obedience of *charity* [I Peter 1:22]. He loves justly and gladly embraces a just command. This love is deservedly acceptable because it is unselfish. It is pure because it is paid neither by word nor tongue, but by deed and truth [I John 3:18]. It is just, since it is paid back as it is received. For he who loves thus undoubtedly loves in no other wise than he is loved; seeking, in his turn, not the things that are his own but the things that are Jesus Christ's [cf. Philippians 2:21], just as He sought the things that are ours, or rather ourselves, and not His own. It is thus He loves who says: "Give praise to the Lord, for He is good" [Psalms 117:1]. He who gives praise to the Lord not because He is good to him but because He is good, he truly loves God for God and not for his own sake. It is not thus that he loves of whom it is said: "he will praise thee when thou shalt do well to him" [Psalms 48:19]. This is the third degree of love by which God is now loved for His very self.

Happy is he who has deserved to attain as high as the fourth degree where a man does not love even himself except for the sake of God. "Thy justice, (O God) is as the mountains of God" [Psalms 35:7]. This love is a mountain and the high mountain of God. In truth, "a curdled mountain, a fat mountain" [Psalms 47:16]. "Who shall ascend into the mountain of the Lord" [Psalms 23:3]: "Who will give me wings like a dove, and I will fly and be at rest" [Psalms 54:7]? This place is in peace: and this abode in Sion [Psalms 65:3]. "Woe is me, that my sojourning is prolonged" [Psalms 119:5]! Flesh and blood, vessel of clay, when will your earthly dwelling place compass this? When will the mind experience such an affection as this so that inebriated with divine love, forgetful of self, and become in its own eyes like "a vessel that is destroyed" [Psalms 30:13], the whole of it may continue on to God and being joined to God, become one spirit with Him [cf. I Corinthians 6: 17], and say: "For Thee my flesh and my heart hath fainted away: thou art the God of my heart, and the God that is my portion forever" [Psalms 72:26]? Blessed and holy, I would say, is he to whom it has been given to experience such a thing in this mortal life at rare intervals or even once, and this suddenly and scarcely for the space of a single moment. In a certain manner to lose yourself as though you were not [cf. Galatians 2:20], and to be utterly unconscious of yourself and to be emptied of yourself and, as it were, brought to nothing, this pertains to heavenly conversation, not to human affection. And if indeed, anyone among mortals is suddenly from time to time (as has been said) even for the space of a moment admitted to this, straightway the wicked world grows envious, the evil of the day throws everything into confusion [cf. Matthew 6:34], the body of death becomes a burden, the necessity of the flesh causes unrest, the fainting away of corruption [cf. Psalms 72:26] offers no support, and what is more vehement than these, fraternal charity calls one back. Alas! he is forced to return to himself, to fall back upon his own, and in his wretchedness to cry out: "Lord, I suffer violence, answer Thou for me [Isaias 38:14]"; and this: "Unhappy man that I am, who shall deliver me from the body of this death" [Romans 7:24]?

Since however, Scripture says God "hath made all things for Himself" [Proverbs 16:4], it will certainly come to pass that the creature will at one time or other conform itself to its Author and be of one mind with Him. We ought therefore be transformed into this same disposition of soul, so that as God has willed that everything should be for Himself, so we too may deliberately desire neither ourselves nor any other thing to have been in the past, or to be in the future, unless it be equally for His sake, to wit, for His sole will, not for our own pleasure. A need allayed, or good fortune received will not delight us so much as that His will is seen perfectly fulfilled in us and by us; which, too, is what we daily ask in prayer when we say: "Thy will be done on earth as it is in heaven" [Matthew 6: 10]. O love, holy and chaste! O sweet and pleasing affection! O pure and undefiled intention of the will! the more surely undefiled and purer, as there is now mixed with it nothing of its own; so much the sweeter and more pleasing, as its every feeling is wholly divine. To be thus affected is to become deified. Just as a little drop of water mixed with a lot of wine seems entirely to lose its own identity, while it takes on the taste of wine and its color; just as iron, heated and glowing, looks very much like fire, having divested itself of its original and characteristic appearance; and just as air flooded with the light of the sun is transformed into the same splendor of light so that it appears not so much lighted up as to be light itself: so it will inevitably happen that in the saints every human affection will then, in some ineffable manner, melt away from self and be entirely transfused into the will of God. Otherwise how will God ". . . be all in all" [I Corinthians 15: 28], if in man there is left anything at all of man himself? The substance, indeed, will remain, but in another form, another glory, and another power. When will this be? Who will see this? Who will possess it? "When shall I come and appear before the face of God" [Psalms 41:3]? O Lord, my God, "My heart hath said to Thee: my face hath sought Thee: Thy face, O Lord, will I still seek" [Psalms 26:8]. Will I, do You think, see Your holy temple?

As for me, I think it will not have come to pass with perfect fulfillment that: "Thou shalt love the Lord thy God with thy whole heart, and with thy whole soul, and with thy whole strength" [Deuteronomy 6:5], until the heart itself is no longer compelled to think about the body, and the soul ceases to have to attend to quickening the body and to providing it with sense-life, and the body's strength freed from vexations is made strong in the power that is of God. For it is impossible wholly to concentrate all these upon God and to hold them fixed upon the Divine Countenance so long as it is necessary for them, absorbed and dissipated, to be subject to this frail and wretched body. And so, in a spiritual and immortal body [cf. Deuteronomy 6:5], in a body perfect, calm, and acceptable, and in all things subject to the spirit, let the soul hope to *apprehend* the fourth degree of love, or, rather, to be *apprehended* in it [cf. Philippians 3:12-13]; for, in truth, it is within the power of God to give it to whomsoever He wishes, not for human diligence to procure by its own efforts. Then, I say, she will easily come into the possession of the highest degree, when, without the slightest delay, as she hastens most eagerly into the joy of her Lord [cf. Matthew 25:21, 23], no allurement of the flesh will now retard her progress, no vexation destroy her peace. Do we think, however, that the holy martyrs actually attained to this grace, even in part, while still detained in those victorious bodies of theirs? Great power of love, certainly, had caught up their souls, within, and thus they had strength so to expose their bodies, without, and condemn their tortures. But, assuredly, the sense of most bitter pain could not but disturb their calm, although it had no power to destroy their peace.

But what of souls already separated from their bodies? We believe that they are completely immersed in that sea of eternal light and of eternity overflowing with light.

ON CHARITY

I remember well that a while ago I wrote a letter to the holy Carthusian brethren and in it, among other matters, I discussed these very grades of love. But, perchance, I there said other things though not foreign to the matter, on the subject of charity, and for this reason certain of those remarks I do not consider it useless to add to this discourse as well, especially since it is easier to transcribe what has already been written than to write something new. That, I say, is true and genuine charity and must be admitted as proceeding entirely from "a pure heart, a good conscience and a faith unfeigned" [I Timothy 1:5], by which we love the good of our neighbor as well as our own. For he who loves only what is his, or loves it more, stands convicted of loving good unchastely, since he loves for his own and not for His sake. And such a one cannot obey the prophet who says: "Give praise to the Lord, for He is good" [Psalms 117: 1]. He gives praise, to be sure, because, perhaps, He is good to him but not because He is good in Himself. Therefore let him understand that it is against him that that reproach was directed by the same prophet: "He will praise thee when thou shalt do well to Him" [Psalms 48:19]. There is a man who gives praise to the Lord because He is powerful, and there is a man who gives praise to Him because He is good to him, and, again, there is a man who gives praise to Him because He is simply good. The first is a servant and fears for himself; the second, a hireling, desires things for his own sake; the third, a son, gives honor to the Father. And so he who is afraid and he who desires things for his own sake, both act for themselves. Only the charity which is found in a son "seeketh not her own" [I Corinthians 13:5]. For this reason I think that it was of charity that it was said: "The law of the Lord is unspotted, converting souls" [Psalms 18:8]; for it is she [Charity] alone which is strong enough to *convert* a soul from love of self and of the world, and direct it to God. For, neither fear nor love of oneself converts the soul. At times they change an expression of countenance or an external act, but an affection, never. Even a servant, to be sure, sometimes does the work of God, but because he does not do it freely he is known still to remain in his hardness. Even the hireling does the work of God, but because he does not do it without recompense he is convicted of being carried along by his own cupidity. Truly, where there is something of one's own there is a distinction between one person and another; where there is a distinction between one person and another there is a corner [reserved for oneself]; and where, to be sure, there is a corner there without doubt there is dirt and moldiness. And so, may that very fear by which he is restrained be his law for the servant; may his cupidity by which he, too, is circumscribed be the hireling's law, since by it he "is tempted . . . being drawn away and allured" [James 1:14]. But neither one of these two can be unspotted, or can convert souls. But charity converts souls whom she makes free agents.

Again, I would call her unspotted because she has accustomed herself to retain for herself nothing of her own. Certainly, in the case of one who has nothing of his own, all that he has is assuredly God's, but what is God's cannot be unclean. Therefore the unspotted law of the Lord is charity, which seeks not what is useful for itself but what is of use to many. For it is called the law of the Lord either because He Himself lives by it or because no one possesses it except as a gift from Him. Nor let it seem absurd that I have said that even God lives by law, since I said by no other law save charity. What in that supreme and blessed Trinity preserves that supreme and unspeakable unity save charity? It is law, then, and charity the law of the Lord which in a certain way holds the Trinity together in unity and binds it "in the bond of peace" [Ephesians 4:3]. Let no one think, however, that I am here taking charity as a quality or as a sort of accident (otherwise I should be saying, which Heaven forbid, that there is in God something which is not God), but as that divine substance which, surely, is neither new nor unusual because John says: "God is charity" [I John 4:8]. Therefore charity is rightly called both God and the gift of God. And so charity gives charity, the substantial gives what is an accident. Where it means the Giver it is the name of substance, where it means the gift it is the name of a quality. This is the eternal law, the Creator and Ruler of the universe. Indeed, "all things" have been made by "her in measure, and number, and weight" [Wisdom 11:21], and nothing is left without a law, since even the very law of all [charity] is not without a law, not, however, any other than itself, by which, although it did not create itself, nevertheless it is its own rule.

THE MEMORARE

REMEMBER, O most gracious Virgin Mary, that never was it known that anyone who fled to thy protection, implored thy help, or sought thy intercession, was left unaided. Inspired with this confidence, I fly unto thee, O Virgin of virgins, my Mother! To thee I come; before thee I stand, sinful and sorrowful. O Mother of the Word Incarnate, despise not my petitions, but, in thy mercy, hear and answer me. Amen.

ST. FRANCIS
OF ASSISI
(1182—1226)

S T. Francis has kindled a great love throughout the world, not only among the million-and-a-half Franciscans who follow his rule and the more than half-a-billion Catholics who venerate him, but also among countless Protestants who have, so to speak, adopted him. So great is that love that those admirers have continued to make up stories about him, as if he were still alive, as if there were not enough factual stories and fact-inspired legends to fill a dozen books. Two of those stories help to explain why Francis is so beloved. One concerns the picture of the Virgin and Child with St. John the Baptist and St. Francis that hangs in the upper church at Assisi. In this painting by Giotto, the Virgin's finger is pointing at St. Francis. The story has it that this is her answer to the question: Which of these two more perfectly resembles her Son?

The second story is told of Blessed Peter Pettinaio, who knew him. "One night when Blessed Peter Pettinaio of the Third Order [of St. Francis] was praying in the Cathedral of Siena, he saw Our Lord Jesus Christ enter the church, followed by a great throng of saints. And each time Christ raised His foot, the form of His foot remained imprinted on the ground. And all the saints tried as hard as they could to place their feet in the traces of His footsteps, but none of them was able to do so perfectly. Then St. Francis came in and set his feet right in the footsteps of Jesus Christ."

These stories imply that St. Francis was the most Christlike of all the saints. Allowing for the extravagance of predilection, we must also admit that St. Francis' life, itself extravagant, gives ample support to the claims of his devotees. He was born at Assisi, a hill town of Umbria in central Italy, in 1182, the son of Pietro di Bernadone, a wealthy linen merchant, and his wife, Pica. A small, lively, graceful, and intelligent boy, he learned Latin at the school attached to the Church of San Giorgio. From his father he learned French, and he sang the troubadour songs of France so well that he came to be known as Francesco (the Frenchman) instead of as Giovanni (John), his baptismal name. From these songs and from the medieval epic poems Francis acquired an ambition to be a knight, loyal to his liege, courteous to all, compassionate to the poor, a defender of the weak.

But his knightly career was short-lived. In the battle between Assisi and its neighbor, Perugia, Francis was taken prisoner. In the Apulian wars, where he fought on the side of the pope, he became ill. Moreover, he came to realize that it was nobler to serve God in poverty than man in glory. Upon his return home, he sold his rich clothes and armor, clad himself in rags and gave himself up to solitary prayer. After a pilgrimage to St. Peter's tomb in Rome, he devoted himself to helping the poor. While praying before a crucifix in the dilapidated Church of San Damiano he heard Christ say, "Francis, go and repair My Church which, as you see, is falling into ruins." At first Francis took these words literally and began to rebuild the church with his own hands and to provide materials through the sale of his family possessions. His father, whose worldly ambitions for his son were hardly being fulfilled while Francis toiled in this manner, became impatient with the boy and brought him before the bishop's court, hoping the bishop would censor such unusual actions. On the day of the hearing, Francis appeared naked, as a sign of his complete rejection of all things material. The bishop was touched by such zeal and the self-debasement of the figure standing naked before him, and he reached out and draped his own cloak about the shoulders of the young man. The act, symbolic of his approval of Francis' activities, finally freed the saint to go on with his work. And Francis continued to serve the poor, and to rebuild the neighboring churches of San Damiano, San Pietro, and St. Mary of the

Angels until, on February 24, 1209, at the bidding of the Gospel injunction to go forth and preach Christ's Word to all nations, he began his apostolic career.

Shortly thereafter, with a few companions, he began to preach in the vicinity of Ancona. By 1210, his followers were sufficiently numerous to require a rule, which Francis composed and took to Rome for the approval of Pope Innocent III. Ordained a deacon (he shrank from the dignity of the priesthood), he returned to Assisi with his companions, now designated Friars Minor, or lesser brothers. They began to live in extreme poverty, first in a shed, then in the Portiuncula Chapel donated by the Benedictines after the community began to grow to amazing numbers. In 1212, St. Clare begged to become a Franciscan, whereupon St. Francis founded a second order, that of cloistered nuns. Dedicated to a missionary life, Francis sent his brothers abroad and himself journeyed to Dalmatia, France, and Spain. In all these countries his new order took root and flourished. In 1219, he joined the Crusaders at the siege of Damietta in Egypt, where, passing alone through the Moslem lines, he confronted the Sultan and attempted to convert him to Christianity. He failed to do this, but so impressed the Sultan that he received a safe-conduct to Palestine, where, with an intensity of devotion now grown to mystical heights, he retraced the steps of his Lord Christ.

Francis was ill when he returned from Palestine in 1221. But neither malaria, nor glaucoma, nor the ravages caused by constant vigils and fasts hurt him as much as the dissensions he found among his now multitudinous brethren. They had compromised, he felt, with his rule of literal poverty to dwell in convents and to vie in learning with the sons of St. Dominic, that vigorous saint whom Francis had met in Rome at the Lateran Council in 1215 and learned to love. He retired from active leadership of his order and devoted himself to prayer, to preaching, to the composition of the rule, and to the founding of the Third Order of St. Francis for laymen and laywomen. Rapt in the vision of God, he rose from grace to grace until, on the feast of the Exaltation of the True Cross, September 15, 1224, he received from God the crowning gift of the stigmata, that is, the five wounds of Christ were imprinted on his own body. His union with the suffering Christ was now complete. He lingered on earth for two years. On his deathbed he composed the joyous Canticle of Brother Sun. He died in his first church, the Portiuncula, on October 3, 1226. Only two years later he was canonized.

St. Francis' writings come to us through unimpeachable sources. *The Fioretti*, or *The Little Flowers of St. Francis*, were written in Italian by an unknown friar who translated selected passages of a larger work in Latin, called *The Actus*, itself a record of the oral testimony of St. Francis' numerous friends and companions. The passages below consist of representative Franciscan thinking. The prose selections convey his love of suffering and of poverty, the poems his spirit of joy and peace.

THE LITTLE FLOWERS
OF ST. FRANCIS

How St. Francis Taught Brother Leo That
Perfect Joy Is Only in the Cross

One winter day St. Francis was coming to St. Mary of the Angels from Perugia with Brother Leo, and the bitter cold made them suffer keenly. St. Francis called to Brother Leo, who was walking a bit ahead of him, and he said: "Brother Leo, even if the Friars Minor in every country give a great example of holiness and integrity and good edification, nevertheless write down and note carefully that perfect joy is not in that."

And when he had walked on a bit, St. Francis called him again, saying: "Brother Leo, even if a Friar Minor gives sight to the blind, heals the paralyzed, drives out devils, gives hearing back to the deaf, makes the lame walk, and restores speech to the dumb, and what is still more, brings back to life a man

107

who has been dead four days, write that perfect joy is not in that."

And going on a bit, St. Francis cried out again in a strong voice: "Brother Leo, if a Friar Minor knew all languages and all sciences and Scripture, if he also knew how to prophesy and to reveal not only the future but also the secrets of the consciences and minds of others, write down and note carefully that perfect joy is not in that."

And as they walked on, after a while St. Francis called again forcefully: "Brother Leo, Little Lamb of God, even if a Friar Minor could speak with the voice of an angel, and knew the courses of the stars and the powers of herbs, and knew all about the treasures in the earth, and if he knew the qualities of birds and fishes, animals, humans, roots, trees, rocks, and waters, write down and note carefully that true joy is not in that."

And going on a bit farther, St. Francis called again strongly: "Brother Leo, even if a Friar Minor could preach so well that he should convert all infidels to the faith of Christ, write that perfect joy is not there."

Now when he had been talking this way for a distance of two miles, Brother Leo in great amazement asked him: "Father, I beg you in God's name to tell me where perfect joy is."

And St. Francis replied: "When we come to St. Mary of the Angels, soaked by the rain and frozen by the cold, all soiled with mud and suffering from hunger, and we ring at the gate of the Place and the brother porter comes and says angrily: 'Who are you?' And we say: 'We are two of your brothers.' And he contradicts us, saying: 'You are not telling the truth. Rather you are two rascals who go around deceiving people and stealing what they give to the poor. Go away!' And he does not open for us, but makes us stand outside in the snow and rain, cold and hungry, until night falls—then if we endure all those insults and cruel rebuffs patiently, without being troubled and without complaining, and if we reflect humbly and charitably that that porter really knows us and that God makes him speak against us, oh, Brother Leo, write that perfect joy is there!

"And if we continue to knock, and the porter comes out in anger, and drives us away with curses and hard blows like bothersome scoundrels, saying: 'Get away from here, you dirty thieves—go to the hospital! Who do you think you are? You certainly won't eat or sleep here!'—and if we bear it patiently and take the insults with joy and love in our hearts, oh, Brother Leo, write that that is perfect joy!

"And if later, suffering intensely from hunger and the painful cold, with night falling, we still knock and call, and crying loudly beg them to open for us and let us come in for the love of God, and he grows still more angry and says: 'Those fellows are bold and shameless ruffians. I'll give them what they deserve!' And he comes out with a knotty club, and grasping us by the cowl throws us onto the ground, rolling us in the mud and snow, and beats us with that club so much that he covers our bodies with wounds—if we endure all those evils and insults and blows with joy and patience, reflecting that we must accept and bear the sufferings of the Blessed Christ patiently for love of Him, oh, Brother Leo, write: that is perfect joy!

"And now hear the conclusion, Brother Leo. Above all the graces and gifts of the Holy Spirit which Christ gives to His friends is that of conquering oneself and willingly enduring sufferings, insults, humiliations, and hardships for the love of Christ. For we cannot glory in all those other marvelous gifts of God, as they are not ours but God's, as the Apostle says: 'What have you that you have not received?'

"But we can glory in the cross of tribulations and afflictions, because that is ours, and so the Apostle says: 'I will not glory save in the Cross of Our Lord Jesus Christ!' "

To whom be honor and glory forever and ever. Amen.

About the Apparition
of the Seraph and the Imprinting of the
Holy Stigmata on St. Francis

Regarding the Third Consideration, that is, the apparition of the Seraph and the imprinting of the Stigmata, you should know that when the Feast of the Cross in September was approaching, Brother Leo went one night at the usual time to say matins with St. Francis.

And after he had called *"Domine, labia mea aperies"* from the end of the bridge, as he usually did and as he had been ordered to do by the Saint, St. Francis did not answer. Now Brother Leo did not go back, as St. Francis had instructed him, but with a good and holy intention he went across the bridge and quietly entered the Saint's cell. By the bright moonlight shining in through the door, he saw that he was not in the cell. Not finding him, he thought that he might be praying outside somewhere in the woods. So he came out and silently walked among the trees looking for him by the light of the moon.

And at last he heard St. Francis' voice speaking, and he went closer to hear what he was saying. In the moonlight he saw St. Francis on his knees, with this face lifted toward the sky and his hands held out to God, saying these words with fervor of spirit: "Who are You, my dearest God? And what am I, your vilest little worm and useless little servant?" And he repeated those words over and over, and he said nothing else.

Brother Leo marveled greatly at this, and he looked up and gazed at the sky. And while he was looking, he saw come down from the heights of Heaven a torch of flaming fire that was very beautiful and bright and pleasing to the eyes and that descended and rested on St. Francis' head. And he heard a voice come out of that flame and speak with St. Francis, and the Saint answered the speaker.

But seeing this and thinking himself unworthy to be so close to that holy spot where this marvelous apparition was taking place, and also fearing to offend St. Francis or to disturb him in his contemplation of such holy secrets, in case the Saint should hear him, he silently went back so that he could not hear what was said. And he stood at a distance, waiting to see the end.

And watching carefully, he saw St. Francis hold his hand

out to the flame three times. And finally, after a long time, he saw the flame return to Heaven.

So Brother Leo went away, feeling reassured and joyful, and began to return quietly to his cell, so that the Saint should not hear him.

But as he was confidently leaving, St. Francis heard the sound of his feet on some twigs and leaves, and he said: "Whoever you are, I command you, in the name of Our Lord Jesus Christ, to stay where you are. Don't move from that spot!"

So Brother Leo obediently stood where he was and waited. And later he told his companions he was so terrified then that he would have preferred that the earth should swallow him up than to wait for St. Francis who, he thought, was angry with him. For Brother Leo took the greatest care not to offend his Father, so that through his fault St. Francis should not deprive him of his companionship. In fact, he felt such faith and love for the Saint that he did not care at all to live without him. And therefore whenever any friars were speaking about the Saints, Brother Leo used to say: "My dear friends, all the Saints are great, but St. Francis is also among the great ones because of the miracles which God performs through him." And he used to speak more willingly about him than about the others. So it is no wonder that he was terrified at his voice.

When St. Francis came up to him, he asked: "Who are you?"

Brother Leo replied, trembling: "I am Brother Leo, Father."

And recognizing him, St. Francis said to him: "Why did you come here, Little Brother Lamb? Did I not tell you many times not to go around watching me? Tell me under holy obedience whether you saw or heard anything?"

Brother Leo answered: "Father, I heard you talking and praying and saying often with great wonder, 'Who are You, my dearest God? And what am I, your vilest little worm and useless little servant?' And then I saw a flame of fire come down from Heaven and speak with you, and you replied several times and held out your hand to it three times, but I don't know what you said."

Then Brother Leo knelt down before St. Francis and confessed the sin of disobedience which he had committed against his order, and with many tears he begged St. Francis to forgive him.

Then he asked very reverently: "Father, please explain to me the words I heard and also tell me those I did not hear."

Now St. Francis loved Brother Leo very much on account of his purity and meekness, and seeing that God had revealed to him or allowed the humble Brother to see some things, St. Francis consented to disclose and explain to him what he was asking.

And he said to him: "Little Brother Lamb of Jesus Christ, in those things which you saw and heard when I said those words, two lights were shown to my soul: one of the knowledge and understanding of the Creator, and the other of the knowledge of myself. When I said, 'Who are You, my dearest God?' then I was in a light of contemplation in which I saw the depths of the infinite goodness and wisdom and power of God. And when I said, 'What am I?' I was in a light of contemplation in which I saw the grievous depths of my vileness and misery, and therefore I said, 'Who are You, the Lord of infinite wisdom and good and mercy, that You deign to visit me, a most vile and abominable and contemptible worm?' And God was in that flame which you saw, and He spoke to me under the form of that flame, as He had formerly spoken to Moses.

"And among other things which He said to me then, He asked me to give Him three gifts. And I replied: 'My Lord, I am entirely Yours. You know that I have nothing but a habit and cord and breeches, and those three things are likewise Yours. So what can I offer or give to Your majesty? For Heaven and earth, fire and water, and everything in them are Yours, Lord. Who indeed has anything that is not Yours? Therefore when we offer You anything, we give You back what is Yours. So what can I offer to You, the Lord God,

King of Heaven and earth and all creation? For what do I have that is not Yours?"

"Then God said to me: 'Put your hand in your bosom and offer me whatever you find there.' I searched and I found there a coin of gold that was so large and bright and beautiful that I had never seen one like it in this world, and then I offered it to God.

"God said to me again: 'Make Me another offering as before.'

"But I said to God: 'Lord, I do not have and do not love and do not want anything but You, and for love of You I have despised gold and all things. So if anything more is found in my breast, You put it there, and I give it back to You, the Ruler of all things.'

"And I did this three times. And after making the third offering, I knelt down and blessed and thanked God, who had given me something to offer. And I was immediately made to understand that those three offerings symbolized the holy golden obedience, the very great poverty, and the very radiant chastity which by His grace God has granted me to observe so perfectly that my conscience reproaches me nothing.

"And just as I put my hand in my bosom and offered and gave those three coins back to God who had placed them there Himself, so God infused into my soul the power always to praise and magnify Him with my voice and heart for all the good things and all the graces which He has granted to me through His very holy goodness.

"So those are the words which you heard when you saw me raise and hold out my hand three times. But be careful, Little Brother Lamb, not to go watching me any more. Now return to your cell with the blessing of God. And take good care of me. For in a few days God will do such astounding and wonderful things on this mountain that the whole world will marvel at them. For He will do something new which He has never done to any other creature in this world."

And after saying those words, he had the Book of the Gospels brought to him, for God had placed in his mind the idea that what God wanted to do with him would be shown to him in opening the Book of the Gospels three times. So when the Book was brought, St. Francis gave himself to prayer. And when he had finished praying, he had Brother Leo open the Book of the Gospels three times in the name of the Holy Trinity. And it pleased Divine Providence that in those three openings the Passion of Christ always appeared before him. Thereby he was given to understand that as he had followed Christ in the acts of his life, so he had to follow Him and be conformed to Him in the afflictions and sufferings of the Passion before he left this world.

And from that time St. Francis began to taste and feel more abundantly the sweetness of divine contemplation and divine visitations.

Among others he had one which immediately preceded and prepared him for the imprinting of the Stigmata, in this way. The day before the Feast of the Cross in September, while St. Francis was praying secretly in his cell, an angel appeared to him and said on God's behalf: "I encourage you and urge you to prepare and dispose yourself humbly to receive with all patience what God wills to do in you."

St. Francis answered: "I am prepared to endure patiently whatever my Lord wants to do to me."

And after he said this, the angel departed.

The next day came, that is, the Feast of the Cross. And St. Francis, sometime before dawn, began to pray outside the entrance of his cell, turning his face toward the east. And he prayed in this way: "My Lord Jesus Christ, I pray You to grant me two graces before I die: the first is that during my life I may feel in my soul and in my body, as much as possible, that pain which You, dear Jesus, sustained in the hour of Your most bitter Passion. The second is that I may feel in my heart, as much as possible, that excessive love with which You, O Son of God, were inflamed in willingly enduring such suffering for us sinners."

And remaining for a long time in that prayer, he understood that God would grant it to him, and that it would soon be conceded to him to feel those things as much as is possible for a mere creature.

Having received this promise, St. Francis began to contemplate with intense devotion the Passion of Christ and His infinite charity. And the fervor of his devotion increased so much within him that he utterly transformed himself into Jesus through love and compassion. And while he was thus inflaming himself in this contemplation, on that same morning he saw coming down from Heaven a Seraph with six resplendent and flaming wings. As the Seraph, flying swiftly, came closer to St. Francis, so that he could perceive Him clearly, he noticed that He had the likeness of a Crucified Man, and His wings were so disposed that two wings extended above His head, two were spread out to fly, and the other two covered His entire body.

On seeing this, St. Francis was very much afraid, and at the same time he was filled with joy and grief and amazement. He felt intense joy from the friendly look of Christ, who appeared to him in a very familiar way and gazed at him very kindly. But on the other hand, seeing Him nailed to the Cross, he felt boundless grief and compassion. Next, he was greatly amazed at such an astounding and extraordinary vision, for he knew well that the affliction of suffering is not in accord with the immortality of the angelic Seraph. And while he was marveling thus, He who was appearing to him revealed to him that this vision was shown to him by Divine Providence in this particular form in order that he should understand that he was to be utterly transformed into the direct likeness of Christ Crucified, not by physical martyrdom, but by enkindling of the mind.

During this marvelous apparition, all of Mount Alverna seemed to be on fire with very bright flames, which shone in the night and illumined the various surrounding mountains and valleys more clearly than if the sun were shining over the earth.

The shepherds who were guarding their flocks in that area witnessed this. And they were gripped by intense fear when they saw the mountain aflame and so much light around it, as they later told the friars, declaring that the fiery light remained above Mount Alverna for an hour or more.

Likewise, because of the brightness of that light, which shone through the windows of the inns in the district, some muleteers who were going to Romagna got up, thinking that the sun had risen, and they saddled and loaded their animals. And while they were on their way, they saw that light cease and the real sun rise.

Now why those holy Stigmata were imprinted on St. Francis is not yet entirely clear. But as he himself told his companions, this great mystery is reserved for the future.

Brother Leo told this account to Brother James of Massa, and Brother James of Massa told it to Brother Ugolino di Monte Santa Maria, and Brother Ugolino, a good and trustworthy man, told it to me who am writing.

During that seraphic apparition, Christ, who appeared to St. Francis, spoke to him certain secret and profound things which the Saint was never willing to reveal to anyone while he was alive, but after his death he revealed them, as is recorded further on. And these were the words: "Do you know what I have done?" said Christ. "I have given you the Stigmata which are the emblems of My Passion, so that you may be My standard-bearer. And as I descended into Limbo on the day when I died and took from there by virtue of these Stigmata of Mine all the souls that I found there, so I grant to you that every year on the day of your death you may go to Purgatory and by virtue of your Stigmata you may take from there and lead to Paradise all the souls of your Three Orders, that is, the Friars Minor, the Sisters, and the Continent, and also others who have been very devoted to you, whom you may find there, so that you may be conformed to Me in death as you are in life."

Now when, after a long time and a secret conversation, this wonderful vision disappeared, it left a most intense ardor and flame of divine love in the heart of St. Francis, and it left a marvelous image and imprint of the Passion of Christ in his flesh. For soon there began to appear in the hands and feet of St. Francis the marks of nails such as he had just seen in the body of Jesus Crucified, who had appeared to him in the form of a Seraph. For his hands and feet seemed to be pierced through the center with nails, the heads of which were in the palms of his hands and in the upper part of his feet outside the flesh, and their points extended through the back of the hands and the soles of the feet so far that they seemed to be bent and beaten back in such a way that underneath their bent and beaten-back point—all of which stood out from the flesh —it would have been easy to put the finger of one's hand as through a ring. And the heads of the nails were round and black. Likewise in his right side appeared the wound of a blow from a spear, which was open, red, and bloody, and from which blood often issued from the holy breast of St. Francis and stained his habit and breeches.

Consequently his companions, before they knew it from him, nevertheless noticed that he did not uncover his hands or feet and that he could not put the soles of his feet on the ground. Later, finding that his habit and breeches were bloody when they washed them for him, they felt sure that he had the image and likeness of Christ Crucified clearly imprinted in his hands and in his feet and likewise in his side.

And although he tried hard to hide and conceal from them those glorious Stigmata, which had thus been clearly imprinted in the flesh, on the other hand he saw that he could scarcely hide them from his intimate companions. Nevertheless he feared to make public the secrets of God. So he was in an agony of doubt as to whether or not he should reveal the vision of the Seraph and the imprinting of the Stigmata.

Finally, urged on by his conscience, he called to himself some of his more intimate companions, and speaking in general terms, he explained his doubt to them without describing what had happened. And he asked for their advice.

Among those friars there was one called Illuminato who was very holy, and he was truly illumined by the grace of God. Realizing that St. Francis must have seen something marvelous, because he seemed almost stunned, he answered this way: "Brother Francis, you must know that God sometimes shows you His divine mysteries not only for yourself but also for the sake of others. So it would seem that you should rightly be afraid of being judged guilty of hiding your talent if you keep hidden something which God has shown you for the future good of many other persons."

Then St. Francis, being moved by these words—although at other times he used to say, "My secret to me"—with very great awe described the above-mentioned vision in detail, adding that Christ, who appeared to him, had said to him certain things which he would never tell anyone while he lived.

Now although those very holy wounds, inasmuch as they were imprinted on him by Christ, gave him very great joy in his heart, nevertheless they gave unbearable pain to his flesh and physical senses.

Consequently, being forced by necessity, he chose Brother Leo, who was simpler and purer than the others. And he revealed everything to him, and he let him see and touch those holy wounds. And St. Francis entrusted his wounds only to him to be touched and rebound with new bandages between those marvelous nails and the remaining flesh, to relieve the pain and absorb the blood which issued and flowed from the wounds. When he was ill, he let the bandages be changed often, even every day in the week, except from Thursday evening all through Friday until Saturday morning, because he did not want the pain of the Passion of Christ which he bore in his body to be eased at all by any man-made remedy or medicine during the time when our Savior Jesus Christ had for us been arrested and crucified, had died and been buried. For the love for Christ, on that day of the Crucifixion he wished to hang, truly crucified with Christ in the sufferings of the Cross.

Sometimes it happened that when Brother Leo was changing the bandage of the wound in the side, St. Francis, because of the pain which he felt from the loosening of the bloody bandage, would put his hand on Brother Leo's chest over his heart. And from the contact of those holy hands on which were imprinted the venerable Stigmata, Brother Leo would feel such sweetness of devotion in his heart that he nearly fainted and fell to the ground. He would begin to sob and be rapt in a life-giving trance.

Lastly, regarding this Third Consideration, when St. Francis had finished the fast of St. Michael the Archangel, by divine revelation he made ready to return to St. Mary of the Angels. So he called Brother Masseo and Brother Angelo, and after many holy words and instructions, he commended to them as strongly as he could that holy mountain, saying that he had to go back to St. Mary of the Angels with Brother Leo. And after this, he said good-by to them and blessed them in the name of Jesus Crucified. And granting their request, he held out to them his very holy hands adorned with those glorious Stigmata, to see and touch and kiss. And leaving them thus consoled, he departed and went down the holy mountain.

To the glory of Our Lord Jesus Christ. Amen.

RHAPSODY
TO LADY POVERTY

O Lord Jesus, show me the paths of Your dearly beloved Poverty. For I know that the Old Testament is the figure of the New, and to them of old You promised that "every place in which your foot will tread, shall be yours" [Deuteronomy 11:24]. To tread on anything is to despise it. Poverty treads on everything, so it is the queen of everything.

But, O dear Lord Jesus Christ, take pity on me and the Lady Poverty, for I am full of anxiety in my love for her and cannot calm myself away from her. You know it, my Lord, for You have enamored me of her. But there she is, sitting in sadness, rejected by everybody. She, "the sovereign Lady of the Nations, has become like a widow woman" [Lamentations 1:1], base and abject though she is Queen of the Virtues, and seated on a dunghill she complains that all her friends have spurned her and become her enemies, showing for so long a time now that they are unfaithful and not true spouses.

See, Lord Jesus, Poverty is to that extent the Queen of the Virtues that You left the haunts of the angels and came down on earth so You could betroth her to You in everlasting love and beget all the children of perfection in Poverty, and of it, and through it. And Poverty clung to You so faithfully that she began her service to You in the very womb of Your Mother, where You had of all living bodies the tiniest. Then too as You came forth from the womb, she welcomed You to the holy manger and the stable, and as You went about in the world, she kept You so despoiled of everything that she had You do without a place to rest Your head.

But also she went with You faithfully as Your most loyal companion when You undertook the battle for our redemption. In the very clash of Your suffering she was there as Your inseparable armor-bearer, and though the disciples deserted You and denied knowing You, she did not abandon You but stayed faithfully at Your side with all the company of her noble peers. Yes, when, because the cross was so high, Your very Mother—and such a Mother!—could not reach You (though she cherished You faithfully even then and remained in union with Your sufferings with anguished affection)—then, I say, Lady Poverty was there like a most welcome handmaiden with all her privations to enfold You more tightly than ever and to share the more feelingly in Your torment.

That is why she took no time to smoothen the cross or to provide it with even crude comfort. The very nails, it is believed, she did not supply in sufficient number for the wounds, nor sharpen them and polish them, but had only three coarse, rough, dull nails ready to add to Your cruel pain. And when You were tortured with that intense thirst, she was there with the concern of a faithful spouse to see that you could have not even a bit of water, but she had the heartless hangmen fix up a drink so bitter that You could rather taste of it than drink it. And so it was that You gave forth Your spirit in the tight embrace of this Your spouse.

Your faithful spouse, however, was not absent either at Your funeral rites, and permitted You to have nothing but what was borrowed for Your tomb, Your ointments and Your burial cloths. Neither was Your holy spouse missing at Your resurrection, since, as You rose gloriously in her embrace, You left all that was loaned and foreign behind You in the tomb. Finally, You took her to Heaven with You, leaving to the people of the world everything that is of the world. And then You consigned to Lady Poverty the seal of the Kingdom of Heaven, to mark with that seal the elect who desire to fare along the path of perfection.

Oh, who would not love this Your Lady Poverty above all others! I entreat You for the favor of being sealed with this privilege, I crave to be enriched with this treasure. I beg You, O Jesus most poor, that it may be the distinction of me and mine forevermore, for Your name's sake to possess nothing under heaven as our own and to be sustained as long as our poor flesh lives only with the closely restricted use of things given us by others.

THE CANTICLE
OF BROTHER SUN

Most High Almighty Good Lord,
Yours are the praises, the glory, the honor, and all blessings!
To You alone, Most High, do they belong,
And no man is worthy to mention You.

Be praised, my Lord, with all Your creatures,
Especially Sir Brother Sun,
By whom You give us the light of day!
And he is beautiful and radiant with great splendor.
Of You, Most High, he is a symbol!

Be praised, my Lord, for Sister Moon and the Stars!
In the sky You formed them bright and lovely and fair.

Be praised, my Lord, for Brother Wind
And for the Air and cloudy and clear and all Weather,
By which You give sustenance to Your creatures!

Be praised, my Lord, for Sister Water,
Who is very useful and humble and lovely and chaste!

121

ST. FRANCIS OF ASSISI

Be praised, my Lord, for Brother Fire,
By whom You give us light at night,
And he is beautiful and merry and mighty and strong!

Be praised, my Lord, for our Sister Mother Earth,
Who sustains and governs us,
And produces fruits with colorful flowers and leaves!

Be praised, my Lord, for those who forgive for love of You
And endure infirmities and tribulations.
Blessed are those who shall endure them in peace,
For by You, Most High, they will be crowned!

Be praised, my Lord, for our Sister Bodily Death,
From whom no living man can escape!
Woe to those who shall die in mortal sin!
Blessed are those whom she will find in Your most holy will,
For the Second Death will not harm them.

Praise and bless my Lord and thank Him
And serve Him with great humility!

ST. FRANCIS'
PEACE PRAYER

Lord, make me an instrument of Your peace.
where there is hatred, let me sow love;
where there is injury, pardon;
where there is doubt, faith;
where there is despair, hope;
where there is darkness, light;
and where there is sadness, joy.

O Divine Master, grant that I may not so much seek
to be consoled as to console,
to be understood as to understand,

to be loved as to love.
For it is in giving that we receive,
it is in pardoning that we are pardoned,
and it is in dying that we are born to eternal life.

ST. THOMAS AQUINAS
(1225–1274)

THE image of St. Thomas as the master theologian and philosopher of the medieval ages of Christendom is so massive that, for many readers, his private personality seems almost to have disappeared. Within the church his authority is often invoked; hence many regard him as an infallible thinking machine who was right so often that his occasional errors, inconsistencies, or ambiguities must be imputed to the incapacities of his readers. Outside the church, the word Thomism is widely regarded as a synonym for all Catholic thinking. But Thomas, despite his legend, was eminently human. His work, far from being the automatic meshing of facts and concepts, in anticipation of our electronic computers, was deeply personal, indeed at times impassioned. And, while he is commonly reputed to be the prince of theologians and philosophers, he would have been the last person on earth to equate his own explanations of the mysteries of the faith with the inexhaustible divine truth that flows through the veins of Christ's Mystical Body, His church. In fact, shortly before his death, after a moment of exalted communion with the Master he was soon to see face to face, he told his faithful companion Reginald, "What I have written seems but straw."

Thomas was born in 1225 at the Castle of Roccasecca, near Acquino, in southern Italy. His father, Landulph, Count of Acquino and Lord of Loretto and Belcastro, was a Lombard who was related to the Emperors Frederick I, Henry VI, and Frederick II. His mother, Theodora, was the daughter of the Count of Theate. Thomas had six elder brothers and two sisters. In 1230 Landulph placed Thomas in the Benedictine Abbey of Monte Cassino. He remained there until 1239, when the Emperor Frederick II, who was at war with the pope, expelled all the students. From Monte Cassino, Thomas was sent to the newly founded University of Naples, where he studied rhetoric under Peter Martin and philosophy under Peter of Hibernia. At Naples, too, he met the Dominicans, then in the spring of their remarkable work as preachers and teachers. In 1244 he became a Dominican—to the horror of his aristocratic family. They sought to dissuade him from this course by procuring for him the Abbey of Monte Cassino itself (with permission to retain his Dominican habit), or the Archbishopric of Naples together with the revenues from many abbeys. But Thomas remained firm in his intention to be, as well as to seem, a Dominican.

Confused and maddened by Thomas' strength of mind, his parents determined to remove him forcibly from his convent in Naples. Hearing of their intentions, Thomas obtained permission to be sent away. Hastily he attempted to reach Paris by way of Rome, but his two brothers, Landulph and Reynold, imperial officers in Tuscany, intercepted him. They returned him to the family castle at Roccasecca where he was to remain for seventeen months. At first, his mother and his sisters tried simply to persuade him to yield to the family wish that he take one of the important positions that could be obtained for him. When these efforts failed, his two hotheaded brothers took charge. They ripped off his Dominican habit, imprisoned him in the tower of the castle, threatened and excoriated; but in vain. Finally, they sent for a beautiful voluptuary and promised her a great deal of money if she could induce Thomas to commit sin, and thereby to weaken, if not ruin, his resolution. But when she came into his chamber, Thomas seized a brand from the fire and drove her away.

Eventually, one of his sisters helped Thomas to escape, by way of a rope dangling from his tower window. But he was not yet free of his family. His mother and brothers used their influence in Rome, so that Thomas had to appear before Pope Innocent IV. After questioning Thomas about his vocation, however, the pope approved his choice. Gratefully, Thomas went to Paris, henceforth to lead the life of the scholar. From 1245 to 1248 he studied under Albert the Great in Paris, and in Cologne. In 1252 he returned to Paris where he became a Master of Theology. Some years later, after a period of teaching, he received the coveted Licentiate. Despite his extreme modesty and his tendency to silence, Thomas was quickly recognized as a man of extraordinary learning and wisdom. Albert the Great, commenting on the remark that his tall, impassive student was a dumb ox, replied prophetically, "The roaring of that ox will be like the bellowing of a bull and fill the whole world."

Soon, indeed, Thomas' voice was filling the world by his teaching and preaching at the papal courts at Agnani, Orvieto, Rome, and Viterbo; by his writings on the intellectual problems that confronted his age in books like the *Summa Contra Gentiles* and the *Summa Theologica;* by his commentaries on the books of Aristotle and of others. Most of his writings were controversial, although modern readers, impressed by Thomas' lucidity, calmness, and charity to his opponents, hardly suspect it. By incorporating within Christian thought the science and philosophy of the ancients, he was striking against those who opposed reason to faith. By the same token, he engaged those who opposed faith to reason. As a result, he drew the fire of both camps, becoming the favorite target of the pure rationalists on the one hand, and the fideists on the other. For all his unruffled logic, Thomas frequently wrote with a sense of urgency. Thus, he concludes his criticism of the Siger of Brabant by the challenge: "Let him reply openly if he dare. He shall find me there confronting him, and not only my negligible self, but many another whose study is truth. We shall do battle with his errors or bring a cure to his ignorance."

St. Thomas' last years underlined the fact that he was not only a scholar, but a man on fire with the love of God. In 1272 he was sent to Naples to found a new house of studies. There, it is recorded, he was kneeling before a crucifix in the convent chapel when he heard a Voice say: "Thou has written well of Me, Thomas. What wouldst thou have as a reward?" Thomas answered: "Only Thyself, Lord." Shortly afterwards he was called by Pope Gregory X to attend the Ecumenical Council at

Lyons. He fell ill on the way and was forced to stop at the Cistercian Abbey at Fossanuova. When his companion, Brother Reginald, heard his last confession, he came from the room weeping. "I have heard the confession of a seven-year-old child," he said. Thomas was meditating on the Canticle of Canticles, the supreme love poem of the Old Testament, when he died in the presence of his companion and his Cistercian hosts.

The passages of St. Thomas' writing set forth below need a word of explanation for the modern reader. St. Thomas' normal mode of composition was that common to the medieval universities, namely the article. At that time the term *article* referred to a professor's summary, final report, or "determination," of a public disputation or debate that had taken place in a kind of seminar composed of students and teachers. The article had a definite five-part structure:

1. The careful statement of the question or issues under consideration.

2. The difficulties or objections raised by various authorities against the position the professor is about to take.

3. Arguments to the contrary, that is, arguments opposed to the difficulties raised in Part Two.

4. The reply, or the presentation of the professor's own arguments in support of his answer to the question or issues presented in Part One.

5. Answers to difficulties or objections, or the professor's response to the viewpoints in Part Two made in the light of his main arguments set forth in Part Four.

Clearly, the medieval article is more formal, condensed, and demanding than the contemporary article found in reviews and magazines of opinion. But if it requires more than usually careful reading, it also offers unusual rewards: the satisfaction of seeing all sides of the question discussed and of expanding the question by considering additional objections and arguments to the contrary. From the medieval article grew the judicial decision, the academic dissertation, and the formal debate.

THE ACT OF FAITH

THIRD ARTICLE
WHETHER IT IS NECESSARY FOR SALVATION TO BELIEVE ANYTHING ABOVE THE NATURAL REASON?

We proceed thus to the Third Article.

Objection 1. Faith does not seem to be necessary for salvation. For the salvation and perfection of a thing seem to be sufficiently ensured by its natural endowments. Now matters of faith surpass man's natural reason, since they are things unseen as stated above [reference to a preceding article of St. Thomas' argument]. Therefore to believe seems unnecessary for salvation.

Objection 2. Further, it is dangerous for man to assent to matters, wherein he cannot judge whether that which is proposed to him be true or false: "Doth not the ear discern words [Job 12:2]?" Now a man cannot form a judgment of this kind in matters of faith, since he cannot trace them back to first principles, by which all our judgments are guided. Therefore it is dangerous to believe in such matters. Therefore to believe is not necessary for salvation.

Objection 3. Further, man's salvation rests on God: "But the salvation of the just is from the Lord. Now the invisible things of God are clearly seen, being understood by the things that are made" [Psalms 36:39]; "His eternal power also and Divinity" [Romans 1:20], and that which is clearly seen by the understanding is not an object of belief. Therefore it is not necessary for man's salvation, that he should believe certain things.

On the contrary, it is written: "Without faith it is impossible to please God" [Hebrews 11:6].

I answer that wherever one nature is subordinate to another, we find that two things concur toward the perfection of the lower nature, one of these being in virtue of the proper motion of that nature, the other coming from the influence of the higher nature. Thus, water by its proper movement moves toward the center (of the earth), while according to the movement of the moon, water is subject to the tidal motion about that center. In like manner the planets have their proper movements from west to east, while in accordance with the movement of the first heaven, they have a movement from east to west. Now the created rational nature alone is immediately subordinate to God, since other creatures do not attain to universal ideas, but only to something particular, while they partake of the divine goodness either in being only, as inanimate things, or also in living, and in knowing individual things as plants and animals; whereas the rational nature, inasmuch as it apprehends the universal notion of good and being, is immediately related to the universal of principle being.

Consequently the perfection of the rational creature consists not only in what belongs to it in respect of its nature, but also in that which it acquires supernaturally by becoming a beneficiary of the divine goodness. Hence it was said above [reference to an earlier article of the argument] that man's ultimate happiness consists in a supernatural vision of God: to which vision man cannot attain unless he be taught by God: "Every one that hath heard of the Father and hath learned cometh to Me" [John 6:45]. Now man gets the benefit of this learning, not indeed all at once, but by little and little, according to the mode of his nature: and every one who learns thus must needs believe, in order that he may acquire science in a perfect degree; thus also Aristotle says that "it behooves a learner to believe."

Hence, in order that a man arrive at the perfect vision of heavenly happiness, he must first of all believe God, as a disciple believes the master who is teaching him.

Reply Objection 1. Since man's nature is dependent on a higher nature, natural knowledge does not suffice for its perfection, and some supernatural knowledge is necessary, as stated above.

Reply Objection 2. Just as man assents to first principles, by the natural light of his intellect, so does a virtuous man, by the habit of virtue, judge aright of things concerning that virtue; and in this way, by the light of faith which God bestows on him, a man assents to truths of faith and not to their contraries. Consequently there is no danger or condemnation to them that are in Christ Jesus, and whom He has enlightened by faith.

Reply Objection 3. In many respects faith perceives the invisible things of God in a higher way than natural reason does in proceeding to God from His creatures. Hence it is written: "Many things are shown to thee above the understanding of man" [Ecclesiasticus 3:25].

QUESTION:
OF THE EFFECTS OF LOVE

We now have to consider the effects of love: under which head there are six points of inquiry: (1) Whether union is an effect of love? (2) Whether mutual indwelling is an effect of love? (3) Whether ecstasy is an effect of love? (4) Whether zeal is an effect of love? (5) Whether love is a passion that is hurtful to the lover? (6) Whether love is cause of all that the lover does?

FIRST ARTICLE
WHETHER UNION IS AN EFFECT OF LOVE?

We proceed thus to the First Article.

Objection 1. It would seem that union is not an effect of love. For absence is incompatible with union. But love is compatible with absence; for the apostle says: "Be zealous for that which is good in a good thing always" (speaking of himself, according to a gloss), "and not only when I am present with you" [Galatians 4:18]. Therefore union is not an effect of love.

Objection 2. Further, every union is either according to essence—thus form is united to matter, accident to subject, and a part to the whole, or to another part in order to make up the whole: or according to likeness, in genus, species, or accident. But love does not cause union of essence; else love could not be between things essentially distinct. On the other hand, love does not cause union of likeness, but rather is caused by it, as stated above. Therefore union is not an effect of love.

Objection 3. Further, the sense in act is the sensible in act, and the intellect in act is the thing actually understood. But the lover in act is not the beloved in act. Therefore, union is the effect of knowledge rather than of love.

On the contrary, Dionysius says that every love is a *unitive force.*

I answer that the union of love and beloved is twofold. The first is real union; for instance, when the beloved is present with the lover. The second is union of affection: and this union must be considered in relation to the preceding apprehension; since movement of the appetite follows apprehension. Now love being twofold, viz. love of concupiscence, and love of friendship; each of these arises from a kind of apprehension of the oneness of the thing loved with the lover. For when we love a thing, by desiring it, we apprehend it as belonging to our well-being. In like manner when a man loves another with the love of friendship, he wills good to him, just as he wills good to himself: wherefore he apprehends him as his other self, in so far, to wit, as he wills good to him as to himself. Hence a friend is called a man's *other self,* and Augustine says: "Well did one say to his friend: Thou half of my soul."

The first of these unions is caused *effectively* by love; because love moves man to desire and seek the presence of the beloved, as of something suitable and belonging to him. The second union is caused *formally* by love; because love itself is this union or bond. In this sense Augustine says that "love is a vital principles uniting, or seeking to unite, two together, the lover, to wit, and the beloved." For in describing it as *uniting* he refers to the union of affection, without which there is no love: and in saying that *it seeks to unite,* he refers to real union.

Reply Objection 1. This argument is true of real union. That is necessary to pleasure as being its cause; desire implies the real absence of the beloved: but love remains whether the beloved be absent or present.

Reply Objection 2. Union has a threefold relation to love. There is a union which causes love; and this is substantial union, as regards the love with which one loves oneself; while as regards the love wherewith one loves other things, it is the union of likeness, as stated above. There is also a union which is essentially love itself. This union is according to a bond of affection, and is likened to substantial union, inasmuch as the lover stands to the object of his love, as to himself, if it be love of friendship; as to something belonging to himself, if it be love of concupiscence. Again there is a union, which is the effect of love. This is real union, which the lover seeks with the object of his love. Moreover this union is in keeping with the demands of love, for as Aristotle relates, "Aristophanes states that lovers would wish to be united both into one, but since this would result in either one or both being destroyed," they seek a suitable and becoming union—to live together, speak together, and be united in other like things.

Reply Objection 3. Knowledge is perfected by the thing known being united, through its likeness, to the knower. But the effect of love is that the thing itself which is loved, is, in a way, united to the lover, as stated above. Consequently the union caused by love is closer than that which is caused by knowledge.

SECOND ARTICLE
WHETHER MUTUAL INDWELLING
IS AN EFFECT OF LOVE?

We proceed thus to the Second Article.

Objection 1. It would seem that love does not cause mutual indwelling, so that the lover be in the beloved and vice versa. For that which is in another is contained in it. But the same cannot be container and contents. Therefore love cannot cause mutual indwelling, so that the lover be in the beloved and vice versa.

Objection 2. Further, nothing can penetrate within a whole,

except by means of a division of the whole. But it is the function of the reason, not of the appetite where love resides, to divide things that are really united. Therefore mutual indwelling is not an effect of love.

Objection 3. Further, if love involves the lover being in the beloved and vice versa, it follows that the beloved is united to the lover, in the same way as the lover is united to the beloved. But the union itself is love, as stated above [First Article]. Therefore it follows that the lover is always loved by the object of his love; which is evidently false. Therefore mutual indwelling is not an effect of love.

On the contrary, it is written: "He that abideth in charity abideth in God, and God in him" [John 4:16]. Now charity is the love of God. Therefore, for the same reason, every love makes the beloved to be in the lover, and vice versa.

I answer that this effect of mutual indwelling may be understood as referring both to the apprehensive and to the appetitive power. Because, as to the apprehensive power, the beloved is said to be in the lover, inasmuch as the beloved abides in the apprehension of the lover, "for that I have you in my heart"[Philippians 1:7]: while the lover is said to be in the beloved, according to apprehension, inasmuch as the lover is not satisfied with a superficial apprehension of the beloved, but strives to gain an intimate knowledge of everything pertaining to the beloved, so as to penetrate into his very soul. Thus it is written concerning the Holy Ghost, Who is God's love, that He "searcheth all things, yea the deep things of God" [I Corinthians 2:10].

As to the appetitive power, the object loved is said to be in the lover, inasmuch as it is in his affections, by a kind of complacency: causing him either to take pleasure in it, or in its good, when present; or, in the absence of the object loved, by his longing, to tend toward it with the love of concupiscence, or toward the good that he wills to the beloved, with the love of friendship: not indeed from any extrinsic cause (as when we desire one thing on account of another, or wish good to another on account of something else), but because the complacency in the beloved is rooted in the lover's heart. For this reason we speak of love as being *intimate;* and of *the bowels of charity.* On the other hand, the lover is in the beloved, by the love of concupiscence and by the love of friendship, but not in the same way. For the love of concupiscence is not satisfied with any external or superficial possession or enjoyment of the beloved; but seeks to possess the beloved perfectly, by penetrating into his heart, as it were. Whereas, in the love of friendship, the lover is in the beloved, inasmuch as he reckons what is good or evil to his friend, as being so to himself; and his friend's will as his own, so that it seems as though he felt the good or suffered the evil in the person of his friend. Hence it is proper to friends "to desire the same things, and to grieve and rejoice at the same," as Aristotle says. Consequently in so far as he reckons what affects his friend as affecting himself, the lover seems to be in the beloved, as though he were become one with him: but in so far as, on the other hand, he wills and acts for his friend's sake as for his own sake, looking on his friend as identified with himself, thus the beloved is in the lover.

In yet a third way, mutual indwelling in the love of friendship can be understood in regard to reciprocal love: inasmuch as friends return love for love, and both desire and do good things for one another.

Reply Objection 1. The beloved is contained in the lover, by being impressed on his heart and thus becoming the object of his complacency. On the other hand, the lover is contained in the beloved, inasmuch as the lover penetrates, so to speak, into the beloved. For nothing hinders a thing from being both container and contents in different ways: just as a genus is contained in its species, and vice versa.

Reply Objection 2. The apprehension of the reason precedes the movement of love. Consequently, just as the reason divides, so does the movement of love penetrate into the beloved, as was explained above.

Reply Objection 3. This argument is true to the third kind of mutual indwelling, which is not to be found in every kind of love.

THIRD ARTICLE
WHETHER ECSTASY IS AN
EFFECT OF LOVE?

We proceed thus to the Third Article.

Objection 1. It would seem that ecstasy is not an effect of love. For ecstasy seems to imply loss of reason. But loves does not always result in loss of reason: for lovers are masters of themselves at times. Therefore love does not cause ecstasy.

Objection 2. Further, the lover desires the beloved to be united to him. Therefore he draws the beloved to himself, rather than betakes himself into the beloved, going forth out from himself as it were.

Objection 3. Further, love unites the beloved to the lover, as stated above [First Article]. If, therefore, the lover goes out from himself, in order to betake himself into the beloved, it follows that the lover always loves the beloved more than himself: which is evidently false. Therefore ecstasy is not an effect of love.

On the contrary, Dionysius says that "the divine love produces ecstasy," and that "God Himself suffered ecstasy through love." Since, therefore, according to the same author, every love is a participated likeness of the divine love, it seems that every love causes ecstasy.

I answer that to suffer ecstasy means to be placed outside oneself. This happens as to the apprehensive power and as to the appetitive power. As to the apprehensive power, a man is said to be placed outside himself, when he is placed outside the knowledge proper to him. This may be due to his being raised to a higher knowledge; thus, a man is said to suffer ecstasy, inasmuch as he is placed outside the connatural apprehension of his sense and reason, when he is raised up so as to comprehend things that surpass sense and reason: or it may be due to his being cast down into a state of debasement; thus a man may be said to suffer ecstasy, when he is overcome by violent passion or madness. As to the appetitive power, a man is said to suffer ecstasy, when that power is borne toward something else, so that it goes forth out from itself, as it were.

135

The first of these ecstasies is caused by love dispositively, in so far, namely, as love makes the lover dwell on the beloved, as stated above, and to dwell intently on one thing draws the mind from other things. The second ecstasy is caused by love directly; by love of friendship, simply; by love of concupiscence, not simply but in a restricted sense. Because in love of concupiscence, the lover is carried out of himself, in a certain sense; in so far, namely, as not being satisfied with enjoying the good that he has, he seeks to enjoy something outside himself. But since he seeks to have this extrinsic good for himself, he does not go out from himself simply, and this movement remains finally within him. On the other hand, in the love of friendship, a man's affection goes out from itself simply; because he wishes and does good to his friend, by caring and providing for him, for his sake.

Reply Objection 1. This argument is true of the first kind of ecstasy.

Reply Objection 2. This argument applies to love of concupiscence, which, as stated above, does not cause ecstasy simply.

Reply Objection 3. He who loves goes out from himself, in so far as he wills the good of his friend and works for it. Yet he does not will the good of his friend more than his own good: and so it does not follow that he loves another more than himself.

THE PANGE LINGUA

This hymn appears in the Holy Thursday Mass.

> Sing, my tongue! Acclaim Christ present,
> Veiled within this sacred Sign:
> Precious blood and risen body,
> Under forms of bread and wine:
> Blood once shed for man's redemption
> By his king, of David's line.

Heaven's promised Gift to mankind,
Born to us of one most pure,
Spends His earthly days among us
Plants the seed of faith secure,
Ends His mission, leaves a symbol
Of the death He will endure:

Dining with His twelve apostles
On the night before He died,
Taking for the Paschal supper
Foods the Law had specified,
Lo, He sets new bread before them,
Handing each—Christ crucified!

Word-made-flesh makes bread His body,
Consecrates it by His word.
Wine becomes the blood of Jesus:
He it is whose voice is heard.
Minds in doubt need faith's assurance:
God who spoke can not have erred.

Bowing low, then, offer homage
To a Sacrament so great!
Here is new and perfect worship;
All the old must terminate.
Senses cannot grasp this marvel:
Faith must serve to compensate.

Praise and glorify the Father,
Bless His Son's life-giving Name,
Singing Their eternal Godhead,
Power, majesty and fame,
Offering Their Holy Spirit
Equal worship and acclaim.

Amen.

THE LAUDA SION

This sequence appears in the Mass for the Feast of Corpus Christi.

> Sion, lift thy voice and sing;
> Praise thy Savior and thy King;
> Praise with hymns thy Shepherd true.
> Strive thy best to praise Him well,
> Yet doth He all praise excel;
> None can ever reach His due.

> See today before us laid
> The living and life-giving Bread,
> Theme for praise and joy profound.
> The same which at the sacred board
> Was by our incarnate Lord,
> Giv'n to His apostles round.

> Let the praise be loud and high;
> Sweet and tranquil be the joy
> Felt today in every breast
> On this festival divine,
> Which records the origin
> Of the glorious Eucharist.

> On this table of the King,
> Our new Paschal offering
> Brings to end the olden rite.
> Here for empty shadows fled,
> Is reality instead;
> Here, instead of darkness, light.

> His own act, at supper seated,
> Christ ordained to be repeated,
> In His memory divine;
> Wherefore now, with adoration,

We the Host of our salvation
Consecrate from bread and wine.

Hear what holy Church maintaineth,
That the bread its substance changeth
Into flesh, the wine to blood.
Doth it pass thy comprehending?
Faith, the law of sight transcending,
Leaps to things not understood.

Here, beneath these signs are hidden
Priceless things, to sense forbidden;
Signs, not things, are all we see
Flesh from bread, and blood from wine,
Yet is Christ in either sign
All entire, confessed to be.

They too who of Him partake,
Sever not, nor rend, nor break,
But entire their Lord receive.
Whether one or thousands eat,
All receive the selfsame meat,
Nor the less for others leave.

Both the wicked and the good
Eat of this celestial food;
But with ends how opposite!
Here 'tis life, and there 'tis death,
The same, yet issuing to each,
In a difference infinite.

Nor a single doubt retain,
When they break the host in twain,
But that in each part remain,
What was in the whole before.

Since the simple sign alone
Suffers change in state or form,

The signified remaining one
And the same for evermore.

Lo! upon the altar lies,
Hidden deep from human eyes,
Bread of angels from the skies,
Made the food of mortal man:

Children's meat, to dogs denied:
In old types foresignified:
In the manna heav'n-supplied,
Isaac, and the Paschal Lamb.

Jesu! Shepherd of the sheep!
Thou Thy flock in safety keep.
Living Bread! thy life supply;
Strengthen us, or else we die;
Fill us with celestial grace:

Thou, who feedest us below!
Source of all we have or know.
Grant that with Thy saints above,
Sitting at the feast of love,
We may see Thee face to face.

Amen, Alleluia.

THE TEACHER

ARTICLE 1
THE QUESTION TREATS OF THE TEACHER,
AND IN THE FIRST ARTICLE WE ASK:
CAN A MAN OR ONLY GOD TEACH AND
BE CALLED TEACHER?

Difficulties:

It seems that only God teaches and should be called a teacher, for

1. In St. Matthew [23:8] we read: "One is your master"; and just before that: "Be not you called Rabbi." On this passage the *Gloss* comments: "Lest you give divine honor to men, or usurp for yourselves what belongs to God." Therefore, it seems that only God is a teacher, or teaches.

2. If a man teaches, he does so only through certain signs. For, even if one seems to teach by means of things, as, when asked what walking is, he walks, this is not sufficient to teach the one who asks, unless some sign be added, as Augustine proves. He does this by showing that there are many factors involved in the same action; hence, one will not know to what factor the demonstration was due, whether to the substance of the action or to some accident of it. Furthermore, one cannot come to a knowledge of things through a sign, for the knowledge of things is more excellent than the knowledge of signs, since the knowledge of signs is directed to knowledge of things as a means to an end. But the effect is not more excellent than its cause. Therefore, no one can impart knowledge of anything to another, and so cannot teach him.

3. If signs of certain things are proposed to someone by a man, the one to whom they are proposed either knows the things which the signs represent or he does not. If he knows the things, he is not taught them. But if he does not know them, he cannot know the meanings of the signs, since he does not know the things. For a man who does not know what a stone is cannot know what the word *stone* means. But if he does not know the meaning of the terms, he cannot learn anything through the signs. Therefore, if a man does nothing else to teach than propose signs, it seems that one man cannot be taught by another.

4. To teach is nothing else than to cause knowledge in another in some way. But our understanding is the subject of knowledge. Now, sensible signs, by which alone, it would seem, man can be taught, do not reach the intellective part, but affect the senses only. Therefore, man cannot be taught by a man.

5. If the knowledge is caused by one person in another, the learner either had it already or he did not. If he did not have

it already and it was caused in him by another, then one man creates knowledge in another, which is impossible. However, if he had it already, it was present either in complete actuality, and thus it cannot be caused, for what already exists does not comes into being, or it was present seminally. But such seminal principles cannot be actualized by any created power, but are implanted in nature by God alone, as Augustine says. So, it remains true that one man can in no way teach another.

6. Knowledge is an accident. But an accident does not change the subject in which it inheres. Therefore, since teaching seems to be nothing else but the transfer of knowledge from teacher to pupil, one cannot teach another.

7. The *Gloss*, on Romans [10:17], "Faith then cometh by hearing," says: "Although God teaches man interiorly, the preacher proclaims it exteriorly." But knowledge is caused interiorly in the mind, not exteriorly in the senses. Therefore, man is taught only by God, not by another man.

8. Augustine says: "God alone, who teaches truth on earth, holds the teacher's chair in heaven, but to this chair another man has the relation which a farmer has to a tree." But the farmer does not make the tree; he cultivates it. And by the same token no man can be said to teach knowledge, but only prepare the mind for it.

9. If man is a real teacher, he must teach the truth. But whoever teaches the truth enlightens the mind, for truth is the light of the mind. If, therefore, man does teach, he enlightens the mind. But this is false, for in the Gospel according to St. John [1:19] we see that it is God who "enlighteneth every man that cometh into this world." Therefore, one man cannot really teach another.

10. If one man teaches another, he must make a potential knower into an actual knower. Therefore, his knowledge must be raised from potency to act. But what is raised from potency to actuality must be changed. Therefore, knowledge or wisdom will be changed. However, this is contrary to Augustine, who says: "In coming to a man, wisdom is not itself changed, but changes the man."

11. Knowledge is nothing else but the representation of

things in the soul, since knowledge is called the assimilation of the knower to the thing known. But one man cannot imprint the likeness of things in the soul of another. For, thus, he would work interiorly in that man, which God alone can do. Therefore, one man cannot teach another.

12. Boethius says that teaching does no more than stimulate the mind to know. But he who stimulates the understanding to know does not make it known, just as one who incites someone to see with the eyes of the body does not make him see. Therefore, one man does not make another know. And so it cannot properly be said that he teaches him.

13. There is no scientific knowledge without certitude. Otherwise, it is not scientific knowledge but opinion or belief, as Augustine says. But one man cannot produce certitude in another by means of the sensible signs which he proposes. For that which is in the sense faculty is less direct than that which is in the understanding, while certainty is always effected by the more direct. Therefore, one man cannot teach another.

14. The intelligible light and a species are all that are needed for knowledge. But neither of these can be caused in one man by another. For it would be necessary for a man to create something, since it seems that simple forms like these can be produced only by creation. Therefore, one man cannot cause knowledge in another and, so, cannot teach.

15. As Augustine says, nothing except God alone can give the mind of man its form. But knowledge is a form of the mind. Therefore, only God can cause knowledge in the soul.

16. Just as guilt is in the mind, so is ignorance. But only God cleanses the mind of guilt, according to Isaias [43:25]: "I am he that blots out thy iniquities for my own sake." Therefore, God alone cleanses the mind of ignorance. And, so, only God teaches.

17. Since science is certain knowledge, one receives science from him whose words give him certainty. However, hearing a man speak does not give anyone certainty. Otherwise, anything that one person says to another would of necessity be clearly certain. Now, one reaches certitude only when he hears the truth speaking within him. And to be certain, he

143

takes counsel with this interior voice even about those things which he hears from men. Therefore, not man but the truth speaking within, which is God, teaches.

18. No one learns through the words of another those things, which, if asked, he would have answered, even before the other spoke. But even before the teacher speaks, the pupil, upon being questioned, would answer about the matters which the teacher proposes. For he would be taught by the words of the teacher only in so far as he knew that matters were such as the teacher claimed. Therefore, one man is not taught by the words of another.

To the Contrary:

1'. In the second Epistle to Timothy [1:11] we read: "Wherein I am appointed a preacher . . . and teacher of the gentiles." Therefore, man can be a teacher and can be called one.

2'. In the second Epistle to Timothy [3:14] it is said: "But continue thou in those things which thou has learned, and which have been committed to thee." Of this the *Gloss* says: "From me as from a true teacher." We conclude as before.

3'. In one place in Matthew [23:8, 9] we find: "One is your Father" and "One is your master." But the fact that God is our Father does not make it impossible for man truly to be called father. Likewise, the fact that God is our teacher does not make it impossible for man truly to be called teacher.

4'. The *Gloss* on Romans [10:15], "How beautiful over the mountains . . . ," reads: "They are the feet who enlighten the Church." Now, it is speaking about the Apostles. Since, then, to enlighten is the act of a teacher, it seems that men are competent to teach.

5'. As is said in the *Meteorology*, each thing is perfect when it can generate things like itself. But scientific knowledge is a kind of perfect knowledge. Therefore, a man who has scientific knowledge can teach another.

6'. Augustine says that just as the earth was watered by a fountain before the coming of sin, and after its coming needed rain from the clouds above, so also the human mind, which is represented by the earth, was made fruitful by the fountain of truth before the coming of sin, but after its coming it needs the teaching of others as rain coming down from the clouds. Therefore, at least since sin came into the world, man is taught by man.

Reply:

There is the same sort of difference of opinion on three issues: on the bringing of forms into existence, on the acquiring of virtues, and on the acquiring of scientific knowledge.

For some have said that all sensible forms come from an external agent, a separated substance or form, which they call the giver of forms or agent intelligence, and that all that lower natural agents do is prepare the matter to receive the form. Similarly, Avicenna says that our activity is not the cause of a good habit, but only keeps out its opposite and prepares us for the habit so that it may come from the substance which perfects the souls of men. This is the agent intelligence or some similar substance.

They also hold that knowledge is caused in us only by an agent free of matter. For this reason Avicenna holds that the intelligible forms flow into our mind from the agent intelligence.

Some have held the opposite opinion, namely, that all three of those are embodied in things and have no external cause, but are only brought to light by external activity. For some have held that all natural forms are in act, lying hidden in matter, and that a natural agent does nothing but draw them from concealment out into the open. In like manner, some hold that all the habits of the virtues are implanted in us by nature. And the practice of their actions removes the obstructions which, as it were, hid these habits, just as rust is removed by filing so that the brightness of the iron is brought to light. Similarly, some also have said that the knowledge of all things is con-created with the soul and that through teaching and the external helps of this type of knowledge all that happens is that the soul is prompted to recall or consider those things which it knew previously. Hence, they say that learning is nothing but remembering.

But both of these positions lack a reasonable basis. For the first opinion excludes proximate causes, attributing solely to first causes all effects which happen in lower natures. In this it derogates from the order of the universe, which is made up of the order and connection of causes, since the first cause, by the pre-eminence of its goodness, gives other beings not only their existence, but also their existence as causes. The second position, too, falls into practically the same difficulty. For, since a thing which removes an obstruction is a mover only accidentally, as is said in the *Physics*, if lower agents do nothing but bring things from concealment into the open, taking away the obstructions which concealed the forms and habits of the virtues and the sciences, it follows that all lower agents act only accidentally.

Therefore, in all that has been said we ought to hold a middle position between these two, according to the teaching of Aristotle. For natural forms pre-exist in matter not actually, as some have said, but only in potency. They are brought to actuality from this state of potency through a proximate external agent, and not through the first agent alone, as one of the opinions maintains. Similarly, according to this opinion of Aristotle, before the habits of virtue are completely formed, they exist in us in certain natural inclinations, which are the beginnings of the virtues. But afterwards, through practice in their actions, they are brought to their proper completion.

We must give a similar explanation of the acquisition of knowledge. For certain seeds of knowledge pre-exist in us, namely, the first concepts of understanding, which by the light of the agent intellect are immediately known through the species abstracted from sensible things. These are either complex, as axioms, or simple, as the notions of being, of the one, and so on, which the understanding grasps immediately. In these general principles, however, all the consequences are included as in certain seminal principles. When, therefore, the mind is led from these general notions to actual knowledge of the particular things, which it knew previously in general and, as it were, potentially, then one is said to acquire knowledge.

We must bear in mind, nevertheless, that in natural things something can pre-exist in potency in two ways. In one, it is in an active and completed potency, as when an intrinsic principle has sufficient power to flow into perfect act. Healing is an obvious example of this, for the sick person is restored to health by the natural power within him. The other appears in a passive potency, as happens when the internal principle does not have sufficient power to bring it into act. This is clear when air becomes fire, for this cannot result from any power existing in the air.

Therefore, when something pre-exists in active completed potency, the external agent acts only by helping the internal agent and providing it with the means by which it can enter into act. Thus, in healing the doctor assists nature, which is the principal agent, by strengthening nature and prescribing medicines, which nature uses as instruments for healing. On the other hand, when something pre-exists only in passive potency, then it is the external agent which is the principal cause of the transition from potency to act. Thus, fire makes actual fire of air, which is potentially fire.

Knowledge, therefore, pre-exists in the learner potentially, not, however, in the purely passive, but in the active, sense. Otherwise, man would not be able to acquire knowledge independently. Therefore, as there are two ways of being cured, that is, either through the activity of unaided nature or by nature with the aid of medicine, so also there are two ways of acquiring knowledge. In one way, natural reason by itself reaches knowledge of unknown things, and this way is called *discovery;* in the other way, when someone else aids the learner's natural reason, and this is called *learning by instruction.*

In effects which are produced by nature and by art, art operates in the same way and through the same means as nature. For, as nature heals one who is suffering from cold by warming him, so also does the doctor. Hence, art is said to imitate nature. A similar thing takes place in acquiring knowl-

147

edge. For the teacher leads the pupil to knowledge of things he does not know in the same way that one directs himself through the process of discovering something he does not know.

Now, in discovery, the procedure of anyone who arrives at the knowledge of something unknown is to apply general self-evident principles to certain definite matters, from these to proceed to particular conclusions and from these to others. Consequently, one person is said to teach another inasmuch as, by signs, he manifests to that other the reasoning process which he himself goes through by his own natural reason. And thus, through the instrumentality, as it were, of what is told him, the natural reason of the pupil arrives at a knowledge of things which he did not know. Therefore, just as the doctor is said to heal a patient through the activity of nature, so a man is said to cause knowledge in another through the activity of the learner's own natural reason, and this is teaching. So, one is said to teach another and be his teacher. This is what the Philosopher means when he says: "Demonstration is a syllogism which makes someone know."

But, if someone proposes to another things which are not included in self-evident principles, or does not make it clear that they are included, he will not cause knowledge in the other but, perhaps, opinion or faith, although even this is in some way caused by inborn first principles, for from these self-evident principles he realizes that what necessarily follows from them is to be held with certitude, and that what is contrary to them is to be rejected completely, and that assent may be given to or withheld from whatever neither follows necessarily from nor is contrary to self-evident principles. Now, the light of reason by which such principles are evident to us is implanted in us by God as a kind of reflected likeness in us of the uncreated truth. So, since all human teaching can be effective only in virtue of that light, it is obvious that God alone teaches interiorly and principally, just as nature alone heals interiorly and principally. Nevertheless, both to heal and to teach can still be used in a proper sense in the way we have explained.

Answers to Difficulties:

1. Since our Lord had ordered the disciples not to be called teachers, the *Gloss* explains how this prohibition is to be understood, lest it be taken absolutely. For we are forbidden to call man a teacher in this sense, that we attribute to him the pre-eminence of teaching, which belongs to God. It would be as if we put our hope in the wisdom of men, and did not rather consult divine truth about those things which we hear from man. And this divine truth speaks in us through the impression of its likeness, by means of which we can judge of all things.

2. Knowledge of things is not produced in us through knowledge of signs, but through knowledge of things more certain, namely, principles. The latter are proposed to us through signs and are applied to other things which were heretofore unknown to us simply, although they were known to us in some respect, as has been said. For knowledge of principles produces in us knowledge of conclusions; knowledge of signs does not.

3. To some extent we know the things we are taught through signs, and to some extent we do not know them. Thus, if we are taught what man is, we must know something about him beforehand, namely, the meaning of animal, or of substance, or at least of being itself, which last concept cannot escape us. Similarly, if we are taught a certain conclusion, we must know beforehand what the subject and predicate are. We must also have previous knowledge of the principles through which the conclusion is taught, for "all teaching comes from pre-existing knowledge," as is said in the *Posterior Analytics*. Hence, the argument does not follow.

4. Our intellect derives intelligible likenesses from sensible signs which are received in the sensitive faculty, and it uses these intelligible forms to produce in itself scientific knowledge. For the signs are not the proximate efficient cause of knowledge, but reason is, in its passage from principles to conclusions, as has been said.

5. In one who is taught, the knowledge did not exist in complete actuality, but, as it were, in seminal principles, in

149

the sense that the universal concepts which we know naturally are, as it were, the seeds of all the knowledge which follows. But, although these seminal principles are not developed to actuality by any created power, as though they were infused by a created power, that which they have in a primitive way and virtually can develop into actuality by means of the activity of a created power.

6. We do not say that a teacher communicates knowledge to the pupil, as though the knowledge which is in the teacher is numerically the same as that which arises in the pupil. It is rather that the knowledge which arises in the pupil through teaching is similar to that which is in the teacher, and this was raised from potency into act, as has been said.

7. As the doctor is said to cause healing, although he works exteriorly, while nature alone works interiorly, so man is said to teach the truth, although he declares it exteriorly, while God teaches interiorly.

8. When Augustine proves that only God teaches, he does not intend to exclude man from teaching exteriorly, but intends to say that God alone teaches interiorly.

9. Man can truly be called a true teacher inasmuch as he teaches the truth and enlightens the mind. This does not mean, however, that he endows the mind with light, but that, as it were, he co-operates with the light of reason by supplying external help to it to reach the perfection of knowledge. This is in accordance with Ephesians [3:8-9]: "To me, the least of all the saints, is given this grace . . . to enlighten all men . . ."

10. Wisdom is twofold, created and uncreated. Man is said to be endowed with both and to improve himself by advancing in them. Uncreated wisdom, however, cannot be changed in any way, whereas in us created wisdom can be changed for some extrinsic reason, though not by reason of anything intrinsic to it. We can consider this capacity for change in two ways. In one way, according to the relation which it has to external things, and in this way it is entirely unchangeable. In the other, according to the existence which it has in the subject it is changed for some extrinsic reason

when the subject which has wisdom in potency is changed into a subject having it in act. For the intelligible forms in which wisdom consists are both likenesses of things and forms perfecting the understanding.

11. In the pupil, the intelligible forms of which knowledge received through teaching is constituted are caused directly by the agent intellect and mediately by the one who teaches. For the teacher sets before the pupil signs of intelligible things, and from these the agent intellect derives the intelligible likenesses and causes them to exist in the possible intellect. Hence, the words of the teacher, heard or seen in writing, have the same efficacy in causing knowledge as things which are outside the soul. For from both the agent intellect receives intelligible likenesses, although the words of the teacher are more proximately posed to cause knowledge than things outside the soul, in so far as they are signs of intelligible forms.

12. Intellectual and bodily sight are not alike, for bodily sight is not a power which compares, so that among its objects it can proceed from one to another. Rather, all the objects of this sight can be seen as soon as it turns to them. Consequently, anyone who has the power of sight can look at all visible things, just as one who has a habit of knowledge can turn his attention to the things which he knows habitually. Therefore, the seeing subject needs no stimulus from another to see something, unless, perhaps, someone else directs the subject's attention to some object by pointing it out or doing something of the sort.

But, since the intellective power can compare, it proceeds from some things to others. As a result, it does not have the same relation to all intelligible objects of consideration. Rather, the mind sees certain things immediately, those which are self-evident, in which are contained certain other things which it can understand only by using reason to unfold those things which are implicitly contained in principles. Thus, before the mind has the habit, it is not only in accidental potency to know these things, but also essential potency. For the mind needs a mover to actualize it through teaching, as is said in the *Physics*. But a man who already knew something habitually would not need this. Therefore, the teacher furnishes the pupil's intellect with a stimulus to knowledge of the things which he teaches, as an indispensable mover, bringing the intellect from potentiality to actuality. But one who shows some thing to bodily sight prompts it to action as a nonessential mover. And one who has the habit of knowledge can in this way receive a stimulus from someone to consider something.

13. The whole certainty of scientific knowledge arises from the certainty of principles. For conclusions are known with certainty when they are reduced to the principles. Therefore, that something is known with certainty is due to the light of reason divinely implanted within us, by which God speaks within us. It comes from man, teaching from without, only in so far as, teaching us, he reduces conclusions to the principles. Nevertheless, we would not attain the certainty of scientific knowledge from this unless there were within us the certainty of the principles to which the conclusions are reduced.

14. Man, teaching from without, does not infuse the intelligible light, but he is in a certain sense a cause of the intelligible species, in so far as he offers us certain signs of intelligible likenesses, which our understanding receives from those signs and keeps within itself.

15. When it is said that nothing but God can form the mind, this is understood of its basic form, without which mind would be considered formless, no matter what other forms it had. This is the form by which it turns toward the Word and clings to Him. It is through this alone that rational nature is called formed, as is clear from Augustine.

16. Guilt is in the affections, on which only God can make an impression, as will appear later. But ignorance is in the understanding, on which even a created power can make an imprint. For the agent intellect impresses the intelligible species on the possible intellect, and through the mediation of this latter, scientific knowledge is caused in our soul by

sensible things and by the teaching of man, as has been said.

17. One has the certainty of scientific knowledge, as has been said, from God alone, who has given us the light of reason, through which we know principles. It is from these that the certainty of scientific knowledge arises. Nevertheless, scientific knowledge can in a certain sense be caused in us by man, as has been said.

18. Before the teacher speaks, the pupil would, if asked, answer about the principles through which he is taught, but not about the conclusions which someone is teaching him. Hence, he does not learn the principles from the teacher, but only the conclusions.

ARTICLE II
IN THE SECOND ARTICLE WE ASK:
CAN ONE BE CALLED HIS OWN TEACHER?

Difficulties:

It seems that he can, for

1. An activity should be ascribed more to the principal cause than to the instrumental cause. But in us the agent intellect is, as it were, the principal cause of the knowledge which is produced in us. But man who teaches another is, as it were, an instrumental cause, furnishing the agent intellect with the instruments by means of which it causes knowledge. Therefore, the agent intellect is more the teacher than another man. If, then, because of what a speaker says we call him the teacher of the one who hears him, the hearer should in a much fuller sense be called his own teacher because of the light of the agent intellect.

2. One learns something only in so far as he acquires certain knowledge. But such certitude is in us by reason of the principles which are naturally known in the light of the agent intellect. Therefore, the agent intellect is especially fitted to teach. We conclude as before.

3. To teach belongs more properly to God than to man.

Hence, it is said in Matthew [23:8]: "For one is your master." But God teaches us in so far as He gives us the light of reason, by means of which we can judge about everything. Therefore, we should attribute the activity of teaching especially to that light. The same conclusion follows as before.

4. It is more perfect to learn something through discovery than to learn it from another, as is clear in the *Ethics*. If, therefore, a man is called a teacher in virtue of that manner of acquiring knowledge by which one learns from another so that the one is called the teacher of the other, he should with much greater reason be called a teacher in virtue of the process of acquiring knowledge through discovery, and so be called his own teacher.

5. Just as one is inspired to virtue by another and by himself, so also he gets to know something by discovering for himself and by learning from another. But those who attain to works of virtue without having another as an instructor or a lawgiver are said to be a law unto themselves, according to Romans [2:14]: "For when the Gentiles, who have not the law, do by nature those things that are of the law . . . they are a law to themselves." Therefore, the man who acquires knowledge by himself ought also to be called his own teacher.

6. The teacher is a cause of knowledge as the doctor is a cause of health, as has been said. But a doctor heals himself. Therefore, one can also teach oneself.

To the Contrary:

1'. The Philosopher says that it is impossible for one who is teaching to learn. For the teacher must have knowledge and the learner must not have it. Therefore, one cannot teach himself or be called his own teacher.

2'. The office of teacher implies a relation of superiority, just as dominion does. But relationships of this sort cannot exist between a person and himself. For one is not his own father or master. Therefore, neither can one be called his own teacher.

Reply:

Through the light of reason implanted in him and without the help of another's instruction, one can undoubtedly acquire knowledge of many things which he does not know. This is clear with all those who acquire knowledge through discovery. Thus, in some sense one can be a cause of his own knowledge, but he cannot be called his own teacher or be said to teach himself.

For in physical reality we find two types of active principles, as is clear from the Philosopher. Now, there is one type of agent which has within itself everything which it produces in the effect, and it has these perfections in the same way as the effect, as happens in univocal agents, or in a higher way than the effect, as in equivocal causes. Then, there is a certain type of agent in which there pre-exists only a part of the effect. An example of this type is a movement which causes health, or some warm medicine, in which warmth exists either actually or virtually. But warmth is not complete health, but a part of it. The first type of agent, therefore, possesses the complete nature of action. But those of the second type do not, for a thing acts in so far as it is in act. Hence, since it actually contains the effect to be produced only partially, it is not an agent in the perfect sense.

But teaching implies the perfect activity of knowledge in the teacher or master. Hence, the teacher or master must have the knowledge which he causes in another explicitly and perfectly, as it is to be received in the one who is learning through instruction. When, however, knowledge is acquired by someone through an internal principle, that which is the active cause of the knowledge has the knowledge to be acquired only partially, that is, in the seminal principles of knowledge, which are the general principles. Therefore, properly speaking, we cannot call a man teacher or master because of such causality.

Answers to Difficulties:

1. Although to some extent the agent intellect is more the principal cause than another's teaching, the knowledge does

not pre-exist in it completely, as it does in the teacher. Hence, the argument does not follow.

2. A like solution should be given to the second difficulty.

3. God knows explicitly everything which man is taught by Him. Hence, the character of teacher can suitably be applied to God. The case is not the same with the agent intellect, for the reason already given.

4. For the one learning a science, to learn it by discovery is the more perfect way of acquiring the knowledge, because it shows that he is more skillful in the acquisition of knowledge. However, for the one causing the knowledge, it is more perfect to cause it by means of instruction. For a teacher who knows the whole science explicitly can teach it to a pupil more readily than the pupil himself could learn it from his own rather general knowledge of the principles of the science.

5. The law has the same relation to matters of action as a principle has to speculative matters, but not the same as a teacher. Consequently, if he is a law unto himself, it does not follow that he can be his own teacher.

6. A doctor heals in so far as he has health, not actually, but in the knowledge of his art. But the teacher teaches in so far as he has knowledge actually. Hence, he who does not have health actually can cause health in himself because he has health in the knowledge of his art. However, it is impossible for one actually to have knowledge and not to have it, in such a way that he could teach himself.

ST. CATHERINE
OF SIENA
(1347—1380)

IF a visitor to Siena had listened to the gossip in the market square, the church porches, the convents, even in the taverns, about 1363, he would have heard two topics repeated over and over again. One was the misery of the times. For it was indeed horrible in Tuscany. The Sienese were oppressed by the constant menace of the plagues, the bitter political rivalry within the city, the anarchy in the countryside, where freebooters and bandits exercised control, and the political enmity of emperor and pope that could result at any moment in siege and slaughter. Yet the same visitor also would have heard of a startling manifestation of Christian love and hope. All Siena was talking about sixteen-year-old Catherine, the twenty-fifth child of the dyer, Giacomo Benincasa, and his wife, Lopa.

Although she wore the mantle of a Dominican tertiary, she was not a nun, nor did she ever become one. She fetched, carried, washed, and cleaned for her family and hid her austerities as best she could; she was known to fast continually and to stay up most of the night in prayer. But it was not what Catherine did that made her extraordinary, it was her inner radiance. She had a tender and compassionate nature that she touched hearts almost immediately.

She could not read or write, yet she possessed gifts of knowledge and wisdom that educated men could not achieve. This was soon revealed in conversations reported by dozens of her followers; in the more than 400 letters she dictated, and in her book, the *Dialogue,* a revelation of her long communions with Christ. As she records in her *Dialogue* Christ

Himself was her teacher and it was He Who guided her life. "Many live in the cell, and yet their thoughts are outside it," He told her, "I will therefore, that thy cell shall be knowledge of thyself and of thy sins." Under His instruction she learned the ways of God: endless humility, patience, perseverance, and joy. She was to become the spiritual mother of countless penitents, the rescuer of hundreds of lost souls, the conscience of popes and kings, the directress of saintly men and women, whose wills, ignited by her ardor, enlightened and warmed the dark, cold Fourteenth Century.

Just what Catherine did during her brief thirty-three years is impossible to summarize. Living in Christ, she loved Him and prayed *to* Him constantly; living in the midst of people, she loved them and prayed *for* them constantly. All her daily activity stemmed from these two loves that were blended into one. She nursed at the hospital; she accompanied condemned men to the block; she brought or sent unhappy sinners to confession; she discoursed with a group of devoted clerical "sons" on the will of God; she fed the poor, she performed miracles of healing; she prophesied—all in the performance of God's will as it was revealed to her from day to day, from moment to moment.

History remembers her chiefly for her zealous insistence on the dignity of the papal office. In this role she is often presented as interfering, imperious, and right. To Gregory XI she wrote long, demanding letters not hesitating to refer to his excessive meekness: "Play the man," she said. "See to it that I do not have to appeal to Christ crucified from you." And when she went to see Gregory in his Babylonian captivity at Avignon, she told him plainly that, if he were unwilling to exercise the power of his office, he should resign. When Urban VI succeeded to the papal throne upon Gregory's death, she defended him against various schismatic cardinals who had voted for him and then switched their loyalties. Nor did her reforming spirit spare lesser clerics who abused their office or led scandalous lives. They, "like men blinded and without the light of reason, have become animals through their sins, and live lasciviously in word and deed."

But even when her days were filled with external activity, as in her last years when she was constantly employed as an envoy and messenger of the beleaguered Urban, Catherine was always more concerned with the love of God and the interior life of the soul. Her *Dialogue*, composed amidst great tumult, is chiefly concerned with revealing the spiritual bridge that all men are invited to cross and in that crossing to share in the unspeakable sufferings and consolations of Christ.

Although Catherine has been established as a great writer in the Tuscan language, she was not a writer at all in the professional sense. She dictated her many letters and counsels to her followers. Sometimes she kept three of them busy simultaneously. Standing in the middle of the room, her eyes aflame with vision and love, she spoke as the spirit moved her. To this day her spirit glows in those letters.

LETTER TO SISTER
DANIELLA OF ORVIETO

Dearest daughter in Christ sweet Jesus:

I, Catherine, servant and slave of the servants of Jesus Christ, write to you in His precious Blood, with desire to see thee in true and very perfect light that thou mayest know the truth in perfection. Oh, how necessary this light is to us, dearest daughter! For without it we cannot walk in the Way of Christ crucified, a shining Way that brings us to life; without it we shall walk among shadows and abide in great storm and bitterness. But if I consider aright, it behooves us to possess two orders of this light. There is a general light, that every rational creature ought to have for recognizing whom he ought to love and obey—perceiving in the light of his mind by the pupil of most holy faith that he is bound to love and serve his Creator, loving Him directly with all his heart and mind, in obeying the commandments of the law to love God above everything and our neighbor as ourselves. These are the principles by which all men besides ourselves are held. This is a general light, which we are all bound by; and without it we shall die and shall follow, deprived of the life of grace, the darkened way of the devil. But there is another light, which is not apart from this, but one with it—nay, by this first, one attains to the second. There are those who, observing the commandments of God, grow into another most perfect light; these rise from imperfection with great and holy desire, and attain unto perfection, observing both commandments and counsels in thought and deed. One should use this light with hungry desire for the honor of God and the salvation of souls, gazing therewith into the light of the sweet and loving Word, where the soul tastes the ineffable love which God has to His creatures, shown to us through that Word, who ran enamored to the shameful death of the Cross, for the honor of the Father and for our salvation.

When the soul has known this truth in the perfect light, it rises above itself, above its natural instincts; with intense, sweet, and loving desires it runs, following the footsteps of Christ crucified, bearing pains, bearing shame, ridicule and insult with much persecution, from the world, and often from the servants of God under pretext of virtue. Hungrily it seeks the honor of God and the salvation of souls; and so much does it delight in this glorious food, that it despises itself and everything else: this alone it seeks, and abandons itself. In this perfect light lived the glorious virgins and the other saints, who delighted only in receiving this food with their Bridegroom, on the table of the Cross. Now to us, dearest daughter and sweet my sister in Christ sweet Jesus, He has shown such grace and mercy that He has placed us in the number of those who have advanced from the general light to the particular—that is, He has made us choose the perfect state of the Counsels; therefore we ought to follow that sweet and straight way perfectly, in true light, not looking back for any reason whatever; not walking in our own fashion but in the fashion of God, enduring sufferings without fault even unto death, rescuing the soul from the hands of devils. For this is the Way and the Rule that the Eternal Truth has given thee; and He wrote it on His body, not with ink, but with His Blood, in letters so big that no one is of such low intelligence as to be excused from reading. Well thou seest the initials of that Book, how great they are and all show the truth of the Eternal Father, the ineffable love with which we were created—this is the truth—only that we might share His highest and eternal good. Thus our Master is lifted up on high upon the pulpit of the Cross in order that we may better study it and should not deceive ourselves saying: "He teaches this to me on earth, and not on high." Not so: for ascended upon the Cross, and uplifted there in pain, He seeks to exalt the honor of the Father, and to restore the beauty of souls. Then let us read heartfelt love, founded in truth, in this Book of Life. Lose thyself wholly, and the more thou shalt lose the more thou shalt find, and God will not despise thy desire. Nay, He will direct thee, and show thee what thou shouldst do, and will enlighten him to whom thou mightest be subject if thou dost according to His counsel. For the soul that prays ought to have a holy jealousy, and let it always rejoice to do whatever it does with the help of prayer and counsel.

TO A PRIEST FRIEND

This is a letter to Raymond of Capua, a spiritual son and later Master General of the Dominicans. It concerns Niccolò di Toldo, a young Perugian aristocrat, who referred to the Sienese government contemptuously. He was arrested and condemned to death. He raged in prison and despaired. He insulted priests who came to visit him. Finally Catherine went to see him and persuaded him to go to confession and communion.

I went to visit him of whom you know, whereby he was so comforted and consoled that he confessed and prepared himself right well. And he made me promise for the love of God that when the time of execution came I would be with him.

And so I promised and did. Then in the morning before the bell tolled I went to him and he was very glad. I took him to hear Mass and he received Holy Communion for the last time. His will was attuned and subject to the will of God and there alone remained a fear of not being brave at the last moment . . . He said to me: "Stay with me and do not leave me. Thus I cannot be other than well and I die content." And he laid his head upon my breast. Then desire increased in my soul and, aware of his fear, I said: "Be comforted, sweet brother, for soon we shall come to the nuptials. You shall go there bathed in the Blood of the Son of God, in the sweet name of Jesus, which must never leave your memory. And I will be waiting for you at the place of execution." Just think, Father, his heart then lost all fear, his face was transfigured from sorrow to joy. He rejoiced, exulted, and said: "Whence comes so much grace to me that the sweetness of my soul will await me at the holy place of execution?" You see what light he had received when he called the scaffold holy! He said: "I will go there all joyous and strong and it will seem a thousand years to me before I reach it, when I think that you are waiting for me there." And he spoke so sweetly about God's goodness that I could scarcely bear it.

I waited for him therefore at the place of execution . . . in continual prayer and in the presence of Mary and Catherine, virgin and martyr. I besought Mary for the grace that he might have light and peace of heart at the last moment and that I might see him safe in God. My soul became then so filled with the sweet promise made to me that I could see no one although there was a great crowd there.

Then he came like a meek lamb and seeing me he laughed. He asked me to make the Sign of the Cross for him. I did so and said, "Up to the nuptials, sweet brother, for you are soon to be in everlasting life." He knelt down with great meekness and I stretched out his neck and bent down over him, reminding him of the Blood of the Lamb. His lips said: *Jesus, Catherine.* So saying, I received his head into my hands, closing my eyes in the Divine Goodness and saying, "I will."

Then I saw God-and-Man, as one sees the splendor of the sun, receiving that soul in the fire of His divine charity. Oh, how ineffably sweet it was to see the goodness of God! With what gentleness and love He waited for that soul as it left the body. . . .

But Niccolò did a gracious act that would draw a thousand hearts. And I do not wonder at it because he already tasted the divine sweetness. He turned back like a new bride who has reached the threshold of her home, who looks round and bows to those accompanying her, showing her gratitude by that sign.

Having had the reply, my soul reposed in peace and quiet in such fragrance of blood that I could not bear to have removed from my garments the blood that had fallen on them. Wretched and miserable, I remained on earth with the greatest envy.

ST. THOMAS MORE
(1478–1535)

THOMAS More appeals to many readers because he seems to be a modern saint. He can be identified with people, places, books, attitudes that are well known to our society. As a boy of fourteen he heard of Columbus' discovery of America. As a student at Oxford and later as a private scholar, he participated in the Renaissance of learning that ushered in the modern world. As a lawyer he argued the case against those who fattened their sheep while other men starved. A new man in the new world of the Sixteenth Century, he resisted the primitive totalitarianism of the Tudor monarchy and resisted to the death, when forced to choose between an omnipotent state and the rights of God and man.

From the moment of his birth in London, when his mother reported she had a vision of him crowned with splendor, Thomas More seemed destined for greatness. His father, Sir John More, one of the judges of the King's bench, sent him to St. Anthony's Grammar School, where he first learned Latin. Then he procured an appointment for him as a page to Cardinal Morton, Archbishop of Canterbury and Lord Chancellor to King Henry VIII. In that household Master More made himself a favorite by his wit, his amiability, and his ceaseless inventiveness. The Cardinal often said to his guests, "This child here waiting at the table, whosoever shall live to see it, will prove a marvelous man." At Canterbury College, Oxford, More studied Greek under Thomas Linacre and perfected his Latin, which he learned to write with a Ciceronian elegance that soon won him the esteem of the learned world.

At sixteen, he entered the New Inn, preparatory to advanced legal study at Lincoln's Inn. After three years he was called to the bar, and began a highly successful career. But for some years, More, the many-sided man, found other outlets for his energies. He lectured on St. Augustine's *The City of God* in St. Lawrence Church before an audience including many learned men. He taught law at Furnival's Inn and spent his spare time at the Charterhouse, where he meditated and prayed to discover whether he should become a Carthusian. Once satisfied that God willed that he should live in the world, he married Joan Colt, by whom he had three daughters and a son. When she died in 1511, he married the redoubtable widow, Alice Middleton, who was a mother to his children and the source of much familial merriment. She may have been, too, something of a hair shirt, no less penitential than the real one he wore most of his life.

More developed into the ideal man that Renaissance writers were always imagining in their conduct books. Intensely human, he was one of the merriest wits in the history of mankind, a delightful companion to his family and his friends. He was also a great intellectual, an intimate friend of Erasmus and of leading scholars at Oxford, Cambridge, Paris, and Louvain. In his house at Chelsea, he presided over an academy where he taught his children, particularly his favorite daughter Margaret, in a manner that was far in advance of the age. His books, the celebrated *Utopia, The History of Richard III, The Dialogue concerning Tyndale,* and *The Confutation of Tyndale's Answer,* advanced him at once to the foremost rank among the serious writers of his day. His prose style, most scholars agree, set the pattern of English for centuries to come. More in addition proved to be an eminent man of affairs. After his initial success at the bar, he became, in rapid succession, a member of parliament, Sheriff of London, Master of Requests to King Henry VIII, and finally Lord Chancellor of England.

Yet he was, above all, God's man. Amidst all his activities he fasted, prayed, and meditated. With the vigilance of an eagle, he descried the enemies of the Christian faith who attacked first the power, and then the authority of the pope. As Henry VIII and his followers pressed the passage of bill after bill abolishing papal rights and privileges and confiscating church revenues, More's position as chancellor became untenable. In May, 1532, he resigned his office.

Immediately Henry's ministers moved to discredit Sir Thomas. First he was accused of corruption, but, since More had no money to speak of, the prosecutors could not bring action. Then the Council, consisting of the most important men in the realm, claimed that More had deliberately misled the king. Years ago, they alleged, Sir Thomas had induced King Henry to write a book that upheld the papal authority— a book for which the pope had awarded Henry the special title, Defender of the Faith. On the contrary, More replied, he had forewarned the king on that occasion that the royal attack against Lutheranism had gone very far in its commitment to papal authority. At that time More simply urged his sovereign to realize the implications of his own writings. But Henry was then vexed by More's cautions. Sir Thomas quoted him as saying: "We are so much bound to the See of Rome, that we cannot do too much honor to it." Once again, a baseless and irrelevant charge fell of its own weight.

More scored heavily on his opponents so long as they sought to trap him by legal means. But he was defenseless against his own conscience. A servile parliament wrote into the Act of Succession a repudiation of the spiritual authority of the pope, and required all priests and More, the layman, to take an oath of obedience to that Act. More refused. He was promptly imprisoned in the Tower. Then began a most fascinating drama. At first the king's men attempted to persuade More to change his mind. They suggested that he swear with the mental reservation, "so far as lawful," as his wife, his daughter, and many others had done. He refused. They expropriated his property and sent his impoverished wife and family to persuade him. Gently, he turned their pleas aside. Persuasion failing, the king's men then sought to extricate a treasonable statement from him. Cromwell, Audley, and others questioned him at great length, but his answers gave them no pretext to bring him to trial. Fraud came to the service of malice when Richard Rich, the solicitor general, falsely reported a conversation between himself and More.

Thomas had said, "Suppose that Parliament would make a law that God should not be God, would you then say that God were not God?" Rich, however, reported that Thomas had added, "No more could the Parliament make the King Supreme Head of the Church." On the basis of this evidence Thomas was brought to trial on July 1, 1535.

Rich, the prosecutor, and hence an illegal witness, testified against him. Before sentence was passed, More had a chance to speak. Prison pale and prematurely aged, he had lost none of his skill. He impugned his prosecutor's credibility before judges who knew Rich to be an infamous timeserver. More asked his judges whether he, More, would be likely to confide in a man like Rich what he refused to reveal to the members of the king's council. Then he reminded his judges that he refused the oath because England had no more right to make laws for the universal Catholic Church than the city of London had the right to legislate for all England. "No more might this realm of England refuse obedience to the See of Rome than might the child refuse obedience to his own natural father."

He died as one prepared to die. Early in his imprisonment he had said to his daughter Margaret: "I find no cause, I thank God, Megg, to reckon myself in worse case here than in mine own house, for me thinketh God maketh me a pet, and getteth me on his lap and dandelleth me."

During his long imprisonment, he finished the *Dialogue of Comfort against Tribulation,* a meditation on the persecution of Christians, and *A Treatise on the Passion,* a section of which appears here.

Later he wrote again to Margaret, sending her his hair shirt as a remembrance. He was put to death on July 6. The king, well aware of More's great eloquence, bid him speak on the scaffold.

He spoke but briefly, jesting with the executioner who trembled at his task. As More laid his head to the block, he placed his beard to one side. Since it had grown in prison, he said, "My beard is not guilty of treason."

On news of his death, the civilized world broke into an

167

agonized moan. Henry heard himself called the Nero who had destroyed the Seneca of Christendom. Unwittingly, he had provided More with a forum of the scaffold from which his noble death spoke even more eloquently than his words.

ON THE REMEMBRANCE
OF DEATH

What profit and commodity cometh unto man's soul by the meditation of death is not only marked of the chosen people of God, but also of such as were the best sort among gentiles and paynims. For some of the old famous philosophers, when they were demanded what faculty philosophy was, answered that it was the meditation or exercise of death. For like as death maketh a severance of the body and the soul, when they by course of nature must needs depart asunder, so (said they) doth the study of philosophy labor to sever the soul from the love and affections of the body while they be together. Now if this be the whole study and labor of philosophy, as the best philosophers said that it is, then may we within short time be well learned in philosophy. For nothing is there that may more effectually withdraw the soul from the wretched affections of the body than may the remembrance of death,—if we do not remember it hoverly, as one heareth a word and let it pass by his ear, without any receiving of the sentence [meaning] into his heart. But if we not only hear this word "death," but also let sink into our hearts the very fantasy and deep imagination thereof, we shall perceive thereby that we were never so greatly moved by the beholding of the Dance of Death pictured in Paul's, as we shall feel ourselves stirred and altered by the feeling of that imagination in our hearts. And no marvel. For those pictures express only the loathly figure of our dead bony bodies, bitten away the flesh; which though it be ugly to behold, yet neither the light thereof, nor the sight of all the dead heads in the charnel house, nor the apparition of a very ghost, is half so grisly as the deep conceived fantasy of death in his nature, by the lively imagination graven in thine own heart. For there seest thou, not one plain grievous sight of the bare bones hanging by the sinews, but thou seest (if thou fantasy thine own death, for so art thou by this counsel advised), thou seest, I say, thyself, if thou die no worse death, yet leastwise lying in thy bed, thy head shooting, thy back aching, thy veins beating, thine heart panting, thy throat rattling, thy flesh trembling, thy mouth gaping, thy nose sharping, thy legs cooling, thy fingers fumbling, thy breath shortening, all thy strength fainting, thy life vanishing, and thy death drawing on.

If thou couldst now call to thy remembrance some of those sicknesses that have most grieved thee and tormented thee in thy days, as every man hath felt some, and then findest thou that some one disease in some one part of thy body, as percase the stone or the strangury, have put thee to thine own mind to no less torment than thou shouldst have felt if one had put up a knife into the same place, and wouldst, as thee then seemed, have been content with such a change,—think what it will be then when thou shalt feel so many such pains in every part of thy body, breaking thy veins and thy life strings, with like pain and grief as thou as many knives as thy body might receive should everywhere enter and meet in the midst. A stroke of a staff, a cut of a knife, the flesh singed with fire, the pain of sundry sickness, many men have essayed in themselves; and they have not yet, somewhat have heard by them that felt it. But what manner dolor and pain, what manner of grievous pangs, what intolerable torment, the silly creature feeleth in the dissolution and severance of the soul from the body, never was there body that yet could tell the tale.

Some conjecture and token of this point we have of the bitter passion and piteous departing of our Savior Jesu Christ, of Whom we nothing read that ever He cried for any pain, neither for the whips and rods beating His blessed body nor the sharp thorns pricking His holy head, or the great, long nails piercing His precious hands and feet. But when the point approached in which His sacred soul should depart out of

His blessed body, at that point He cried loud once or twice to His Father in heaven, into Whose mighty and merciful hands, at the extreme point, with a great loud cry He gave up the ghost (Matthew 27:50; Mark 15:37; Luke 23:96). Now if that death was so painful and ragious to our Savior Christ, Whose joy and comfort of His godhead, if He would have suffered it, might in such wise have redounded into His soul, and so forth into His body, that it should not only have supped up all His pain, but also have transformed His holy body into a glorious form and made it impossible,—what intolerable torment will death be then to us miserable wretches, of which the mere part among the pangs of our passage shall have yet so painful twitches of our own conscience that the fear of hell, the dread of the devil, and sorrow at our heart at the sight of our sins, shall pass and exceed the deadly pains of our body.

Other things are there which will peradventure seem no great matter to them that feel them not, but unto him that shall lie in that case, they shall be tedious out of all measure.

Have ye not ere this, in a sore sickness, felt it very grievous to have folk babble to you, and namely such things as ye should answer to, when it was pain to speak? Think ye not now that it will be a gentle pleasure, when we lie dying, all our body in pain, all our mind in trouble, our soul in sorrow, our heart all in dread while our life walketh awayward, while our death draweth toward, while the devil is busy about us, while we lack stomach and strength to bear any one of so manifold heinous troubles, will it not be, as I was about to say, a pleasant thing to see before thine eyes and hear at thine ear a rabble of fleshly friends, or rather of flesh flies, skipping about thy bed and thy sick body, like ravens about thy corpse, now almost carrion, crying to thee on every side, "What shall I have? What shall I have?" Then shall come thy children and cry for their parts; then shall come thy sweet wife, and where in thine health haply she spake thee not one sweet word in six weeks, now shall she call thee sweet husband and weep with much work and ask thee what shall she have; then shall thine executors ask for the keys, and ask what money is owing thee, ask what substance thou hast, and ask where thy money lieth. And while thou liest in that case, their words shall be so tedious that thou wilt wish all that they ask for upon a red fire, so thou mightest lie one half-hour in rest.

Now is there one thing which a little I touched before, I wot not whether more painful or more perilous,—the marvellous intent business and solicitation of our ghostly enemy the devil, not only in one fashion present, but surely never absent from him that draweth towards death. For since that of his pestilent envy conceived from the beginning of man's creation, by which he lay in wait to take our first mother, Eve, in a train, and thereby drawing our former father, Adam, into the breach of God's behest, found the means not without the grievous increase of his own damnation, to deprive us of paradise and bereave us our immortality, making us into subjection not only of temporal death but also of his eternal tormentry, were we not by the great bounty of God and Christ's painful passion, restored to the possibility of everlasting life, he never ceased since to run about like a ramping lion (Psalms 21:14; I Peter 5:8), looking whom he might devour—it can be no doubt but he most busily travaileth in that behalf at the time that he perceiveth us about to depart hence. For well he knoweth that then he either winneth a man forever, or forever loseth him; for have he him never so fast afore, yet if he break from him then he can after his death never get him again. Well he may, peradventure, have him as his gaoler in his prison of purgatory for the time of his punition temporal; but as he would have him for his perpetual slave, shall he never have him after, how sure soever he had him afore, if he get from him at the time of his death. For so lost he suddenly the thief that hung on the right hand of Christ. And on the other side, if he catch a man fast at the time of his death, he is sure to keep him forever. For as the Scripture saith, "Wheresoever the stone falleth, there shall it abide" (Ecclesiastes 11:3). And since he knoweth this for very surety and is of malice so venomous and envious that he had liefer double his own pain than suffer us to escape from pain, he, when we draw to death, doth his uttermost endeavor to bring us to damnation, never ceasing to minister, by subtle and incogitable (incalculable) means, first unlawful longing to live and horror to go gladly to God at His calling.

Then giveth he some false glade (opening) of escaping that sickness, and thereby putteth in our mind a love yet and cleaving to the world, keeping of our goods, loathsomeness of shrift, sloth towards good works. And if we be so far gone that we see we cannot recover, then he casteth in our minds presumption and security of salvation as a thing well won by our own works, of which, if we have any done well, he casteth them into our minds with over great liking and thereby withdraweth us from the haste of doing any more, as a thing that either needeth not or may be done by our executors. And instead of sorrow for our sins and care of heaven, he putteth us in mind of provision for some honorable burying,— so many torches, so many tapers, so many black gowns, so many merry mourners laughing under black hoods, and a gay hearse, with the delight of goodly and honorable funerals: in which the foolish sick man is sometimes occupied as though he thought that he should stand in a window and see how worshipfully he shall be brought to church.

And thus inveigleth he them that either be good, or but meetly (moderately) bad.

But as for those that he hath known for special wretches, whose whole life hath in effect been all bestowed in his service, whom he hath brought into great and horrible sins by the horror whereof he hath kept them from confession, these folk at their end he handleth in another fashion. For into their minds he bringeth their shameful sins by heap, and by the abominable sight thereof draweth them into desperation. For the aggrieving whereof our Lord, after their deserving, suffereth him to show himself to them for their more discomfort in some fearful figure and terrible likeness, by the beholding whereof they conceive, sometimes despair of their salvation and yield themselves as captives quick, beginning their hell in this world, as hath appeared by the words and wretched behavior of many that of a shameful, sinful life have died and departed with heavy desperate death. Now death being such as I have described, or rather much more horrible than any man can describe, it is not to be doubted but if we busily remembered the terror and grief thereof, it must needs be so bitter to the fleshly mind that it could not fail to take away the vain delight of all worldly vanities. But the thing that letteth us to consider death in his kind, and to take great profit that would arise of the remembrance thereof is that for by the hope of long life, we look upon death either so far off that we see him not at all, or but a slight and uncertain sight, as a man may see a thing so far off that he wotteth not whether it be a bush or a beast. And surely so fare we by death, looking thereat afar off through a great long space of as many years as we hope to live,—and those we imagine many, and perilously and foolishly beguile ourselves. For likewise as wives would their husbands should ween by the example of Sarah that there were no woman so old but she might have a child, so is there none old man so old but that, as Tully [Cicero] saith, he trusteth to live one year yet. And as for young folk, they look not how many be dead in their own days younger than themselves, but who is the oldest man in the town, and upon his years they make their reckoning,—where the wiser way were to reckon that a young man may die soon, and an old man cannot live long, but within a little while die the one may, the other must. And with this reckoning shall they look upon death much nearer hand, and better perceive him in his own likeness, and thereby take the more fruit of the remembrance and make themselves the more ready thereto.

Thou wouldst somewhat remember death the more effectually, and look upon him somewhat the more nearly, if thou knewest thyself sick, and specially of any perilous sickness that would make an end of thee though thou feltest yet little pain. For commonly when we be sick than begin we to know ourselves, then pain bringeth us home, then we think how merry a thing it were to be praying in health, which we cannot now do for grief. Then care we little for our gay gear, then desire we no delicate dainties; and as for Lady Lechery, then abhor we to think on. And then we think in ourselves that if ever we recover and mend in body, we will amend in soul, leave all vices and be virtuously occupied the remnant of our life. Insomuch that very true we find the words of the epistle that the well-learned man, Plinius Secundus, after his sickness wrote unto his friend, wherein after the description of men's fantasies in their disease, he closeth up his letter in this wise: "Look," saith he, "all the good counsel and precepts that all the philosophers and wise men in this world give us for instruction of virtuous living, all that can I compendiously give to myself and thee in few words: no more, lo, but let us be such when we be whole, as we think we will be when we be sick."

Now then if thou be ever sick, and ever sick of a perilous sickness, wouldst thou not, if thou knewest thyself in such case, have better remembrance of death than thou hast? It would be hard, peradventure, to make thee believe thyself sick while thou feelest no harm, and yet is that no sure knowledge of health. Trow ye not that many a man is infected with the great sickness a good while ere he perceive it, and the body sore corrupt within ere he feel the grief? How many men have there been that have gone about with God's marks on their body, never perceiving themselves to be sick, but as merry as ever they were in their lives, till other men gave them warning how near they were their deaths? And therefore never reckon thyself whole, though thou feel no grief.

But thou wilt haply say, "Be it that I cannot surely reckon myself whole, yet ye show me not why I should reckon myself sick." Thou sayest right well, and that shall I show thee now. Tell me, if one were in case that he must be fain once or twice a day to swaddle and plaster his leg and else he could not keep his life, wouldst thou reckon his leg sick or whole? I ween (imagine) ye will agree that his leg is not well at ease, nor the owner neither. Now if ye felt your belly in such case that ye must be fain all day to tend it with warm clothes (hot compresses) or else ye were not able to abide the pain, would ye reckon your belly sick or whole? I ween (imagine) ye would reckon your belly not in good quart (condition). If thou shouldst see one in such case that he could not hold up his head, that he could not stand on his feet, that he should be fain to lie down alone and there lie speechless as a dead stock an hour or two every day, wouldst thou not say that he were perilously sick and had good cause to remember death, when he lieth every day in such case as though he were dead already?

Now then I pray thee consider me that our bodies be ever in such case so tender of themselves that except we lapped them continually with warm clothes, we were not able to live one winter week. Consider that our bodies have so sore a sickness and such a continual consumption in themselves that the strongest were not able to endure and continue ten days together, were it not that once or twice a day we be fain to take medicines inward to clout them up withal and keep them as long as we can. For what is our meat and drink but medicines against hunger and thirst, that give us warning of that we daily lose by our inward consumption? And of that consumption shall we die in conclusion, for all the medicines that we use, though never other sickness came at us.

Consider also that all our swaddling and tending with warm clothes and daily medicines, yet can our bodies not bear themselves but that almost half our time ever in twenty-four hours we be fain to fall in a swoon which we call sleep, and there lie like dead stocks by a long space ere we come to ourselves again: insomuch that among all wise men of old it is agreed that sleep is the very image of death.

Now thou wilt peradventure say that this is but a fantasy. For though we call this hunger sickness and meat a medicine, yet men know well enough what very real sickness is and what very medicines be, and thereby we know well enough that they be none.

If thou think this, then would I wit of thee what thou callest a sickness. Is not that a sickness that will make an end of thee if it be not helped? If that be so, then I suppose thou bearest ever thy sickness with thee,—for very sure art thou that it will make an end of thee if thou be not helped.

What callest thou, then, a medicine? Is it not such a thing as either applied outwardly to thy body, or received inward, shall preserve thee against that sore or sickness that else would put thee or some part of thee in peril? What can be, then, more properly and more verily a medicine than is our meat and drink, by which is resisted the peril and undoubted death that else should in so few days follow, by the inward sickness of our own nature continually consuming us within? For as for that ye reckon that we know which be sickness, that is but a custom of calling, by which we call no sickness by that name but such as be casual and come and go. For that that is common to all men, and never from any man, because we reckon it natural, we give it not the name of sickness, but we name sickness a passion (suffering) that cometh seldomer and, as we reckon, against nature, whereas the conflict of the divers qualified elements tempered in our body, continually laboring each to vanquish other and thereby to dissolve the whole, though it be as sore against the continuance of our nature and as sore laboreth to the dissolution of the whole body as other sickness do, yet we neither call it sickness, nor the meat that resisteth it we call no medicine, and that for none other cause but for the continual familiarity that we have therewith.

But now consider, if it were so that one whole country were born all lepers, which is a sickness rather foul and perilous than painful, or all an whole country born with the falling sickness, so that never any of them had ever in their lives known or heard either themselves or any other void of those diseases, trow ye this, then, that they would ever have reckoned them for sickness? Nay surely, but they would have counted for sickness the colic and the stone and such other like as come and go. But as for their leprosy and falling evil, they would never account it other than we account hunger or sleep. For as for that thy hunger doth thee pleasure when it is fed, so doth sometimes the itch of a sore leg when thou clawest about the brinks (edges).

And thus mayest thou surely see that all our whole life is but a sickness never curable, but as an incurable canker, with continual swaddling and plastering blotched up to live as long as we may, and in conclusion undoubtedly to die of the same sickness, and though there never came other. So that, if you consider this well, thou mayest look upon death, not as a stranger, but as a nigh neighbor. For as the flame is next the smoke, so is death next an incurable sickness; and such is all our life.

And yet if this move you little, but that ye think for all this that death is far from you, I will go somewhat nearer you. Thou reckonest every man near his death when he is dying. Then if thyself be now already dying, how canst thou reckon thyself far from death? Some man saith merrily to his fellow, "Be merry, man,—thou shalt never die as long as thou livest." And albeit he seem to say true, yet saith he more than he can make good. For if that were true, I could make him much merrier, for then he should never die. Ye will peradventure marvel of this, but it is easy to prove. For I think ye will grant me that there is no time after that a man hath once life, but he is either alive or dead. Then will there no man say that one can die either before he get life or after that he hath lost it, and so hath he no time left to die in but while he hath life. Wherefore, if we neither die before our life nor when we be dead already, needs must it follow that we never die but while we live.

It is not all one to die and to be dead. Truth it is that we be never dead while we live; and it is, meseemeth, as true, not only that we die while we live, but also that we die all the while we live. What thing is dying? Is it any other thing than the passage and going out of this present life?

Now tell me, then, if thou wert going out of an house, whether art thou going out only when thy foot is on the uttermost inch of the threshold, thy body half out of the door, or else when thou beginnest to set the first foot forward to go out, in what place of the house soever ye stand when ye buskle (start) forward? I would say that ye be going out of the house from the first foot ye set forward to go forth. No man will think other, as I suppose, but all is one reason in going hence and coming hither. Now if one were coming hither to this town, he were not only coming hither while he were entering in at the gate, but all the way also from whence he came hitherward. Nor, in likewise, in going hence from this town,— a man is not only going from this town while he hath his body in the gate going outward, but also while he setteth his foot out of his host's house to go forward. And therefore, if a man met him by the way, far yet within the town, and asked him whither he were going, he should truly answer that he were going out of the town, all were the town so long that he had ten miles to go ere he came at the gate.

And surely, methinketh that in likewise a man is not only dying, that is to say, going in his way out of this life, while he lieth drawing on, but also all the while that he is going towards his end,—which is by all the whole time of his life, since the first moment in which he began to live, until the last moment of his life, or rather the first in which he is fully dead.

Now if this be thus, as meseemeth that reason proveth, a man is always dying from afore his birth, and every hour of our age, as it passeth by, cutteth his own length out of our life and maketh it shorter by so much, and our death so much the nearer. Which measuring of time and diminishing of life, with approaching towards death, is nothing else but from our beginning to our ending, one continual dying: so that wake we, sleep we, eat we, drink we, mourn we, sing we, in what wise soever live we, all the same while die we. So that we never ought to look towards death as a thing far off, considering that although he made no haste towards us, yet we never cease ourselves to make haste towards him.

Now if thou think this reason but a sophistical subtlety, and thinkest while thou art a young man thou mayest for all this think thy death far off, that is to wit, as far as thou hast by likelihood of nature many years to live, then will I put thee an homely example, not very pleasant, but none the less very true and very fit for the matter.

If there were two, both condemned to death, both carried out at once towards execution; of which two, the one were sure that the place of his execution were within one mile, the other twenty miles off, yea an hundred, and ye will, he that were in the cart to be carried an hundred miles would not take much more pleasure than his fellow in the length of his way, notwithstanding that it were an hundred times as long as his fellow's and that he had thereby a hundred times as long to live, being sure and out of all question to die at the end.

Reckon me now yourself a young man in your best lust, twenty years of age, if ye will. Let there be another, ninety. Both must ye die, both be ye in the cart carrying forward. His gallows and death standeth within ten miles at the farthest, and yours within eighty. I see not why ye should reckon much less of your death than he, though your way be longer, since ye be sure ye shall never cease riding till ye come at it. And this is true, although ye were sure that the place of your execution stood so far beyond his. But what if there were to the place of your execution two ways, of which the one were four score miles farther about than your fellow's, the other nearer by five miles than his; and when ye were put in the cart, had warning of both; and though ye were showed that it were likely that ye should be carried the longer way, yet it might hap ye should go the shorter, and whether ye were carried the one or the other, ye should never know till ye come to the place: I trow ye could not in this case make much longer of your life than of your fellow's.

Now in this case are we all. For our Lord hath not indented (entered into an agreement) with us of the time [Job 14:13]. He hath appointed what we may not pass, but not how soon we shall go, nor where, not in what wise. And therefore if thou wilt consider how little cause thou hast to reckon thy death so far off by reason of thy youth, reckon how many as young as thou have been drowned in the selfsame waters in which thou rowest. And thus shalt thou well see that thou hast no cause to look upon thy death as a thing far off, but a thing undoubtedly nigh thee, and ever walking with thee. By which, not a false imagination but a very true contemplation, thou shalt behold him and advise (heed) him such as he is, and thereby take occasion to flee vain pleasures of the flesh that keep out the very (true) pleasures of the soul.

ST. IGNATIUS LOYOLA

(1492—1556)

IGNATIUS of Loyola, baptized Iñigo, is perhaps less known for his own sake than he is through that remarkable extension of his personality, the Society of Jesus, the order he founded and guided to swift and unique eminence. The Jesuits, as the society is popularly called, were, and are, a paradoxical order. Their members vow to obey a single head, yet they are encouraged to exercise a maximum of personal liberty in their individual tasks. Their organization is a military one, yet the members are wholly dedicated to the missions of peace. As the name implies, the society aspires to be the companions of Jesus Christ and to unite all men in that companionship.

While the founder did surrender himself entirely to God and sought to give himself to the work of his society, he was never other than himself—an outstanding individual, a man of great charm, courtesy, and compassion. Indeed, it was because he was such a gentleman that he succeeded in winning men to the order, and in and through that order, he attracted countless others to membership in Christ's Church.

He was the youngest of eleven children born to Maria Saez de Balde and Don Beltran, lord of the small fief of Loyola, in Guipuzcoa in the north of Spain. The family was noble, but neither rich nor important. Traditionally, its men were soldiers. Ignatius grew up dreaming of glory on the field of battle, his head stuffed with the romances of chivalry that spurred knights to unheard-of gallantries but provoked in Cervantes the satirical thoughts that animated *Don Quixote*.

Ignatius became a page at the court of Ferdinand of Aragon, where he learned the arts of the caballero—military proficiency, and music, dancing and the manners and fashions of gentility. He joined the army in 1517 and lived gaily, in the style of his caste.

In 1521, when Francis I of France declared war on King Charles V to recover the province of Navarre, Ignatius was sent to Pamplona to resist the invasion. Under the Count de la Foix the French army marched on Pamplona. Outnumbered ten to one by the French, the Spanish viceroy withdrew, leaving Ignatius with a small garrison in the citadel. The city surrendered, but not Ignatius. He stirred up the men to an heroic resistance. When the French artillery blasted a breach in the wall, Ignatius, sword in hand, led his men in defense of the gap until a cannon ball, ricocheting from a bastion, shattered his right leg. The citadel fell and Ignatius, freed in acknowledgment of his heroism, was sent home on a litter.

The shattered leg had been badly set and the doctors at Loyola had to break it and set it again. It became infected and Ignatius nearly died of gangrene. When he recovered and found that the bone stuck out under his knee, he demanded a third break and a sawing of the bone. He did not mind the limp from the shortened right leg, but he did want to be able to wear his stockings neatly and to pull on his fashionable military boots. This was perhaps his last and most painful concession to vanity. For during his long convalescence, he began to read, first, *The Golden Legend*, a collection of the lives of the saints, and later a life of Christ. Gradually he realized that Christ, as well as kings, had his knights. Vowed now to a Christian knighthood, he set out on a pilgrimage to the monastery and shrine at Montserrat. There he made a general confession and left his sword at the altar as a symbol of his new devotion. For a year he stayed at Manresa, near Montserrat, where he meditated, prayed, and fasted. In a cave at Manresa he began to make notes on his spiritual experiences, notes that, expanded and corrected throughout the years, came to be known as *The Spiritual Exercises*.

Life now shone with a new meaning. "It is not enough that I serve the Lord," he said to himself. "All hearts ought to love Him, and all tongues ought to praise Him." To prepare for his mission of kindling men's love of God, he set out for Palestine, where for several enraptured months he retraced Christ's footsteps in the holy places. Returning to Spain, he began simultaneously to offer the peace of Christ to his neighbors and to study, for this pilgrim-hermit-knight errant of the Lord was a poorly educated man by the high standards of the flourishing Renaissance. At thirty-three, he went to a grammar school in Barcelona and for two years endured the jeers of ten-year-old boys. By 1526 he had acquired enough knowledge to enter the University of Alcala. There the religious instructions he gave to the people of the town were misrepresented as heretical, and he spent over a month in prison. He studied another two years at Salamanca, was again imprisoned, and then moved on to Paris where, in 1535, after seven laborious years and much private tutoring, he finally won his Master of Arts degree.

For Ignatius, learning was necessary to help the many penitents who sought him out wherever he went. At Paris, the first of his converts was his tutor, the brilliant and holy Peter Faber of Savoy, who found that his pupil could teach him a wisdom he had hitherto sought in vain. His most important convert was Francis Xavier, a Spanish nobleman like himself, but intellectually proud and ambitious. Ignatius followed Francis Xavier like a holy hound, sensing in this compatriot a power that, rightly directed, could set the world on fire. Others sought out the limping saint to learn from him the sweetness of Christ's love. Altogether there were seven—a priest among them—who vowed in the chapel at Montmartre to finish their studies and then offer themselves to the pope for whatever services he might require.

Before the company left Paris in 1537 three doctors of divinity had joined the band. With holy joy and no plans beyond their vow, the ten set out for Venice where they worked in a hospital. In the same year those who were not priests were ordained and the pope summoned them to Rome. Some taught in the seminaries, some instructed the people of Rome, others, Xavier among them, went to convert the heathen overseas. In an incredibly short time, Ignatius' band grew from ten to sixty, later to thousands. The informal association became a regular order, and a constitution was drawn up by Ignatius.

In 1541, Ignatius was elected general of the Society of Jesus. He held this office until his death in 1556.

At the heart of the incredible expansion of Jesuit activity was Ignatius himself and the most direct way to know the man is through *The Spiritual Exercises*. The *Exercises* are what the word implies—spiritual efforts, a striving to see, to know, and to understand God's will. In a series of meditations, arranged in periods of four weeks, the Christian is invited to think about God in order, first, to reform what needs reforming, then to progress in his knowledge of God attained by Christ's example, and finally to unite himself with God by spiritual love. Ever respectful of human intelligence and liberty, Ignatius does not attempt to meditate for his readers. Rather, he sets down points for contemplation. He persuades only by suggesting examples of virtue recorded in the Gospels. He seeks to make the reader seek for himself, to hear by himself, the revelations of the Holy Spirit.

THE SPIRITUAL EXERCISES
(The Fourth Day of the Second Week)

A MEDITATION ON TWO STANDARDS

The one of Christ, our supreme Captain and Lord; the other of Lucifer, the mortal enemy of our human nature.

Preparatory prayer. [To ask God our Lord for grace that all my intentions, actions, and operations may be ordered purely to the service and praise of His divine Majesty.]

First prelude. The history: here it will be how Christ calls and desires all to come under His Standard; and Lucifer, on the contrary, under his.

Second prelude. The composition, seeing the place: here it will be to see a vast plain embracing the whole region of Jerusalem, where the supreme Captain-General of the good is Christ our Lord; and another plain, in the region of Babylon, where the chief of the enemy is Lucifer.

Third prelude. To ask for what I desire; and here it will be to ask for knowledge of the deceits of the wicked chieftain, and for help to guard myself against them; and for knowledge of the true life which the supreme and true Captain reveals, and for grace to imitate Him.

First point. To picture to myself how the chieftain of all the enemy seats himself in the midst of that great plain of Babylon as on a lofty throne of fire and smoke—horrible and terrible to behold.

Second point. To consider how he calls together innumerable demons and how he disperses them some to one city, some to another, and so on throughout the whole world, omitting no provinces, places, states of life, nor any single individual.

Third point. To consider the harangue which he makes to them and how he admonishes them to ensnare men in nets and bind them with chains, bidding them first to tempt them with the lust of riches (as he is wont to do in most cases), in order that thereby they may more easily come to the vain honor of the world, and afterwards to unbounded pride: the first step is that of riches, the second of honor, the third of pride; and from these three steps he leads on to all other vices.

In like manner, on the other hand, we are to picture the supreme and true Captain Who is Christ our Lord.

First point. To consider how Christ our Lord takes His stand on a great plain near Jerusalem, in a lowly place, fair and gracious to behold.

Second point. Consider how the Lord of the whole world chooses so many persons, Apostles, Disciples, and so forth, and sends them throughout the whole world, to spread abroad His sacred doctrine among all states and conditions of persons.

Third point. Consider the address which Christ our Lord makes to all His servants and friends, whom He sends on this expedition, charging them that they should desire to help all, by drawing them first to a most perfect spiritual poverty, and (if it should please His divine Majesty and He should will to choose them) not less to actual poverty. Secondly, to a desire of reproaches and contempt; because from these two things results humility. There are three steps: the first, poverty, opposed to riches; the second, shame or contempt, opposed to worldly honor; the third, humility opposed to pride; and from these three steps let them lead them on to all the other virtues.

First Colloquy. A colloquy addressed to our Lady to obtain for me grace from her Son and Lord, that I may be received under His Standard: first, in most perfect spiritual poverty, and (if it should please His divine Majesty, and He should will to elect and receive me) not less in actual poverty; secondly, in bearing reproaches and injuries, the better to imitate Him in these, provided only I can suffer them without sin on the part of any person or displeasure of His divine Majesty; and after this a "Hail Mary."

Second colloquy. To ask the same of the Son, that He may obtain it for me from the Father; and to say an "Anima Christi."

Third colloquy. To ask the same of the Father, that He may grant it to me; and to say an "Our Father."

Let this Exercise be made at midnight, and afterwards a second time in the morning; and let two repetitions of the same be made about the hours of Mass and Vespers, always ending with the three colloquies with our Lady, with the Son, and with the Father; and let the meditation on the Three Classes which follows be made during the hour before supper.

THREE CLASSES OF MEN

On the same fourth day let there be made a meditation on three classes of men, in order that we may embrace the best.

Preparatory prayer. The usual preparatory prayer.

First prelude. The history concerning three classes of men, each of which has acquired ten thousand ducats not purely or duly for the love of God. They all desire to save their souls, and to find in peace, God our Lord, by ridding themselves of the weight and impediment to this end which they find in their affection to the thing acquired.

Second prelude. The composition, seeing the place: it will be here to behold myself, how I stand in the presence of God

185

our Lord and all His saints, that I may desire and know that which is more pleasing to His divine Goodness.

Third prelude. To ask for what I desire: it will be here to beg for grace to choose that which may be more for the glory of His divine Majesty and the salvation of my soul.

First class. The first class would wish to get rid of the affection which they have for the thing acquired, in order to find in peace, God our Lord, and be able to save their souls; but up to the hour of death they do not take the means.

Second class. The second class desires to get rid of the affection, but they desire to do so in such a way as to remain in possession of what they have gained, so that God should come to what they desire. They do not resolve to relinquish the thing in order to go to God, although this should be the best state for them.

Third class. The third class desires to get rid of the affection, but they desire to get rid of it in such a way as to be no more inclined to retain the thing acquired than not to retain it, desiring to will its retention or not to will it, only according as God our Lord shall give them to will, and according as it shall seem to them better for the service and praise of His divine Majesty. Meanwhile, they wish to consider that they do actually leave all, striving with all their might not to wish for that or for any other thing unless it be solely the service of God our Lord that moves them; so that the desire of being better able to serve God our Lord may be what moves them to take or to leave the thing.

Colloquies. Make the same three colloquies as were made in the preceding contemplation on the Two Standards.

It is to be observed, that when we feel a shrinking from, or repugnance to actual poverty, when in fact we are not indifferent to poverty or riches, it is a great help, in order to overcome such an inordinate affection, to beg in the colloquies (even though it be against the flesh) that our Lord would elect us to actual poverty; to protest that we desire, beg, and supplicate it, provided only it may be to the service and praise of His divine goodness.

THE FIFTH DAY

A contemplation on the departure of Christ our Lord from Nazareth to the River Jordan, and how He was Baptized.

This contemplation will be made once at midnight, and again in the morning and two repetitions of it at the hour of Mass and Vespers, and before supper the application of the five senses to it; in each of these five Exercises prefixing the usual preparatory prayer, and the three preludes, according as all this has been explained in the contemplations on the Incarnation and the Nativity, and concluding with the three colloquies of the Three Classes or according to the note which follows the Three Classes.

The particular examination, after dinner and supper, will be made on the defects and negligences regarding the Exercises and Additions of this day; and so likewise on the succeeding days.

THE SIXTH DAY

A contemplation on how Christ our Lord went from the River Jordan to the wilderness, inclusively (including what happened there), keeping in everything the same form as on the fifth day.

THE SEVENTH DAY

How St. Andrew and others followed Christ our Lord.

THE EIGHTH DAY

Of the Sermon on the Mount; concerning the eight Beatitudes.

THE NINTH DAY

How Christ our Lord appeared to His disciples on the waves of the sea.

THE TENTH DAY

How our Lord preached in the temple.

THE ELEVENTH DAY

Of the raising of Lazarus.

THE TWELFTH DAY

Of the Day of Palms.

THREE OBSERVATIONS

In the contemplations of this second week, each one according to the time he wishes to give, or the progress he makes, can prolong or shorten the week. If he should wish to prolong it, let him take the Mysteries of the Visitation of our Lady to St. Elizabeth, the Shepherds, the Circumcision of the Infant Jesus, and the three kings and so of others; if to shorten it, let him omit even some of those which are set down above; because this is intended only to give an introduction and method, in order afterwards to contemplate better and more completely.

The matter of the Elections will be begun from the contemplation of Christ's departure from Nazareth for the Jordan inclusively, that is to say, on the fifth day, as is explained in what follows.

Before anyone enters upon the Elections, in order that he may be well affected towards the true doctrine of Christ our Lord, it will be very helpful to consider attentively the following three Modes of Humility, considering them from time to time during the whole day, and also making the colloquies in accordance with what will be said below.

THREE MODES OF HUMILITY

First mode. Necessary to eternal salvation: that I so abase and humble myself as far as lies in my power, as in all things to obey the law of God our Lord, in such sort that though men would make me Lord of all created things in the world, or for the preservation of my own temporal life, I would not enter into deliberation about breaking a commandment, whether divine or human, that binds me under mortal sin.

Second mode. More perfect humility: when I find myself in such a point that I do not desire, nor feel myself attached to, riches more than poverty, honor more than dishonor, a long life more than a short one, when the service of God our Lord and the salvation of my soul are equal; and furthermore that not for all created things, nor should my life be endangered, would I enter into deliberation about committing a venial sin.

Third mode. Most perfect humility: when the first and second Modes being included, and the praise and glory of the divine Majesty being equal, in order better to imitate Christ our Lord and to become actually more like to Him, I desire and choose poverty with Christ poor rather than riches; reproaches with Christ laden therewith, rather than honor; and I desire to be accounted as worthless and a fool for Christ, Who was first held to be such, rather than wise and prudent in this world.

It will be very profitable for him who desires to obtain this third Mode of Humility to make the above-mentioned three colloquies of the classes, imploring our Lord to be pleased to elect him to this third Mode of greater and more perfect humility, in order the better to imitate and serve Him, if it be for the equal or greater service and praise of His divine Majesty.

THE ELECTION

Preamble to making the election.

In every good Election, so far as regards our part, the eye of our intention ought to be single, looking only to the end for which I was created, namely, for the praise of God our Lord, and the salvation of my soul. Therefore, whatever I choose ought to be for this, that it may help me towards the end for which I am created: not ordering or drawing the end to the means, but the means to the end. As, for example, it happens that many first choose to marry, which is a means, and in the second place to serve God our Lord in the married state, which service of God is the end. In the same way there are others who first desire to possess benefices, and then to serve

God in them. So that these persons do not go straight to God, but rather wish that God should come straight over to this inordinate affection, and consequently they make the end a means, and of the means an end, so that what they ought to choose first they choose last. For first we ought to make it our object to desire to serve God, which is the end; and secondarily to accept the benefice, or to marry (if that should be more fitting for me), which is the means to the end. Nothing therefore ought to move me to take such means, or to deprive myself of them, except only the service and praise of God our Lord, and the eternal salvation of my soul.

A CONSIDERATION

For the purpose of obtaining knowledge of the matters about which an Election ought to be made; it contains four points and a note.

First point. It is necessary that all matters about which we wish to make an Election should be indifferent or good in themselves, and such as are approved within our Holy Mother, the hierarchical Church, and not bad, nor repugnant to her.

Second point. There are some that fall under an immutable Election, such as are the priesthood, matrimony, and so forth; there are others which fall under a mutable Election, as, for instance, accepting or relinquishing benefices, accepting or renouncing temporal goods.

Third point. In an immutable Election when once it has been made, there is no room for choosing, because it cannot be undone, as is the case with matrimony, the priesthood, etc. Only this is to be noticed, that if anyone has not made his Election duly and in order, without inordinate affections, let him repent and take care to lead a good life in that which he has chosen. Such an Election, however, does not seem to be a divine vocation, since it was an ill-ordered and perverted Election. Many err in this respect taking a perverted or bad Election for a divine vocation; whereas every divine vocation is always pure, clear, and without admixture of the flesh, or of any other inordinate affection.

Fourth point. If anyone has made an Election duly and in order, in matters which fall under a mutable Election, not having inclined to the flesh or to the world, he has no cause to make a fresh Election, but only to perfect himself in what he has chosen as much as he can.

It is to be observed that if such a mutable Election has not been made sincerely and in due order, then it is expedient to make it duly, if one desires to bring forth notable fruits and such as shall be very pleasing to God our Lord.

THREE TIMES
in each of which a sound and good Election may be made.

The first time is when God our Lord so moves and attracts the will, that without doubting or being able to doubt, such a devout soul follows what has been pointed out to it; as St. Paul and St. Matthew did when they followed Christ our Lord.

The second time is when much light and knowledge is obtained by experience of consolations and desolations, and by experience of the discernment of various spirits.

The third time is one of tranquillity, in which a man, considering first for what end he is born, namely, to praise God our Lord and to save his soul. Desiring this, he chooses as the means to this end, a certain kind or state of life within the bounds of the Church, in order that he may be helped by it in the service of his Lord, and the salvation of his soul.

I call it a time of tranquillity, when the soul is not agitated by different spirits, and enjoys the use of its natural powers freely and quietly.

If an Election is not made in the first or second time, there follow two methods of making it according to this third time.

THE FIRST METHOD
of making a good and sound Election.

First Point. To propose to myself the matter about which I wish to make an Election, as, for example, an office or benefice which is to be accepted or left, or any other thing which falls under a mutable Election.

Second point. It is necessary to keep before my eyes the end for which I am created, which is to praise God our Lord, and to save my soul; and at the same time to find myself indifferent, without any inordinate affection; so that I am not more inclined or disposed to take the thing proposed than to leave it, nor to leave it more than to take it; but that I find myself, as it were, exactly balanced, ready to follow that which I shall feel to be more for the glory and praise of God our Lord, and for the salvation of my soul.

Third point. To beg of God our Lord that He may be pleased to move my will and place in my soul that which I ought to do in regard to the matter proposed, namely, that which may be more to His praise and glory, considering the matter well and faithfully with my understanding, and choosing in conformity with His most holy will and good pleasure.

Fourth point. To consider the matter, reckoning the advantages and benefits which accrue to me if I hold the proposed office or benefice, solely with reference to the praise of our Lord God and the salvation of my soul; and on the other hand to consider likewise the disadvantages and dangers which there are in holding it. And then, secondly, acting in the same manner, to look at the advantages and benefits in not holding it, and likewise, on the other hand, at the disadvantages and dangers in not holding it.

Fifth point. After I have considered and reasoned on every aspect of the matter proposed, to see to which side reason more inclines; and thus according to the preponderating movement of reason, and not according to any sensual inclination, a decision ought to be made about the matter proposed.

Sixth point. After such an Election or decision has been made, he who has made it ought with great diligence to go to prayer in the presence of God our Lord, and to offer Him the said Election, to the end that His divine Majesty may be pleased to receive and confirm it, if it should be to his greater service and praise.

THE SECOND METHOD

of making a sound and good Election.
It contains in itself four rules and one note.

First rule. The love which moves me and makes me choose the said thing, should descend from on high, from the love of God: in such a manner that he who chooses should first feel in himself that the love which he has more or less for the thing which he chooses is solely for the sake of his Creator and Lord.

Second rule. To place before my eyes a man whom I have never seen or known, and, desiring his highest perfection, to consider what I would tell him to do and choose for the greater glory of God our Lord, and the greater perfection of his soul; and acting myself in a similar manner, to keep the rule which I lay down for another.

Third rule. To consider, as if I were at the point of death, the form and measure which I should then desire to have observed in the method of the present Election; and regulating myself according to that, let me make my decision on the whole matter.

Fourth rule. Considering attentively in what condition I shall find myself at the Day of Judgment, to think how I shall then wish to have decided in regard to the present matter; and the rule which I should then wish to have observed, I will observe now, that I may then find myself full of joy and gladness.

Having observed all the above-mentioned rules in order to secure my salvation and eternal rest, I will make my Election and oblation to God our Lord, according to the sixth point of the first method of making an Election.

METHOD of Amending and
Reforming One's Present Life and State.

It is to be noted, with regard to those who hold office in the Church, or are settled in matrimony (whether rich in temporal goods or not), that where they have no opportunity, or no very ready will for making an Election in things which fall under mutual Election, it is very profitable in place of making an Election, to give them a form and method of amending and reforming each his own life and state, namely, by setting before himself his creation, and directing his life and state to the glory and praise of God our Lord and the salvation of his soul. In order to arrive at and attain this end, he ought by means of the Exercises and methods of Election, as above explained, to consider and examine carefully how large a house and establishment he ought to keep up, how he ought to regulate and govern it, how he ought to instruct it by word and example. Likewise with regard to his means: what proportion he ought to take for his family and household, and how much for distribution among the poor and for other pious objects; not desiring nor seeking anything else except in all and through all the greater praise and glory of God our Lord. For let each reflect that he will make progress in all spiritual matters just so far as he shall have divested himself of his self-love, self-will, and self-interest.

ST. PETER
OF ALCANTARA
(1499—1562)

ONE day in October, 1559, Pedro of Alcantara, the head of the order of Reformed Franciscans, arrived at the city of Avila to visit several monasteries under his jurisdiction. He was by that time an almost legendary figure throughout Spain and the whole Christian world. A former scholar at the University of Salamanca and a canon lawyer, he had retired from the world to enter the austere branch of the Franciscans. With uncompromising logic, he aimed early in life to subdue all his inordinate cravings the better to prepare his soul for communion with Christ. He fasted. He ate—once a day, sometimes less often—bread moistened in water and boiled herbs. He slept one hour and a half a night in a cell so small that he could only kneel or crouch. He kept such close custody over his eyes that he could not recognize his friar companions save by their voices, nor could he describe the architecture of the convent church, for he never raised his eyes in what he would have regarded as superfluous curiosity. He kept closing doors on distractions until he was completely alone with the God and All of his desire.

What he thought about in those wilderness monasteries and hermitages in his native Estremadura he set down in three books, *Mental Prayer*, *On the Peace of the Soul*, and *On the Interior Life*. Here are contemplations of the Divine Love, particularly of the Incarnation and the Blessed Sacrament, a prolonged invitation to a union with Christ, the life of heaven on earth. Yet the greater his joy in heaven the more uncompromising became his austerities, for he believed passionately that it was hypocritical to seek God without denying oneself.

Penance was not his end, but the straight and narrow path to Heaven.

People were attracted to him as they had been long before to his divine master. John III, the King of Portugal, prevailed upon the Franciscan provincial to send Peter to Lisbon. There he felt suffocated by the surfeit of honors and conveniences and left as soon as he could. His native town of Alcantara summoned him to be the peacemaker in a public dispute. His brethren elected him provincial both in Spain and Portugal. Although ever seeking solitude, all manner of men—princes, scholars, penitents—continued to seek him out. Finally, after long but reluctant service in the higher offices of his order, Peter decided to found a still stricter congregation, called the Discalced (barefooted) Franciscans. Near Pedroso in the diocese of Plasencia, he founded a monastery thirty-two feet long and twenty-eight feet wide, with cells no bigger than tombs. Here he lived in poverty and joy. Still, people tracked him down. In 1555, the Emperor Charles V had abdicated his throne and retired to the great monastery at Juste to prepare for death. He wanted Peter as his confessor, but Peter begged to be allowed to cling to his solitude. Had he not won the Emperor over to his request, he would not have been in Avila on that day in 1559 to meet with, console, and direct a sister saint who at that moment was facing one of the great crises of her life.

Teresa of Avila had but lately experienced a second conversion in which, after a long illness, she began to aspire to a life of greater perfection. Moreover, she had been receiving visions and inspirations from the Lord, gifts of such extraordinary nature that her quite ordinary confessors and advisers accused her of deluding herself. Harassed by many anxieties and scruples, she had obtained permission to spend eight days at the house of Doña Guiomar de Ulloa, a learned, holy widow and intimate friend. Guiomar, hearing of Peter's arrival, arranged for a meeting between the two. It turned out to be a momentous spiritual encounter. On her part, Teresa poured out her soul "without duplicity and concealment." She told him how horrified she was at the suggestion that her visions and inspirations were considered by some to be the work of the devil. St. Peter listened, his eyes cast down. At long last he spoke. Out of his own long experience in mystical contemplation, he assured her it was the Holy Spirit that guided her. With great joy he recognized her as a kindred soul to whom he could disclose without fear the secrets of God's own long loving discourses with himself. As St. Teresa wrote, "For if the Lord brings anyone to this state he will find no pleasure or comfort equal to that of meeting another whom he believes He has brought along the first part of the same road. . . ."

Peter recognized true sanctity in Teresa. He went to see her confessor and explain to him the manifestations of divine grace that the confessor had not rightly assessed. He encouraged Teresa to continue in her resolve to reform the Carmelite order and, a few years later, he lent his great authority to her own request to begin her work of reform at the convent of St. Joseph. They parted agreeing to exchange letters on the spiritual matters that lay closest to their hearts. So closely were they joined in their love of God that, although physically they never met again, they were nevertheless in each other's presence. In her *Autobiography,* St. Teresa tells us how she saw Peter in a vision just before his death, and many times thereafter. He died at his monastery at Arenas, on his knees, just after reciting, "We shall go into the house of the Lord." Teresa's comments on St. Peter remain St. Peter's best epitaph:

"Since his death it has been the Lord's good pleasure that I should have more intercourse with him than I had during his life and that he should advise me on many subjects. I have often beheld him in the greatest bliss. The first time he appeared to me he said, 'Oh happy penance that hath obtained for me so great a reward. . . .' See then how this austere life has ended in great glory."

ON THE MISERIES
OF THIS LIFE

Today you will meditate upon the miseries of human life. Thus you will see how vain is the glory of the world, how fit to be despised, for it has no other frail foundation than this miserable life. The defects and miseries of this life are, as it were, innumerable. You may consider especially the seven following.

Consider, first, that this life is short, some seventy or eighty years at most, and, if it stretches beyond, is, as the Prophet says, "but labor and sorrow" [Psalms 1:10]. Take from this the period of infancy, which is more an animal than a human life, and the time spent in sleep, during which we neither use our senses nor that reason of ours which is proper to man, and you will see that life is even shorter than at first appears, If, moreover, you compare it with the eternity of the life to come, it will seem to you hardly a speck. Thus you will perceive how infatuated those are who, to enjoy so short a breath of life, expose themselves to lose the repose of that which is to last for ever.

Secondly, consider how uncertain this life is. Here is another misery to add to the former, for, as though it were not enough that it is so short, it is also without security and uncertain. How many reach those seventy or eighty years I mentioned? For how many the strands are broken when they would begin to weave! How many pass away in the flower of their age—as we put it—or before they reach maturity! "You know not," as the Savior says, "at what hour your Lord will come, in the morning or at midday, at midnight or at the cock-crowing" [Mark 13:35]. Better to appreciate this truth, think of the deaths of the many persons you have known in this world, especially of your friends and comrades, and of persons who have been famous and admired. At varying ages in life has death struck them and swept away all their schemes and hopes.

Thirdly, consider how frail and delicate this life is, and you will see how no vessel of glass is as fragile. A breeze, or a hot sun, a draught of cold water, or the breath of a sick person: these are enough to despoil us of it, as everyday experience shows. How many a man is cut down in the flower of his age from one or other of these causes.

In the fourth place, see how mutable this life is, never the same for long. Think how our bodies change; they do not remain permanently in the one same regular state of health; much less do our souls. Like the sea are these, always restless under the varying winds and waves of passion, of craving, of desire, which trouble us at every hour. Think, finally, of the changes of fortune: no one willingly consents to remain in the same state of life, with the same measure of prosperity, the same joy, but human life is like a wheel, forever rolling on. Above all, dwell on the unceasing movement of life: day or night, it never pauses, lessening as it moves. What is our life but a torch which is forever consuming itself? The more resplendently it burns, the more rapidly will it fail. What is our life but a flower, which opens out in the morning, and blooms at midday, and in the evening withers? [Job 14:2]. It is by reason of this continuous change that God says, by the mouth of Isaias, "All flesh is grass, and all the glory thereof as the flower of the field" [Isaias 40: 6]. Saint Jerome comments thus upon these words: "Truly, when we consider the frailty of our flesh, and how at every point and moment of time we increase and decrease, without ever remaining in the same state, and how that which at this very instant forms the subject of our discourse, of our schemes and meditations, is so much cut off from our life, we shall not hesitate to speak of our flesh as a little grass, and all its glory as the flower of the field." The infant at the breast, how quickly does it grow into a child, and the child into a big lad, and lo and behold, the big lad is soon well on in years, and, when on the verge of old age, marvels to find himself no longer young! The woman, whose beauty attracted the attention of so many young men, soon finds herself with wrinkled brow, and she

199

who was once so attractive quickly becomes an object of aversion.

Fifthly, consider how deceitful is life. This is perhaps the worst feature of all, so many does she lead astray, so many cling to her in blind affection. She is ugly, and we fancy her beautiful; bitter, and she appears to us sweet; short, and each one esteems her enduring; she seems spacious, and is narrow; she seems so lovable that there is no peril nor labor men will not face for her, even at the risk of life eternal, doing such things as lead them to the loss of the life which knows no end.

Sixthly, consider how this life, already burdened with those miseries we have mentioned, is subject also to so many misfortunes both of soul and body. Nothing else is it than a valley of tears and sea of measureless sorrow. St. Jerome relates how Xerxes, that mighty monarch, who leveled out the mountains and filled in the seas, found himself one day looking down from an eminence upon a countless host of armed men. He admired them for some time and then began to weep. Questioned on the cause of his tears, he replied: "I weep because a hundred years hence not one of those I see before me will be alive." "Would that we," adds St. Jerome, "could mount to some such height whence we might view all the world at our feet. Then might we see the falls and disasters of all the world, nations destroyed one by the other, and kingdom by kingdom. Here would we see torments, and in another place massacre; some perishing at sea, others led away captive; here a wedding, there a death; some dying by violence, others in peace; some abounding in wealth, others in beggary. Finally, we should see not merely the army of Xerxes, but all men in the world, living today, and doomed, in a few days, to vanish" [Funeral Oration on Nepotian].

Think of all the infirmities and labors of man's body, all the afflictions and anxieties of his soul, all the perils that accompany man in every state and in every period of his life, and you will see well enough the miseries of human life, and, clearly too, how little the world can give. Thus will you easily come to hold in little esteem all that there is in it.

To all these miseries succeeds the last, which is death. For body and soul alike this is the final terror. In an instant the body is stripped of all, and the soul fixed for ever in its eternity.

This meditation will help to make you understand how short and wretched is the glory of the world—yet it is on this that a worldly life relies—and in consequence how reasonable it is to disdain and scorn it.

ST. FRANCIS XAVIER

(1506—1552)

IT is said of the English poet, Samuel Taylor Coleridge, that he left his greatest masterpieces unfinished, including Wordsworth, whose powers seemed to decline when Coleridge was no longer present to inspire them. It is said of St. Ignatius Loyola that his greatest achievement was St. Francis Xavier, whose powers were enlarged when he went his own way, precisely because Ignatius had led him to the source of all personal power and liberty—God's love.

When Francis Xavier first met Loyola at the University of Paris in 1529, he was not, in the words of a mutual friend, "very much addicted to him." Ignatius, but recently arrived from Spain, was a battered, limping, half-educated, poverty-stricken bird of passage, absolutely propertyless save for a donkey-load of books and a worn manuscript of *The Spiritual Exercises*. The wits of the university laughed at him. Already thirty-six years old, he still did not know enough Latin to study philosophy, so back he went with the schoolboys at the College Montaigne. Francis Xavier, almost ready for his licentiate at twenty-three, was brilliant, ambitious, worldly, handsome, and athletic. Today we would describe him as intellectually venturesome rather than scholarly; he was fairly certain of endless fellowships and ultimately a place at the top, a professorship, a bishopric, or office in the Empire. Yet both men were cut from the same stone. Like Ignatius, Francis was born of sturdy Basque minor nobility, of a family rich in piety, pride, and military prowess. Unlike him, Xavier was well educated by the three chaplains attached to the Xavier household in Navarre, and had come on to Paris to win his spurs rather than to save souls.

Francis seemed plainly put out when his countryman Ignatius, after being publicly sentenced to flogging by the principal of the College de St. Barbe, Xavier's own college, was cleared of the charge against him—turning young rakes into men of piety. Worse still Ignatius was actually admitted to the college and assigned the same room as Francis and his scholarly friend, Peter Faber. Faber, already resolved to become a priest, immediately found in Ignatius a father and a friend. But Xavier ignored, or pretended to ignore, the lively, prescient eyes of his new roommate and the new-found peace that flooded Peter Faber's soul. When he won his licentiate Francis began teaching. He could not fail to notice how, subtly, Ignatius was knitting their lives together. For students came to him at Loyola's suggestion, and the older man, penniless though he was, always managed to provide Francis' desperate need for money.

What Ignatius saw in Francis Xavier, who saw so little in him, was an immense capacity for the love and service of God. Xavier's very resistance was a clue to his as yet unacknowledged dissatisfaction with his own irresolution. By taste, as well as by grace, Xavier shunned the bawdy and the dissolute life of Parisian students. But he was not yet ready for the decision to break completely with world and to dedicate himself to Christ—a decision that the patient Ignatius evidently hoped he would make. In the summer of 1533, Peter Faber decided to visit his home in Savoy, so that Francis and Ignatius were left alone in the room at the College de Sainte Barbe. Somehow, by the time Peter returned at the beginning of the next year, Ignatius had accomplished his long-sought design. Francis was no longer the gentleman-scholar-athlete hankering after human glory. He was one with Ignatius in his desire to win all men to Christ. How this happened we do not know. Later, Ignatius said that Francis "was the lumpiest dough he had ever kneaded."

Henceforth, Francis' life was marked by a burning zeal to save men's souls. When the yet unorganized band of Jesuits left Paris (France and Spain were again at war and the predominantly Spanish group may well have felt the chill of antagonism), they went first to Venice, where Xavier, with a singular charm and graciousness, tended the sick in the hospitals. Ordained with Ignatius in 1537, he accompanied that brother of his soul to Rome, where he quickly became known for his sermons and his multitude of charities. But he was destined for other work. Portugal, then in the flood-tide of its empire, had petitioned the pope for missionaries to take care of her vast territories in the Indies. Ignatius chose two of his followers for the task: Rodriguez and Bobadilla, but the latter was gravely stricken and Xavier was sent in his place.

Xavier left Lisbon in 1541 aboard the flagship *Santiago* for a voyage around Cape Horn to India that was to take over a year. Aboard the lumbering carrack there were seven hundred men: the new Governor of Goa, Martin Affonso, and his retinue of officials, some merchants, soldiers, black slaves, and criminals on their way to penal colonies on the East African coast. Xavier could not have asked for greater opportunity to serve God and man. On the voyage he took care of the poor and sick, heard confessions, endured cheerfully the stench, the alternate heat and cold, the lack of water, and the putrid food. The ship's surgeon, Cosme Saraiva, later wrote, "Everybody held him for a saint, and that was my own fixed opinion."

Once in Goa, the capital of Portuguese India, Xavier immediately made for the hospital, described in a contemporary report as "the filthiest and foulest den on this earth," where there was work to be done among "the slaves, galley-birds, and other scum." Soon after, in his mission as Papal Nuncio "to help the colonists, to instruct the newly converted Indians, and to work for the salvation of the unbelievers," Xavier was walking up and down the streets of Goa, singing the creed, the Ten Commandments, and other lessons in simple rhymes, dramatizing the catechism and drawing after him enormous crowds. Goa could not contain him. Spurred by a divine impatience, he went alone down the coast to Cape Comorin and then northward on the East Coast, instructing and baptizing thousands. He agonized because his thousands of Christians had none to care for them, and thousands more failed to become Christians because there was no one to preach to them.

In a famous letter, dated January 15, 1544, he wrote to his brothers in Rome:

"Multitudes out here fail to become Christians only because there is nobody prepared for the holy task of instructing them. I have often felt strongly moved to descend on the Universities of Europe, especially of Paris and its Sorbonne, and say aloud like a madman to those who have more learning than good will to employ it advantageously, telling them how many souls miss Heaven and fall into Hell through their negligence! If, while they studied their humanities, they would study also the account which God will demand of them for the talent He gave, many might feel the need to engage in spiritual exercises that would lead them to discover and embrace the Divine Will, as against their own proclivities, and cry to God, 'Lord, here I am. What wouldst Thou have me to do? Send me where Thou willest, yea, even to India? . . .' Out here people flock into the Churches in such numbers that my arms are almost paralyzed with baptizing, and my voice gives out completely through repeating endlessly in their tongue the Creed, the commandments, the prayers, and a sermon on Heaven and Hell. . . ."

Soon this letter, translated into Latin and distributed throughout the world, stimulated a vast missionary activity. In the meantime, however, Francis was alone and other horizons beckoned. In 1545 he sailed to Malacca, then a great center of trade and even more in need of his help than Goa. From his base there he visited the Moluccas and other islands, and finally Japan, where he landed in 1549. For two years he preached in Japan with great success, although against difficult odds. Discovering that the Japanese imitated the superior culture of the Chinese, Francis decided to convert China. He returned to Goa, where a company of Jesuits was now consolidating his pioneer missions, and assembled an embassy to the emperor of China. But this embassy failed. On the island of Sancian, off the Chinese coast, while waiting with a faithful companion for a ship to take him to China, he died with the name of Jesus on his lips.

Francis wrote no treatise for publication. But his many letters are replete with a wisdom that combines the cunning of the serpent with the simplicity of the dove. His longest and most revealing letter is addressed to Father Gaspar Baertz, whom he desired to be his successor as Rector of the Jesuit community in Goa, India. Instead he sent Baertz to Ormuz, a sink of iniquity on the Kirmanian coast at the mouth of the Persian Gulf. While his instructions to his well-loved disciple apply chiefly to the work of a sixteenth-century missionary, they are, for the most part, of equal interest to the modern reader. Above all they stress the "indispensable need of experience and acquaintance with the human heart" in matters touching upon religion.

LETTER LXIX TO FATHER GASPAR BAERTZ

Above all things be mindful of yourself, and of discharging faithfully what you owe first to God, and then to your own conscience; for by means of these two duties you will find yourself become more capable of serving your neighbors and of gaining souls. Take care always to incline, even beyond moderation, to the practice of the most abject employments. By exercising yourself in them, you will acquire humility, and daily advance in that virtue. For this reason I would have you not leave to any other, but yourself take charge of, the teaching the ignorant those prayers, which every Christian ought to have by heart: an employment certainly by no means ostentatious. Have yourself the patience to make the children and slaves of the Portuguese repeat them word by word after you. Do the same thing to the children of the native Christians. Those who behold you thus diligently employed will never suspect you of any arrogance—they will be edified by your modesty; and as modest persons easily attract the esteem of others, they will judge you more fit to instruct themselves in those mysteries of the Christian religion of which they are ignorant.

You must frequently visit the poor in the hospitals and poorhouses, and from time to time exhort them to confess themselves, and to communicate; giving them to understand that confession is the remedy for past sins, and holy communion a preservation against relapses—that both of them destroy the causes of the miseries which they now suffer, and which they fear for the future, inasmuch as the ills they suffer are only the punishment of their offenses. On this account, when they are willing to confess, you should hear their confessions with all the leisure you can afford them. After this care taken of their souls, do what you can to help the poor creatures in what they want for their bodies; recommend them with all diligence and affection to the administrators of the establishment in which they are, or else procure them from others who can help them the relief which they need.

You must also visit and preach to the prisoners, and exhort them earnestly to make a general confession of their lives. They have more need than others to be stirred up to this, because many or most people of that sort have never made an exact confession since they were born. After this, ask the Brotherhood of Mercy to have pity on those poor wretches, and to labor with the judges to look into their causes and to provide daily food for the most necessitous, who oftentimes have not the wherewithal to subsist. You must be of all the service you can to the Brotherhood of Mercy, showing yourself devoted to it, promoting it, commending it, and most readily working in every way in your power to help it.

If in that great port of Ormuz you have to hear the confession of any rich merchants whom you find to have the possession of ill-gotten goods on their consciences, and who are bound and willing to restore them, but yet cannot make restitution to the persons who have been injured, either because they are dead, or because of themselves they know not who or where they are, even though they force upon you the money for restitution, remit the whole thereof into the hands of the Brotherhood of Mercy, even though you may

207

think of some necessitous persons on whom such charity might be well employed. Thus you will not expose yourself to be deceived by the insidious tricks of wicked men, who affect an air of innocence and poverty; men full to the throat of imposture and wickedness, but who cannot so easily deceive the Brotherhood of Mercy, to whom it will be much safer and more seemly for you to transfer the invidious and perplexing office of making all due inquiries; thus the alms will reach those who are truly poor, and the greedy lying of these avaricious impostors will be defeated. And besides, you will gain the more leisure for those functions which in a more especial manner belong to your state of life, which is devoted to the assistance of souls: otherwise this frequent and manifold care of the distribution of alms would deprive you of no small part of the leisure which you will need so much. In fine, by this means you will prevent the complaints and suspicion of men, who are from their own common badness, would be ready to think evil of you, as if, under the pretense of serving others, you were cunningly playing a game for yourself, and withdrawing for your own use a part of the money intrusted to you to give away, thus cheating the necessities of the poor and practicing a wicked theft upon them.

In dealing with those whom in the various intercourse of life you come across, whether in spiritual or secular things, whether at home or abroad, whether it be in the way of speech or of company, whether their familiarity or friendship with you be only ordinary or of the highest degree, always bear yourself as if you had it in your mind that they might one day become enemies instead of your friends. By this management of yourself, you will never let them be aware of any act or word of yours which, if they were to bring out at any time when in a passion, might make you blush for it as an exposure of yourself, or be sorry for it on account of mischief it might cause to your work and business. This perpetual watchfulness and care is made necessary for us on account of the wickedness of this corrupt world, whose children are continually observing the children of light with mistrustful and malignant eyes. And the same care is due also for the sake of your own spiritual advancement, which will make great progress if you regulate all your words and actions by continual and most attentive prudence.

By this same precaution you will guard the inconstant minds of your friends against the danger of change. In any case you will prepare for yourself in their minds many things which will be your defenders, for they will remember the uprightness of your conduct, and they will conceive a reverence for you which will put them to confusion if ever they become your enemies. This consideration of the instability of men will also make you look more to God, despise yourself more, and cling to God, Who is ever present to us, with extreme humility and great sweetness of soul: practices which if we omit, we find a number of things stealing upon us which hurt the eyes of people who see us, and gradually alienate from us their good will. The examen, which we call particular, will do a great deal as to keeping up this carefulness. Take care never to fail to make it twice a day, or once at least, according to our common method, whatsoever business you have upon your hands.

Before all things, devote your first and principal care to cleansing your own conscience and keeping it without stain. Let your diligence in preserving or in cleansing the consciences of others come after this of your own; for how can a man be of use to others who takes no care for himself? Preach to the people as frequently as ever you can: for the usefulness of preaching spreads far and wide everywhere; and amongst all evangelical employments there is none from which greater fruit for the service of God and the good of men can be expected.

In your sermons beware of admitting any doubtful propositions as to which there is difficulty, because doctors are divided. For the subjects of sermons should be chosen from clear and unquestionable truths, which tend to the regulation of manners and the reprehension of vices. Set forth the enormity of sin, enlarge on the atrocity of the offense to God's infinite Majesty which is committed by the sinner. Imprint in souls a lively horror of that sentence which shall be thundered out against guilty sinners at the last judgment. Represent with all the colors of your eloquence those most bitter pains which the damned are eternally to suffer in hell. In fine, threaten them with death, and especially with sudden and unexpected death, those particularly who neglect the service of God, and who, having their conscience loaded with many most grievous sins, think nothing of sleeping on in supine negligence in such a condition. You are to mingle with all these considerations the remembrance of the cross, the wounds, and death of Christ, by which He vouchsafed to atone for our sins; but you are to do this in as moving and pathetical a manner as possible, by figures and colloquies proper to excite emotions in the mind, such as cause in our hearts a deep sorrow for our sins, on account of the offense done to God thereby, even so as to draw tears from the eyes of your audience, who are then to be led to make resolutions of cleansing their consciences as soon as possible by confession, and of celebrating their reconciliation to God by due reception of the holy Communion. This is the one true idea which I wish you would propose to yourself for preaching profitably.

When you reprove vices in the pulpit be careful never to speak against or attack any person by name, especially those who are officers or magistrates. If they do anything which you disapprove, and of which you think convenient to admonish them, make them a visit, and speak to them in private; or when they come of themselves to confession, whisper to them in the secret tribunal of penance, what you have to say to them. But altogether avoid the speaking against them openly; for they are a sort of people who are commonly difficult and irritable, and they are so far from amending upon such public admonitions that they are stung by them, and become furious, like bulls under a gadfly, and rush headlong to perdition.

Moreover, before you take upon you to give even private admonitions take care that you know them a little first, and have some familiarity with the people whom you wish to correct, so to prepare your way: and then make your admonition either more gentle or more strong in tone according to the measure of your favor or authority with the friend you are reproving, so as to be more free and severe with the one who is more bound to you, and more sparing and cautious with one with whom you are less familiar. Take care always to temper the sternness of your reproof with the serenity of your air, a smiling countenance, and gentle glances, and much more by the civility of well-mannered words, and the sincere protestation of your love, which is the only thing which forces on you that unpleasant but necessary attempt to deliver a friend from the stain which disfigures him. It is good also to add to the pleasantness of your discourse marks of submissive reverence, with tender embraces, and all other fitting marks of the sincere good will and unquestionable respect which you have for the person of him whom you are correcting. These things are the honey and preserves which are mixed with and which season the bitterness of the dose; unpleasant in itself, and which will turn out of no use if it be administered without some such condiment to men whose stomachs are likely to be turned by it. For if a harsh voice, a rigid countenance, or threatening aspect and a lowering brow should be added to the natural disagreeableness of so unpleasant a matter as a reprehension, I am very much afraid that men of such fastidious delicacy and sensitive ears will not be able to restrain their bile. They have power at their back, they are accustomed to adulation; and it is more likely, in such cases, that they will shake off all restraint and moderation, and send their inopportune censor about his business, with a good deal of abuse into the bargain.

For what concerns confession, how you are to advise others, and they practice it, this is the method which I judge the fittest for these quarters of the world, where the license of sin is very great, and the use of penance very rare. Whenever you find a person who wishes to unburthen in confession a conscience laden with a long accumulation of sin, exhort him in the first place to take two or three days of preparation, to examine his conscience thoroughly, to go back to the first recollections of his childhood, then through all the various stages of age and occupation which he has passed through in all his life up to this time, making up the account of all his sins in deed, word, or thought, and if his memory require it, writing it down and reading it over. When he is thus prepared, you can hear his confession, after which it will generally be well that you should not give him absolution at once, but persuade him to think it over for two or three days, to withdraw his mind from his ordinary occupations, and by means of meditations adapted to excite him to sorrow for his sins, out of love of God Whom he has offended, to prepare himself to gain greater fruit from his sacramental absolution. During those three days you shall exercise your penitent in some of the meditations of the first week of the Exercises, giving him the points, and teaching him the method of meditation and prayer, and you shall counsel him also to help himself, by means of some voluntary penance, for example, of fasting or disciplining himself, to conceive in his inmost heart a true detestation for his offenses, and even shed tears of repentance.

Besides this, you must take care, if the penitents have unjust possession of anything belonging to others, that they make restitution in this interval of time; or if they have injured the reputation of any one, that they retract what they have said; or if they are engaged in unlawful attachments and have been living in sin, cause them to break off those criminal engagements, and remove at once the occasions of their crime. However solemnly and seriously they may promise to do these things at a future time, it is not safe to trust them without the actual performance of their engagement. Let them perform beforehand what they declare that they will do. There is not any time more proper to exact from sinners these duties, the performance of which is as necessary as it is difficult. For when once their fervor and excitement of mind have grown cold, and their familiar enticements have begun to drag them back with fatal persuasiveness to the sins to which they have been accustomed and which they have but just left off for the time, it will be in vain to ask them to keep their promise. Before, therefore, you send them away absolved from all their sins, insist by all means on their anticipating these dangers. Otherwise, so frail is human nature, you will have to bewail to no purpose their speedy relapse towards the precipice, from the slippery declivity of which you have not far enough removed them.

In dealing with sinners in the sacred tribunal of penance, take heed lest by any hasty severity you frighten away those who have begun to discover the wounds of their souls to you. How enormous soever their sins may be, hear them, not only with patience, but with mildness; help out their bashfulness when they find it difficult to confess, testifying to them your compassion, and seeming not to be surprised at what you hear, as having heard in confession sins much more grievous and foul than theirs. And, lest they should despair of pardon for their faults, speak to them of the treasures of the infinite mercies of God. Sometimes when they have confessed some crime with great trouble of mind, hint to them that their sin is not altogether so great as they may think; that by God's assistance you can heal even more mortal wounds of the soul; bid them go on without any apprehension, and make no difficulty of telling all. It is necessary to use this motherly indulgence, so to speak, in order to assist these poor souls in bringing forth their sins, for in truth it is a most painful labor which they undergo in bringing to birth the spirit of salvation, until at last they have emptied the whole terrible sink of their conscience.

You will find some of them whom the weakness either of their age or sex will make them feel more ashamed as to revealing to you the foul lusts with which they have stained themselves. When you perceive that, meet them more than half way, telling them that they are neither the only nor the first persons who have fallen into such foul sins, that you have met with far worse sins of that kind than those can be which they want the confidence to tell you. Impute a great part of their offenses to the violence of the temptation, the seductiveness of the occasion, and the concupiscence innate in all men. More than this, I tell you that in dealing with such persons, we must sometimes go so far and so low, in order to loosen the chains of this miserable shame in these unhappy persons whose tongues the devil has by his cunning tied up, as of our own accord to indicate in general the sins of our own past lives, so to elicit from these guilty souls the confession of the sin which they will otherwise hide, to their irreparable loss. For what can a true and fervent charity refuse to pay for the safety of those souls who have been redeemed with the blood of Jesus Christ? But to understand when this is proper to be done, how far to proceed, and with what precautions, is what the guidance of the Spirit and your own experience must teach you at the time in each particular conjuncture.

You will sometimes meet with men—and I would that they may be few—who doubt of the power and efficacy of the holy sacraments, and especially as to the Presence of the Body of Christ in the Eucharist. This comes from their not frequenting those sacred mysteries, from their continual intercourse with pagans, Mahometans, and heretics, or from the bad example given them by some Christians, and even (which I speak with shame and sorrow) by some of our own priestly order; for when they see some priests, whose life is not more holy than that of the common multitude, still go rashly and almost as a pastime to the altar, they imagine that it is in vain that we teach that Jesus Christ is present in the holy sacrifice of the Mass, for that if He were there present, He would never suffer such impure hands to touch Him with impunity.

The way you should take to set these people right is as follows. First establish yourself in their friendship by courteous speeches and kind manners, and then endeavor by familiar questions to elicit their private thoughts. If you find in them the errors I have mentioned, then search out their causes, occasions, and beginnings. You will thus understand where to apply your remedy, and then do this with all diligence and vigor, alleging whatever, as the occasion suggests, may seem to be of use; take great pains to prove clearly the truth of the sacred dogma, and never leave off till you have conquered, and till they protest that they are most firmly persuaded with a faith certain beyond all doubt that the Body and Blood of Christ our Lord and Redeemer are most truly present under the species of bread and wine duly consecrated. After that it will not be difficult to lead them to cleanse their souls in good faith by confession, and to receive more frequently the sacred banquet of the table of God with due devotion. . . .

Whenever you are preparing yourself to talk with any one concerning the things which belong to the worship of God and the salvation of the soul, put in practice this precaution—not to say a word before you have divined and discovered by any sign you can note what is the interior state of the man's mind. I mean whether he is quiet or under the influence of some strong passion—whether he is ready to follow the right path when it is shown him, or whether he is in error with his eyes open, irrevocably wedded to low cares and objects, to which he has been hitherto in the habit of postponing his religious duties, and seems likely to do the same for the future; whether he is the subject of temptations from the devil, or whether he is left to himself and his own nature—in fine, whether he is disposed to listen to an admonition, or whether he is rough and irritable to the touch, so that it may be feared that he will break out into a rage if he be handled too incautiously.

When you have got some presumptive knowledge on these points, you must adapt your address to the person accordingly. Speak gently to the angry, quietly to the troubled, use some appropriate artifice to insinuate your business into the mind of the preoccupied; be more free and expansive with well-disposed persons, who are likely to be docile and easily led to anything that is good. At the same time, never be foolishly fawning to any one, never stop short at mere compliments, always skillfully mix up some wholesome medicine in what you give to the sick man, however much he may turn from it, so that by degrees he may be disposed to a better state. When any one is all on fire with excitement from a keen sense of recent injury, then do you also blame the deed of which he complains. If it be bad in itself, then use what reasonings

215

you can to persuade him that the doer has fallen out of imprudence, and not sinned through malice. When you see that your man listens to you, and is not altogether displeased, you may add that God has perhaps permitted this in order to punish him for some similar offense which he has himself committed. Then ask him familiarly, whether he remembers ever to have injured any one in word or deed. Whether, at least, in his youth, he was not somewhat ill-tempered with his parents, disobedient to his teachers, quarrelsome with his companions, and may not have given some one or other just cause to complain of him? And when he acknowledges this, tell him that he must think it fair that he is now paid off in kind. For now he has offered him by God a very precious opportunity of wiping out his former fault. If, on the other hand, his complaint be not just, take him in hand gently and gradually, pull to pieces the false arguments by which he persuades himself of what is so far from being the case. Then increase your boldness little by little, show him a little gentle anger, as he really deserves, and then, at last, when you feel you can do it safely, give him a more serious scolding. These artifices, by the blessing of God, sometimes charm away the ill-humors of men so overwhelmed with troubles, and dissolve the sort of spell by which they have been bound, so as to leave them free and able to do what is right. When you have thus made your way easy, you must go on with confidence, and bring your work to the greatest perfection in your power, spending yourself to the utmost in your desire to do honor to God, and win for Him the love and reverence of the souls which He has created to love and to praise Him.

The injunction which I have given above—namely, that you should find out from men who are well acquainted with the matter what are the commercial frauds most common at Ormuz—I would not have confined either to that place in particular, or to those specific heads of which I spoke. Wherever you are, even if it be only in passing and on a journey, always make it a point to try to find out as exactly as possible from good men who know the ways of common life, not only what are the prevalent crimes or customary tricks of cheating in such places, but the whole manners of the people there, the opinions and prejudices of the populace, what the nation is intent upon, what are the peculiar customs of the country, the mode of government, the method of the courts, the forms of suits, the quibbles of lawyers, and whatever has any sort of bearing upon the character of the state or of civil society there. Believe my experience, nothing of all this is useless for the physician of souls to know, in order that he may at once understand their diseases, may easily provide remedies, and may always have at command a power of readily and quickly meeting all necessities.

This will teach you what to dwell upon most frequently in your sermons, and what to insist on urgently with your penitents. This knowledge will arm you and prepare you for your promiscuous conversations with men, and you will be so fortified by it, as never to be amazed at anything as new, never to be put into a ferment at any unforeseen occurrence: it will make you feel at home in all the variety of questions that will arise one after another, it will make you dexterous in the multiplied business you will have to transact with men of all sorts, and also give you authority with all. When men of the world are admonished of anything by religous persons, they generally despise them, because they think that they have no experience of affairs. But if they find that any one is quite as well versed as they are and has as much experience as themselves, in the common usages of civil life, they will hold such a one in admiration, trust themselves to him, and will not hesitate when he urges them even to do violence to themselves, and to carry out whatever he advises them, even though it be arduous. So you see what good fruit may come from such knowledge, and therefore you must now consider that it is your business to labor in acquiring it as much as in old days you labored to learn philosophy or theology. And it must be sought, not from dead books—that is, from men who have had experience in affairs, and who know well the manners of the people. With this knowledge you will do more good than if you poured forth upon the crowd whole libraries of speculation. . . .

The truth is, that men listen attentively to those things above all which reach their inmost conscience. Sublime speculations, perplexed questions, scholastic controversies, soar not only above the intelligence of those who are creeping along on the ground, but also above their interest. They make a great deal of empty thunder and vanish away without any fruit. You must show men clearly to themselves, if you wish to have them hanging upon the words of your mouth. But to set forth what their own interior feelings are, you must first know them; and the only way to know them is to be much in their company, to study them, observe them, pray with them. So turn over and over again these living books; it is from these that you will gain everything—how to teach them with efficacy, how easily to act on and affect and turn and move sinners whither it behooves them to be moved for their souls' salvation.

Do not neglect the study of dead books on account of this. Holy Scripture, the Fathers of the Church, the sacred canons, ascetical books, and those which treat of moral subjects, duties, rights, and their distinctions—all these must be diligently consulted at proper times. It is in them that we find how to remedy temptations, the arguments by which to persuade, the motives of heroic affections, and examples of all that is praiseworthy taken from the lives of the Saints. But after all, these things have no warmth or life, and are of little avail, unless the minds of the audience are first opened so as to admit them into their own depths. And the certain key thus to open them is that picture and representation of each one's interior state of which I have spoken, skillfully drawn by a preacher who has full knowledge of the ways of men, and set in a good light before the eyes of everybody. . . .

MY GOD, I LOVE THEE

My God, I love Thee! not because
    I hope for heaven thereby;
Nor because those who love Thee not
    Must burn eternally.

Thus, O my Jesus, Thou didst me
    Upon the cross embrace!
For me didst bear the nails and spear
    And manifold disgrace.

And griefs and torments numberless
    And sweat of agony,
Yea, death itself—and all for one
    That was Thy enemy.

Then why, O blessèd Jesus Christ,
    Should I not love Thee well!
Not for the hope of winning heaven
    Nor of escaping hell!

Not with the hope of gaining aught,
    Not seeking a reward;
But as Thyself hast loved me
    O everlasting Lord!

E'en so I love Thee and will love
    And in Thy praise will sing—
Solely because Thou art my God
    And my eternal King!

Attributed to St. Francis Xavier
From the Latin by Edward Caswell

ST. TERESA
OF AVILA
(1515—1582)

TERESA de Cepeda y Ahumada was born of a noble family, well to do but not rich, in the Castilian town of Avila, just after the conquest of the Moors. Her father, Don Alonso Sanchez de Cepeda, was the archetypal Spanish gentleman; pious, conservative, learned. He had three children of his first wife and nine of Doña Beatriz de Ahumada, his second wife. Teresa was Doña Beatriz' third child, a lively, affectionate, intelligent girl as much given to playing games with her brother Rodrigo as she was to drinking in the good example and instructions of her parents.

Her *Autobiography*, a book that ranks with St. Augustine's *Confessions*, tells us how in her earliest years she combined piety and play. Rodrigo and Teresa both conceived an ardent desire to see God. The surest way, they knew from their father's stories, was to die for their faith. Soon the two children decided to go to the land of the Moors, where, with God's help, they hoped to be captured and put to death. Alas! They had just reached the bridge outside the town when an uncle and an aunt met them and returned them to their harassed mother. Deprived of this opportunity for martyrdom, they then decided to become hermits at home. They built little cells in the garden, where Teresa especially spent long hours by herself, praying the rosary in the manner her mother had taught her.

When Teresa was thirteen Doña Beatriz died. The child dawdled about the house, reading romances of chivalry, curling her hair, and trying out perfumes. Don Alonso took note of this adolescent vanity and sent her to a nearby convent school of St. Mary of Grace conducted by the Augustinian nuns. There Teresa repaired the broken thread of her early devotion. Once again she wanted to do what God wanted her to do. It seemed at first that He wanted her to learn patience, for after eighteen months she suffered the first of her many serious sicknesses. Upon her recovery she entered the Carmelite convent of the Incarnation. Shortly after her profession in 1538 her illness returned. For three years she suffered violent headaches, fever, comas, paralysis. During her sufferings she began to learn about the importance of mental prayer. "In the midst of sickness," she wrote, "the best of prayer may be made; and it is a mistake to think that it can only be made in solitude."

Gradually, Teresa began to regard all her prayers in the first twenty years of her religious life as imperfect and herself as a sinner. Touched by the visions of Christ and His revelations of what favors she had received, she craved the most complete abandonment to His will. "Oh Joy of the Angels, my Lord and my God, I cannot think of conversing with You without desiring to melt like wax in the fire of Your divine love, and to consume all that is earthly in me by loving You. . . . Even the wicked, whose affections have no conformity to Your spirit, ought to approach You, that they may become good, even though they first abide with You, sometimes with a thousand distractions, as I did." She was moving, on the rush of God's grace, from the ordinary prayers of words and thoughts to the prayer of quiet, or passive, watchful love in the presence of God, and to the prayer of union, where the soul is in direct and immediate contact with God Himself.

Her ecstasy and joy were unbounded. But so, too, in moments of reflection were her fears. She could not conceive how she, a miserable creature, could deserve such an excess of love. Moreover, she knew of many deluded women who, confusing supernatural vision with natural hallucinations, or even with the suggestions of the devil, had merited the condemnation of the church. Thus began her search for advice. The first priest she consulted said that, judging from the imperfections she had admitted to him, she was most surely deluded by the devil. Fortunately, she found more learned advisers, several Jesuits, among them St. Francis Borgia, to give her more prudent counsel. But it was the visit of St. Peter of Alcantara, whose own holiness and learning were so overwhelming, that resulted in the ultimate clarification of her doubts. Henceforth, Teresa of Avila was no longer the uncertain nun but the masterful, joyous, foundress of the Reformed Carmelites, the Mother of Saints, and by virtue of her writings a Doctor of Mystical Theology.

Her first foundation of the Reform was St. Joseph's Convent at Avila in 1562. By 1567 her work began to spread. In a pilgrimage of love she erected convents and monasteries at Barcelona, Medina del Campo, Malagon, Valladolid, Pastrana, Salamanca, Alba de Tormes, Caravaca, Seville. Not a corner of Spain but feels the impulse of her love. In all she founded sixteen convents and fourteen monasteries during her lifetime.

St. Teresa would have laughed in derision at the thought that she was a writer, much less a learned theologian. She regarded herself as an ignorant, hardly literate woman who had received great gifts from God, but who was not meant to write. But write she did at the command of her confessors. Her first book, the *Life*, or the *Autobiography*, was begun in 1562 when Father Garcia de Toledo, her current confessor, sought to have at hand evidence of her orthodoxy. Revised and expanded from time to time, it was finished in 1566. During the next few years it was read by many theologians, including the official examiners of the Inquisition. All of them pronounced in its favor. By that time, her reform of the Carmelites was well under way and there were numerous requests from the foundress for spiritual guidance. Again under orders, she composed her *Way of Perfection*, and then between 1573 and 1582, *The Foundations*; and in 1577 *The Interior Castle*, besides a number of minor works.

All of her books have the same theme: how God leads the generous soul from the lower level of prayer, the purgative way, to the highest level where the soul experiences joys akin to those of heaven. All of them reflect Teresa's uninhibited personality—her wit, her racy colloquial manner of speech, her homely realism, her impatience with pretense, her independence of books, and her reliance on the experience of God's action in her own soul. As befits a mother, she is practical, shrewd, sometimes caustic, yet always compassionate, tender and inexhaustibly loving, true at once to the kindred places of heaven and home. No one has excelled her in the candor of her self-revelations. Small wonder that her *Life* is at once a great literary classic, rivalled only by St. Augustine's *Confessions,* and a source book of Christian meditation and devotion. "This truth I am referring to and which was taught me," Teresa writes of the revelations in the *Life,* "is truth in itself, and is without beginning or end, and upon this truth all other truths depend, just as all other loves depend upon this love and all other greatnesses upon this greatness."

THE LIFE OF
ST. TERESA OF JESUS

CHAPTER VIII: The Great Advantage of Prayer

It is not without reason that I have dwelt so long on this portion of my life. I see clearly that it will give no one pleasure to see anything so base; and certainly I wish those who may read this to have me in abhorrence, as a soul so obstinate and so ungrateful to Him Who did so much for me. I could wish, too, I had permission to say how often at this time I failed in my duty to God, because I was not leaning on the strong pillar of prayer. I passed nearly twenty years on this stormy sea, falling and rising, but rising to no good purpose, seeing that I went and fell again. My life was one of perfection; but it was so mean, that I scarcely made any account whatever of venial sins; and though of mortal sins I was afraid, I was not so afraid of them as I ought to have been, because I did not avoid the perilous occasions of them.

I may say that it was the most painful life that can be imagined, because I had no sweetness in God, and no pleasure in the world.

When I was in the midst of the pleasures of the world, the remembrance of what I owed to God made me sad; and when I was praying to God, my worldly affections disturbed me. This is so painful a struggle, that I know not how I could have borne it for a month, let alone for so many years. Nevertheless, I can trace distinctly the great mercy of our Lord to me, while thus immersed in the world, in that I had still the courage to pray. I say courage, because I know of nothing in the whole world which requires greater courage than plotting treason against the King, knowing that He knows it, and yet never withdrawing from His presence; for, granting that we are always in the presence of God, yet it seems to me that those who pray are in His presence in a very different sense: for they, as it were, see that He is looking upon them; while others may be for days together without even once recollecting that God sees them.

It is true, indeed, that during these years there were many months, and, I believe, occasionally a whole year, in which I so kept guard over myself that I did not offend our Lord, gave myself much to prayer, and took some pains, and that successfully, not to offend Him. I speak of this now, because all I am saying is strictly true; but I remember very little of those good days, and so they must have been few, while my evil days were many. Still, the days that passed over without my spending a great part of them in prayer were few, unless I was very ill, or very much occupied.

When I was ill, I was well with God. I contrived that those about me should be so, too, and I made supplications to Our Lord for this grace, and spoke frequently of Him. Thus, with the exception of that year of which I have been speaking, during eight-and-twenty years of prayer, I spent more than eighteen in that strife and contention which arose out of my attempts to reconcile God and the world. As to the other years, of which I have now to speak, in them the grounds of the warfare, though it was not slight, were changed; but inasmuch as I was—at least, I think so—serving God, and aware of the vanity of the world, all has been pleasant, as I shall show hereafter.

The reason, then, of my telling this at so great a length is that, as I have just said, the mercy of God and my ingratitude, on the one hand, may become known; and, on the other, that men may understand how great is the good which God works in a soul when He gives it a disposition to pray in earnest, though it may not be so well prepared as it ought to be. If that soul perseveres in spite of sins, temptations, and relapses, brought about in a thousand ways by Satan, our Lord will bring it at last—I am certain of it— to the harbor of salvation, as He has brought me myself; for so it seems to me now. May His Majesty grant I may never go back and be lost! He who gives himself to prayer is in possession of a great blessing, of which many saintly and good men have written—I am speaking of mental prayer— glory be to God for it; and, if they had not done so, I am not proud enough, though I have but little humility, to presume to discuss it.

I may speak of that which I know by experience; and so I say, let him never cease from prayer who has once begun it, be his life ever so wicked; for prayer is the way to amend it, and without prayer such amendment will be much more difficult. Let him not be tempted by Satan, as I was, to give it up, on the pretense of humility; let him rather believe that His words are true Who says that, if we truly repent, and resolve never to offend Him, He will take us into His favor again, give us the graces He gave us before, and occasionally even greater, if our repentance deserve it [Ezchiel 18:21]. And as to him who has not begun to pray, I implore him by the love of our Lord not to deprive himself of so great a good.

Herein there is nothing to be afraid of, but everything to hope for. Granting that such a one does not advance, nor make an effort to become perfect, so as to merit the joys and consolations which the perfect receive from God, yet he will by little and little attain to a knowledge of the road which leads to heaven. And if he perseveres, I hope in the mercy of God for him, seeing that no one ever took Him for his friend that was not amply rewarded; for mental prayer is nothing else, in my opinion, but being on terms of friendship with God, frequently conversing in secret with Him Who, we know, loves us. Now, true love and lasting friendship require certain dispositions: those of our Lord, we know, are absolutely perfect; ours, vicious, sensual, and thankless; and you cannot, therefore, bring yourselves to love Him as He loves you, because you have not the disposition to do so; and if you do not love Him, yet, seeing how much it concerns you to have His friendship, and how great is His love for you, rise above that pain you feel at being much with Him Who is so different from you.

O infinite goodness of my God! I seem to see Thee and myself in this relation to one another. O Joy of the angels! When I consider it, I wish I could wholly die of love! How true it is that Thou endurest those who will not endure Thee! Oh, how good a friend art Thou, O my Lord! How Thou comfortest and endurest, and also waitest for them to make themselves like unto Thee, and yet, in the meanwhile, art Thyself so patient of the state they are in! Thou takest into account the occasions during which they seek Thee, and for a moment of penitence forgettest their offenses against Thyself.

I have seen this distinctly in my own case, and I cannot tell why the whole world does not labor to draw near to Thee in this particular friendship. The wicked, who do not resemble Thee, ought to do so, in order that Thou mayest make them good, and for that purpose should permit Thee to remain with them at least for two hours daily, even though they may not remain with Thee but, as I used to do, with a thousand distractions, and with worldly thoughts. In return for this violence which they offer to themselves for the purpose of remaining in a company so good as Thine—for at first they can do no more, and even afterwards at times— Thou, O Lord, defendest them against the assaults of evil spirits, whose power Thou restrainest, and even lessenest daily, giving to them the victory over these their enemies. So it is, O Life of all lives, Thou slayest none that put their trust in Thee, and seek Thy friendship; yea, rather, Thou sustainest their bodily life in greater vigor, and makest their soul to live.

I do not understand what there can be to make them afraid who are afraid to begin mental prayer, nor do I know what it is they dread. The Devil does well to bring this fear upon us, that he may really hurt us; if, by putting me in fear, he can make me cease from thinking of my offenses against God, of the great debt I owe Him, of the existence of heaven and hell, and of the great sorrows and trials He underwent for me. That was all my prayer, and had been, when I was in this dangerous state, and it was on those subjects I dwelt whenever I could; and very often, for some years, I was more occupied with the wish to see the end of the time I had appointed for myself to spend in prayer, and in watching the hourglass, than with other thoughts that were good. If a sharp penance had been laid upon me, I know of none that I would not very often have willingly undertaken, rather than prepare myself for prayer by self-recollection. And certainly the violence with which Satan assailed me was so irresistible, or my evil habits were so strong, that I did not betake myself to prayer; and the sadness I felt on entering the oratory was so great, that it required all the courage I had to force myself in. They say of me that my courage is not slight, and it is known that God has given me a courage beyond that of a woman; but I have made a bad use of it. In the end, our Lord came to my help; and then, when I had done this violence to myself, I found greater peace and joy than I sometimes had when I had a desire to pray.

If, then, our Lord bore so long with me, who was so wicked —and it is plain that it was by prayer all my evil was corrected—why should any one, how wicked soever he may be, have any fear? Let him be ever so wicked, he will not remain in his wickedness so many years as I did, after receiving so many graces from our Lord. Is there any one who can despair, when He bore so long with me, only because I desired

227

and contrived to find some place and some opportunities for Him to be alone with me—and that very often against my will? For I did violence to myself, or rather our Lord Himself did violence to me.

If, then, to those who do not serve God, but rather offend Him, prayer be all this, and so necessary, and if no one can really find out any harm it can do him, and if the omission of it be not a still greater harm, why, then, should they abstain from it who serve and desire to serve God? Certainly I cannot comprehend it, unless it be that men have a mind to go through the troubles of this life in greater misery, and to shut the door in the face of God, so that He shall give them no comfort in it. I am most truly sorry for them, because they serve God at their own cost; for of those who pray, God Himself defrays the charges, seeing that for a little trouble He gives sweetness, in order that, by the help it supplies, they may bear their trials.

But because I have much to say hereafter of this sweetness, which our Lord gives to those who persevere in prayer, I do not speak of it here; only this will I say: prayer is the door to those great graces which our Lord bestowed upon me. If this door be shut, I do not see how He can bestow them; for even if He entered into a soul to take His delight therein, and to make that soul also delight in Him, there is no way by which He can do so; for His will is, that such a soul should be lonely and pure, with a great desire to receive His graces. If we put many hindrances in the way, and take no pains whatever to remove them, how can He come to us, and how can we have any desire that He should show us His great mercies?

I will speak now—for it is very important to understand it—of the assaults which Satan directs against a soul for the purpose of taking it, and of the contrivances and compassion wherewith our Lord labors to convert it to Himself, in order that men may behold His mercy, and the great good it was for me that I did not give up prayer and spiritual reading, and that they may be on their guard against the dangers against which I was not on my guard myself. And, above all, I implore them for the love of our Lord, and for the great love with which He goeth about seeking our conversion to Himself, to beware of the occasions of sin; for once placed therein, we have no ground to rest on—so many enemies then assail us, and our own weakness is such, that we cannot defend ourselves.

Oh, that I knew how to describe the captivity of my soul in those days! I understood perfectly that I was in captivity, but I could not understand the nature of it; neither could I entirely believe that those things which my confessors did not make so much of were so wrong as I in my soul felt them to be. One of them—I had gone to him with a scruple —told me that, even if I were raised to high contemplation, those occasions and conversations were not unfitting for me. This was towards the end, when, by the grace of God, I was withdrawing more and more from those great dangers, but not wholly from the occasions of them.

When they saw my good desires, and how I occupied myself in prayer, I seemed to them to have done much; but my soul knew that this was not doing what I was bound to do for Him to Whom I owed so much. I am sorry for my poor soul even now, because of its great sufferings, and the little help it had from any one except God, and for the wide door that man opened for it, that it might go forth to its pastimes and pleasures, when they said that these things were lawful.

Then there was the torture of sermons, and that not a slight one; for I was very fond of them. If I heard any one preach well and with unction, I felt, without my seeking it, a particular affection for him, neither do I know whence it came. Thus, no sermon ever seemed to me so bad, but that I listened to it with pleasure; though, according to others who heard it, the preaching was not good. If it was a good sermon, it was to me a most special refreshment. To speak of God, or to hear Him spoken of, never wearied me. I am speaking of the time after I gave myself to prayer. At one time I had great comfort in sermons, at another they distressed me, because they made me feel that I was very far from being what I ought to have been.

I used to pray to our Lord for help; but, as it now seems to me, I must have committed the fault of not putting my whole trust in His Majesty, and of not thoroughly distrusting myself. I sought for help, took great pains; but it must be that I did not understand how all is of little profit if we do not root out all confidence in ourselves, and place it wholly in God. I wished to live, but I saw clearly that I was not living, but rather wrestling with the shadow of death; there was no one to give me life, and I was not able to take it. He Who could have given it me had good reasons for not coming to my aid, seeing that He had brought me back to Himself so many times, and I as often had left Him.

CHAPTER IX: Light in Her Darkness

My soul was now grown weary; and the miserable habits it had contracted would not suffer it to rest, though it was desirous of doing so. It came to pass one day, when I went into the oratory, that I saw a picture which they had put by there, and which had been procured for a certain feast observed in the house. It was a representation of Christ most grievously wounded; and so devotional, that the very sight of it, when I saw it, moved me—so well did it show forth that which He suffered for us. So keenly did I feel the evil return I had made for those Wounds, that I thought my heart was breaking. I threw myself on the ground beside it, my tears flowing plenteously, and implored Him to strengthen me once for all, so that I might never offend Him any more.

I had a very great devotion to the glorious Magdalene, and very frequently used to think of her conversion—especially when I went to Communion. As I knew for certain that our Lord was then within me, I used to place myself at His feet, thinking that my tears would not be despised. I did not know what I was saying; only He did great things for me, in that He was pleased I should shed those tears, seeing that I so soon forgot that impression. I used to recommend myself to that glorious saint, that she might obtain my pardon.

But this last time, before that picture of which I am speaking, I seem to have made greater progress; for I was now very distrustful of myself, placing all my confidence in God. It seems to me that I said to Him then that I would not rise up till He granted my petition. I do certainly believe that this was of great service to me, because I have grown better ever since.

This was my method of prayer: as I could not make reflections with my understanding, I contrived to picture Christ as within me; and I used to find myself the better for thinking of those mysteries of His life during which He was most lonely. It seemed to me that the being alone and afflicted, like a person in trouble, must needs permit me to come near to Him.

I did many simple things of this kind; and in particular I used to find myself most at home in the prayer in the garden, whither I went in His company. I thought of the bloody sweat, and of the affliction He endured there; I wished, if it had been possible, to wipe away that painful sweat from His face; but I remember that I never dared to form such a resolution—my sins stood before me so grievously. I used to remain with Him there as long as my thoughts allowed me, and I had many thoughts to torment me. For many years, nearly every night before I fell asleep, when I recommended myself to God, that I might sleep in peace, I used always to think a little of this mystery of the prayer in the garden—yea, even before I was a nun, because I had been told that many indulgences were to be gained thereby. For my part, I believe that my soul gained very much in this way, because I began to practise prayer without knowing what it was; and now that it had become my constant habit, I was saved from omitting it, as I was from omitting to bless myself with the sign of the cross before I slept.

And now to go back to what I was saying of the torture which my thoughts inflicted upon me. This method of praying, in which the understanding makes no reflections, hath this property: the soul must gain much, or lose. I mean, that those who advance without meditation, make great progress, because it is done by love. But to attain to this involves great labor, except to those persons whom it is our Lord's good pleasure to lead quickly to the prayer of quiet. I know of some. For those who walk in this way, a book is profitable, that by the help thereof they may the more quickly recollect themselves. It was a help to me also to look on fields, water, and flowers. In them I saw traces of the Creator—I mean, that the sight of these things was as a book unto me; it roused me, made me recollected, and reminded me of my ingratitude and of my sins. My understanding was so dull, that I could never represent in the imagination either heavenly or high things in any form whatever until our Lord placed them before me in another way.

I was so little able to put things before me by the help of my understanding, that, unless I saw a thing with my eyes, my imagination was of no use whatever. I could not do as others do, who can put matters before themselves so as to become thereby recollected. I was able to think of Christ only as man. But so it was; and I never could form any image of Him to myself, though I read much of His beauty, and looked at pictures of Him. I was like one who is blind, or in the dark, who, though speaking to a person present, and feeling his presence, because he knows for certain that he is present—I mean, that he understands him to be present, and believes it—yet does not see him. It was thus with me when I used to think of our Lord. This is why I was so fond of images. Wretched are they who, through their own fault, have lost this blessing; it is clear enough that they do not love our Lord—for if they loved Him, they would rejoice at the sight of His picture, just as men find pleasure when they see the portrait of one they love.

At this time, the *Confessions* of St. Augustine were given me. Our Lord seems to have so ordained it, for I did not seek them myself, neither had I ever seen them before. I had a very great devotion to St. Augustine, because the monastery in which I lived when I was yet in the world was of his order; and also because he had been a sinner—for I used to find great comfort in those saints whom, after they had sinned, our Lord converted to Himself. I thought they would help me, and that, as our Lord had forgiven them, so also He would forgive me. One thing, however, there was that troubled me—I have spoken of it before—our Lord had called them but once, and they never relapsed; while my relapses were now so many. This it was that vexed me. But calling to mind the love that He bore me, I took courage again. Of His mercy I never doubted once, but I did very often of myself.

O my God, I am amazed at the hardness of my heart amidst so many succors from Thee. I am filled with dread when I see how little I could do with myself, and how I was clogged, so that I could not resolve to give myself entirely to God. When I began to read the *Confessions*, I thought I saw myself there described, and began to recommend myself greatly to this glorious saint. When I came to his conversion, and read how he heard that voice in the garden, it seemed to me nothing less than that our Lord had uttered it for me: I felt so in my heart. I remained for some time lost in tears, in great inward affliction and distress. O my God, what a soul has to suffer because it has lost the liberty it had of being mistress over itself! and what torments it has to endure! I wonder now how I could live in torments so great: God be praised Who gave me life, so that I might escape from so fatal a death! I believe that my soul obtained great strength from His divine Majesty, and that He must have heard my cry, and had compassion upon so many tears.

A desire to spend more time with Him began to grow within me, and also to withdraw from the occasions of sin: for as soon as I had done so, I turned lovingly to His Majesty at once. I understood clearly, as I thought, that I loved Him; but I did not understand, as I ought to have understood it, wherein the true love of God consists. I do not think I had yet perfectly disposed myself to seek His service when

His Majesty turned towards me with His consolations. What others strive after with great labor, our Lord seems to have looked out for a way to make me willing to accept—that is, in these later years to give me joy and comfort. But as for asking our Lord to give me either these things or sweetness in devotion, I never dared to do it; the only thing I prayed Him to give me was the grace never to offend Him, together with the forgiveness of my great sins. When I saw that my sins were so great, I never ventured deliberately to ask for consolation or for sweetness. He had compassion enough upon me, I think—and, in truth, He dealt with me according to His great mercy—when He allowed me to stand before Him, and when He drew me into His presence; for I saw that, if He had not drawn me, I should not have come at all.

Once only in my life do I remember asking for consolation, being at the time in great aridities. When I considered what I had done, I was so confounded, that the very distress I suffered from seeing how little humility I had, brought me that which I had been so bold as to ask for. I knew well that it was lawful to pray for it; but it seemed to me that it is lawful only for those who are in good dispositions, who have sought with all their might to attain to true devotion—that is, not to offend God, and to be disposed and resolved for all goodness. I looked upon those tears of mine as womanish and weak, seeing that I did not obtain my desires by them; nevertheless, I believe that they did me some service; for, especially after those two occasions of great compunction and sorrow of heart, accompanied by tears, of which I am speaking, I began in a special way to give myself more to prayer, and to occupy myself less with those things which did me harm—though I did not give them up altogether. But God Himself, as I have just said, came to my aid, and helped me to turn away from them. As His Majesty was only waiting for some preparation on my part, the spiritual graces grew in me as I shall now explain. It is not the custom of our Lord to give these graces to any but to those who keep their consciences in greater pureness.

CHAPTER X: Four Degrees of Prayer

I speak now of those who begin to be the servants of love; that seems to me to be nothing else but to resolve to follow Him in the way of prayer, who has loved us so much. It is a dignity so great, that I have a strange joy in thinking of it; for servile fear vanishes at once, if we are, as we ought to be, in the first degree. O Lord of my soul, and my good, how is it that, when a soul is determined to love Thee—doing all it can, by forsaking all things, in order that it may the better occupy itself with the love of God—it is not Thy Will it should have the joy of ascending at once to the possession of perfect love? I have spoken amiss; I ought to have said, and my complaint should have been, why is it we do not? for the fault is wholly our own that we do not rejoice at once in a dignity so great, seeing that the attaining to the perfect possession of this true love brings all blessings with it. . . .

A beginner must look upon himself as making a garden, wherein our Lord may take His delight, but in a soil unfruitful, and abounding in weeds. His Majesty roots up the weeds, and has to plant good herbs. Let us, then, take for granted that this is already done when a soul is determined to give itself to prayer, and has begun the practice of it. We have, then, as good gardeners, by the help of God, to see that the plants grow, to water them carefully, that they may not die, but produce blossoms, which shall send forth much fragrance, refreshing to our Lord, so that He may come often for His pleasure into this garden, and delight Himself in the midst of these virtues.

Let us now see how this garden is to be watered, that we may understand what we have to do: how much trouble it will cost us, whether the gain be greater than the trouble, or how long a time it will take us. It seems to me that the garden may be watered in four ways: by water taken out of a well, which is very laborious; or with water raised by means of an engine and buckets, drawn by a windlass—I have drawn it this way sometimes—it is a less troublesome way than the first, and gives more water; or by a stream or brook, whereby the garden is watered in a much better way—for the soil is more thoroughly saturated, and there is no necessity to water it so often, and the labor of the gardener is much less; or by showers of rain, when our Lord Himself waters it, without labor on our part—and this way is incomparably better than all the others of which I have spoken.

Now, then, for the application of these four ways of irrigation by which the garden is to be maintained; for without water it must fail. The comparison is to my purpose, and it seems to me that by the help of it I shall be able to explain, in some measure, the four degrees of prayer to which our Lord, of His goodness, has occasionally raised my soul. May He graciously grant that I may so speak as to be of some service to one of those who has commanded me to write, whom our Lord has raised in four months to a greater height than I have reached in seventeen years! He prepared himself better than I did, and therefore is his garden, without labor on his part, irrigated by these four waters—though the last of them is only drop by drop; but it is growing in such a way, that soon, by the help of our Lord, he will be swallowed up therein, and it will be a pleasure to me, if he finds my explanation absurd, that he should laugh at it.

Of those who are beginners in prayer, we may say, that they are those who draw the water up out of the well—a process which, as I have said, is very laborious; for they must be wearied in keeping the senses recollected, and this is a great labor, because the senses have been hitherto accustomed to distractions. It is necessary for beginners to accustom themselves to disregard what they hear or see, and to put it away from them during the time of prayer; they must be alone, and in retirement think over their past life. Though all must do this many times, beginners as well as those more advanced; all, however, must not do so equally, as I shall show hereafter. Beginners at first suffer much, because they are not convinced that they are penitent for their sins; and yet they are, because they are so sincerely resolved on serving God. They must strive to meditate on the life of

Christ, and the understanding is wearied thereby. Thus far we can advance of ourselves—that is, by the grace of God—for without that, as everyone knows, we never can have one good thought.

This is beginning to draw water up out of the well. God grant there may be water in it! That, however, does not depend on us; we are drawing it, and doing what we can towards watering the flowers. So good is God, that when, for reasons known to His Majesty—perhaps for our greater good—it is His will the well should be dry, He Himself preserves the flowers without water—we, like good gardeners, doing what lies in our power—and makes our virtues grow. By water here I mean tears, and if there be none, then tenderness and an inward feeling of devotion.

What, then, will he do here who sees that, for many days, he is conscious only of aridity, disgust, dislike, and so great an unwillingness to go to the well for water, that he would give it up altogether, if he did not remember that he has to please and serve the Lord of the garden; if he did not trust that his service was not in vain, and did not hope for some gain by a labor so great as that of lowering the bucket into the well so often, and drawing it up without water in it? It will happen that he is often unable to move his arms for that purpose, or to have one good thought: working with the understanding is drawing water out of the well.

What, then, once more, will the gardener do now? He must rejoice and take comfort, and consider it as the greatest favor to labor in the garden of so great an Emperor; and as he knows that he is pleasing Him in the matter—and his purpose must not be to please himself, but Him—let him praise Him greatly for the trust He has in him—for He sees that, without any recompense, he is taking so much care of that which has been confided to him; let him help Him to carry the Cross, and let him think how He carried it all His life long; let him not seek his kingdom here, nor ever intermit his prayer; and so let him resolve, if this aridity should last even his whole life long, never to let Christ fall down beneath the Cross.

The time will come when he shall be paid once for all. Let him have no fear that his labor is in vain: he serves a good Master, Whose eyes are upon him. Let him make no account of evil thoughts, but remember that Satan suggested them to St. Jerome also in the desert [Epistle 22, *ad Eustochium*]. These labors have their reward, I know it; for I am one who underwent them for many years. When I drew but one drop of water out of this blessed well, I considered it was a mercy of God. I know these labors are very great, and require, I think, greater courage than many others in this world; but I have seen clearly that God does not leave them without a great recompense, even in this life; for it is very certain that in one hour, during which our Lord gave me to taste His sweetness, all the anxieties which I had to bear when persevering in prayer seem to me ever afterwards perfectly rewarded.

I believe that it is our Lord's good pleasure frequently in the beginning, and at times in the end, to send these torments, and many other incidental temptations, to try those who love Him, and to ascertain if they will drink the chalice [St. Matthew xx.22:], and help Him to carry the Cross, before He intrusts them with His great treasures. I believe it to be for our good that His Majesty should lead us by this way, so that we may perfectly understand how worthless we are; for the graces which He gives afterwards are of a dignity so great, that He will have us by experience know our wretchedness before He grants them, that it may not be with us as it was with Lucifer.

What canst Thou do, O my Lord, that is not for the greater good of that soul which Thou knowest to be already Thine, and which gives itself up to Thee to follow Thee whithersoever Thou goest, even to the death of the Cross; and which is determined to help Thee to carry that Cross, and not to leave Thee alone with it? He who shall discern this resolution in himself has nothing to fear: no, no; spiritual people have nothing to fear. There is no reason why he should be distressed who is already raised to so high a degree as this is of wishing to converse in solitude with God, and to abandon the amusements of the world. The greater part of the work is done; give praise to His Majesty for it, and trust in His goodness who has never failed those who love Him. Close the eyes of your imagination, and do not ask why He gives devotion to this person in so short a time, and none to me after so many years. Let us believe that all is for our greater good; let His Majesty guide us whithersoever He will: we are not our own, but His. He shows us mercy enough when it is His pleasure we should be willing to dig in His garden, and to be so near the Lord of it: He certainly is near to us. If it be His Will that these plants and flowers should grow— some of them when He gives water we may draw from the well, others when He gives none—what is that to me? Do Thou, O Lord, accomplish Thy will; let me never offend Thee, nor let my virtues perish; if Thou hast given me any, it is out of Thy mere goodness. I wish to suffer, because Thou, O Lord, hast suffered; do Thou in every way fulfill Thy Will in me, and may it never be the pleasure of Thy Majesty that a gift of so high a price as that of Thy love, be given to people who serve Thee only because of the sweetness they find thereby.

It is much to be observed, and I say so because I know by experience, that the soul which begins to walk in the way of mental prayer with resolution, and is determined not to care much, neither to rejoice nor to be greatly afflicted, whether sweetness and tenderness fail it, or our Lord grants them, has already traveled a great part of the road. Let that soul, then, have no fear that it is going back, though it may frequently stumble; for the building is begun on a firm foundation. It is certain that the love of God does not consist in tears, nor in this sweetness and tenderness which we for the most part desire, and with which we console ourselves; but rather in serving Him in justice, fortitude, and humility. That seems to me to be a receiving rather than a giving of anything on our part.

ST. TERESA OF AVILA

LINES WRITTEN
IN HER BREVIARY

Let nothing disturb thee,
Nothing affright thee;
All things are passing;
God never changeth;
Patient endurance
Attaineth to all things;
Who God possesseth
In nothing is wanting;
Alone God sufficeth.

From the Spanish
by Henry Wadsworth Longfellow

ST. JOHN
OF THE CROSS
(1542–1591)

THIRTY-five miles north and west of Avila, in the wind-swept Castilian village of Fontiveros, there was born on June 24, 1542, to a weaver and his wife a son, Juan de Yepes. When Juan was seven his father died, and his mother moved with himself and his brother to Arévalo and then to the large, prosperous, royal city of Medina del Campo, the better to support her family. At first young Juan was apprenticed to a carpenter, a tailor, and a sculptor. But he showed such remarkable aptitude for study that his mother sent him to a local grammar school. There Juan succeeded so well that he was adopted by a local philanthropist, Don Antonio Alvarez de Toledo, who had retired from business to devote himself to the management of a hospital. Don Alvarez brought the boy to live with him in the hospital with the hope of training him for the priesthood and, in due course, of providing his hospital with a chaplain.

To this end he sent Juan to the college conducted by the Jesuits where the young man studied with great diligence and immense enthusiasm. In 1563 he entered the Carmelite monastery at Medina and, after his novitiate, went to the University of Salamanca to complete the course in arts and theology. In 1567 Juan was ordained a priest and returned to Medina to make his vows.

St. Teresa, who had just received official permission to begin her work of reforming the Carmelites, was in Medina to found a convent of the Reform. The two saints met. Teresa was then fifty-two, a shrewd, humorous, trained judge of men. Juan was twenty-five, small of stature but with a singularly high forehead, and amazing self-possession. Young enough to be her son, he had advanced far along the same road she had taken. For him, too, the road led to complete dedication to God. Like herself, he thought the mitigated Carmelite rule too relaxed. He had already consulted his prior with a view of transferring to the Carthusians, who sought contemplation through solitude and penance. Here was a man to gladden her heart. She proposed that he join her Discalced Reform and join in founding a monastery for monks. He agreed, provided that the work would begin soon, and then returned to Salamanca for further work in theology.

Upon his return Teresa presented him with a broken-down house outside Duruelo. It was so bad that, as she reported in her *Foundations,* one of her most austere nuns said, "Mother, I am certain that nobody, however good and spiritual could endure this. You must not consider it." Yet Juan and two companions were supremely happy at Duruelo, rising early for devotions, then walking barefoot, winter and summer, to preach and hear confessions in the countryside. Soon Duruelo attracted its flow of penitents, and the growing community moved to Mancera where recruits kept coming. Juan founded a second monastery of the Reform at Partrana in 1570 and a third in the university town of Alcala de Henares in 1571.

Reform is like the breaking and resetting of a bone. There is no way to do it save by hurting the patient. It is not surprising then that the Calced (sandaled)—those who abided by the mitigated rule—Carmelites began to regard Teresa and her reformed group (the Discalced) as dissidents, especially after Teresa had petitioned that the Discalced become a separate province in 1575. Some angry Carmelites openly persecuted the Reformers. Teresa herself was forbidden to live the life she had vowed to follow. Juan, now recognized as a leader as important as Teresa, was importuned to abandon the Reform. This he refused to do, although he yearned with all his heart to bring harmony to his order.

Incensed by his refusal, the enemies of the Reform broke into Juan's dwelling at Avila and hauled him off to the local monastery where he was flogged, and then they dragged him off to Toledo. There, from the night of December 3, 1577, to August 16, 1578, he was imprisoned in a cell ten feet by six, lit by a hole high in the wall. His food was bread, water, and scraps of salt fish. At first Juan was whipped daily, but when it became clear he would not change his mind, he was beaten at irregular intervals. Worse than the physical mistreatment, were the unceasing efforts of his captors to persuade him of his errors and disobedience, and the constant repetition of the rumor that the Reform was soon to be suppressed by ecclesiastical authority. When Teresa heard of these sufferings she wrote, "I don't know how God tolerates such things."

Yet out of his miseries, Juan was to distill the perfume of his poetry and his mystical writings. Permitted pen, ink, and a little paper, he wrote a little book in which he composed a good part of "The Spiritual Canticle" and other poems that are not only masterpieces of Spanish literature, but also the occasion of those treatises on mystical theology that won for him the title, "Doctor of the Universal Church." Moreover, prison gave him an experience of privation that, viewed with the eye of faith, brought him closer to the sufferings of Christ, who also had suffered at the hands of His own people. Juan's soul expanded in prison, yet he dreamed of freedom. On the night of the Feast of the Assumption, August 15, 1578, he had a vision of Our Lady in which she commanded him to escape. The next night he made a rope of his bed clothes and, opening the door that was insecurely bolted, slid down the monastery wall. He dropped into an areaway and ran to the adjoining building. It turned out to be his one refuge in Toledo— the convent of Reformed Carmelites. The nuns took him in, fed him, gave him clothes and sent him to the house of a sympathetic Canon of the Cathedral. A short time later Juan slipped out of Toledo.

The next dozen years Juan spent in various monasteries chiefly in the south of Spain. There he composed his treatises —*The Ascent of Mt. Carmel, The Dark Night of the Soul, The Spiritual Canticle,* and *The Living Flame of Love.* Originally these were expositions of his poems, but after revision they developed into a systematic account of ascetical and mystical theology. What distinguishes these books is not only their extraordinary dimensions, but also the degree of excellence within each dimension. They express the height of divine contemplation achieved only by St. Augustine and St. Teresa. They have a depth of learning that is comparable to that of St. Thomas. To these qualities they add that of poetry, for Juan's prose, disciplined and exact, sings its way to the heart as it penetrates the mind. Listen, for example, to the lines below, from *The Ascent of Mt. Carmel*, that describe a woodcut he made to illustrate the spiritual mountain he would have his readers climb:

In order to arrive at having pleasure in everything,
Desire to have pleasure in nothing.
  In order to arrive at possessing everything,
Desire to possess nothing.
  In order to arrive at being everything,
Desire to be nothing.
  In order to arrive at knowing everything,
Desire to know nothing.
  In order to arrive at that wherein thou hast no pleasure,
Thou must go by a way wherein thou hast no pleasure.
  In order to arrive at that which thou knowest not,
Thou must go by a way that thou knowest not.
  In order to arrive at that which thou possessest not,
Thou must go by a way that thou possessest not.
  In order to arrive at that which thou are not,
Thou must go through that which thou art not.

THE WAY NOT TO
IMPEDE THE ALL

When thou thinkest upon anything,
Thou ceasest to cast thyself upon the All.
  For, in order to pass from the all to the All,
Thou hast to deny thyself wholly in all.
  And, when thou comest to possess it wholly,

Thou must possess it without desiring anything.
    For, if thou wilt have anything in all,
Thou hast not thy treasure purely in God.

Juan had taken for himself the name Juan of the Cross, a name that signified his will to accept the sufferings of Christ. Suffer he did, to the very end. In the last years of his life, a new superior of his order resented Juan's defense of the Teresian reforms. As a result, he was sent off to a lonely friary at La Peñuela, where, with intense joy, he welcomed the humiliations visited upon him. His last days were spent at Ubeda, still a virtual exile, but consoled by his own maxim that even the harshest of our trials is a source of glory: "Where there is no love, put love in, and you will draw love out."

ST. JOHN
OF THE CROSS

CHAPTER XX

The spiritual man, then, must see to it carefully that his heart and his rejoicing begin not to lay hold upon temporal things; he must fear lest from being little it should grow to be great, and should increase from one degree to another. For little things do indeed become great; and from a small beginning there comes in the end a great matter, even as a spark suffices to set a mountain on fire and to burn up the whole world. And let him never be self-confident because his attachment is small, and fail to uproot it instantly because he thinks that he will do so later. For if, when it is so small and in its beginnings, he has not the courage to make an end of it, how does he suppose, and presume, that he will be able to do so when it is great and more deeply rooted. The more so since Our Lord said in the Gospel: He that is unfaithful in little will be unfaithful also in much [Luke 16:10]. For he that avoids the small sin will not fall into the great sin; but great evil is inherent in the small sin, since it has already penetrated within the fence and wall of the heart; and as the proverb says: Once begun, half done. Wherefore David warns us, saying: "Though riches abound, let us not apply our heart to them" [Psalms 61:2].

Although a man might not do this for the sake of God and of the obligations of Christian perfection, he should nevertheless do it because of the temporal advantages that result from it, to say nothing of the spiritual advantages, and he should free his heart completely from all rejoicing in the things mentioned above. And thus, not only will he free himself from the pestilent evils which we have described in the last chapter, but, besides this, he will withdraw his joy from temporal blessings and acquire the virtue of liberality, which is one of the principal attributes of God, and can in no wise coexist with covetousness. Apart from this, he will acquire liberty of soul, clarity of reason, rest, tranquillity and peaceful confidence in God and a true reverence and worship of God which comes from the will. He will find greater joy and recreation in the creatures through his detachment from them, for he cannot rejoice in them if he look upon them with attachment to them as to his own. Attachment is an anxiety that, like a bond, ties the spirit down to the earth and allows it no enlargement of heart. He will also acquire, in his detachment from things, a clear conception of them, so that he can well understand the truths relating to them, both naturally and supernaturally. He will therefore enjoy them after a very different fashion from that of one who is attached to them, and he will have a great advantage and superiority over such a one. For, while he enjoys them according to their truth, the other enjoys them according to their deceptiveness; the one appreciates the best side of them and the other the worst; the one rejoices in their substance; the other, whose sense is bound to them, in their accident. For sense cannot grasp or attain to more than the accident, but the spirit, purged of the clouds and species of accident, penetrates the truth and worth of things, for this is its object. Wherefore joy, like a cloud, darkens the judgment, since there can be no voluntary joy in creatures without voluntary attachment, even as there can be no joy which is passion when there is no habitual attachment in the heart; and the renunciation and purgation of such joy leave the judgment clear, even as the mists leave the air clear when they are scattered.

This man, then, rejoices in all things—since his joy is dependent upon none of them—as if he had them all; and this other, through looking upon them with a particular sense of ownership, loses all the pleasure of them in general. This former man, having none of them in his heart, possesses them all, as St. Paul says, in great freedom [II Corinthians 6:10]. This latter man, inasmuch as he has something of them through the attachment of his will, neither has nor possesses anything; it is rather they that have possessed his heart, and he is, as it were, a sorrowing captive. Wherefore, if he desire to have a certain degree of joy in creatures, he must of necessity have an equal degree of disquietude and grief in his heart, since it is seized and possessed by them. But he that is detached is untroubled by anxieties, whether in prayer or apart from it; and thus, without losing time, he readily gains great spiritual treasure. But the other man loses everything, running to and fro upon the chain by which his heart is attached and bound; and with all his diligence he can still hardly free himself for a short time from this bond of thought and rejoicing by which his heart is bound. The spiritual man, then, at the first motion of his heart toward creatures, must restrain it, remembering the truth which we have here laid down, that there is naught wherein a man must rejoice, save in his service of God, and in his striving for His glory and honor in all things, directing all things solely to this end and turning aside from vanity in them, looking in them neither for his own joy nor for his consolation.

There is another very great and important benefit in this detachment of the rejoicing from creatures—namely, that it leaves the heart free for God. This is the dispositive foundation of all the favors which God will grant to the soul, and without this disposition He grants them not. And they are such that, even from the temporal standpoint, for one joy which the soul renounces for love of Him and for the perfection of the Gospel, He will give him a hundred in this life, as His Majesty promises in the same Gospel [Matthew 19:29]. But, even were there not so high a rate of interest, the spiritual man should quench these creature joys in his soul because of the displeasure which they give to God. For we see in the Gospel that, simply because that rich man rejoiced at having goods for many years, God was so greatly angered that He told him that his soul would be brought to account on that very night [Luke 12:20]. Therefore, we must believe that, whensoever we rejoice vainly, God is beholding us and preparing some punishment and bitter draught according to our deserts, so that the pain which results from the joy may sometimes be a hundred times greater than the joy. For, although it is true, as St. John says on this matter, in the Apocalypse, concerning Babylon, that as much as she had rejoiced and lived in delights, so much torment and sorrow [Revelation 18:7] should be given her, yet this is not to say that the pain will not be greater than the joy, which indeed it will be, since for brief pleasures are given eternal torments. The words mean that there shall be nothing without its particular punishment, for He Who will punish the idle word will not pardon vain rejoicing.

CHAPTER XXI

By natural blessings we here understand beauty, grace, comeliness, bodily constitution and all other bodily endowments; and likewise, in the soul, good understanding, discretion and other things that pertain to reason. Many a man sets his rejoicing upon all these gifts, to the end that he himself, or those that belong to him, may possess them, and for no other reason, and gives no thanks to God Who bestows them on him so that He may be the better known and loved by him because of them. But it is vanity and deception to rejoice for this cause alone, as Solomon says in these words: Deceitful is grace and vain in beauty; the woman who fears God, she shall be praised [Proverbs 31:30]. Here he teaches us that a man ought rather to be fearful because of these natural gifts, since he may easily be distracted by them from the love of God, and, if he be attracted by them, he may fall into vanity and be deceived. For this reason bodily grace is said to be deceptive because it deceives a man in the way and attracts him to that which beseems him not, through vain joy and complacency, either in himself or in others that have such grace. And it is said that beauty is vain because it causes a man to fall in many ways when he esteems it and rejoices in it, for he should only rejoice if he serves God or others through it. But he ought rather to fear and harbor misgivings lest perchance his natural graces and gifts should be a cause of his offending God, either by his vain presumption or by the extreme affection with which he regards them. Wherefore he that has such gifts should be cautious and live carefully, lest, by his vain ostentation, he give cause to any man to withdraw his heart in the smallest degree from God. For these graces and gifts of nature are so full of provocation and occasion of evil, both to him that possesses them and to him that looks upon them, that there is hardly any who entirely escapes from binding and entangling his heart in them. We have heard that many spiritual persons, who had certain of these gifts, had such fear of this that they prayed God to disfigure them, lest they should be a cause and occasion of any vain joy or affection to themselves or to others, and God granted their prayer.

The spiritual man, then, must purge his will, and make it to be blind to this vain rejoicing, bearing in mind that beauty and all other natural gifts are but earth, and that they come from the earth and will return thither; and that grace and beauty are smoke and vapor of this same earth; and that they must be held and esteemed as such by a man that desires not to fall into vanity, but will direct his heart to God in these matters, with rejoicing and gladness, because God is in Himself all these beauties and graces in the most eminent degree, and is infinitely high above all created things. And, as David says, they are all like a garment and shall grow old and pass away, and He alone remains immutable forever [Psalms 101:27]. Wherefore, if in all these matters a man direct not his rejoicing to God, it will ever be false and deceptive. For of such a man is that saying of Solomon to be understood, where he addresses joy in the creatures, saying: To joy I said: "Wherefore art thou vainly deceived?" [Ecclesiastes 2:2] That is, when the heart allows itself to be attracted by the creatures.

CHAPTER XXII

Although many of these evils and benefits that I am describing in treating of these kinds of joy are common to all, yet, because they follow directly from joy and detachment from joy (although comprised under any one of these six divisions which I am treating), therefore I speak under each heading of some evils and benefits which are also found under another, since these, as I say, are connected with that joy which belongs to them all. But my principal intent is to speak of the particular evils and benefits which come to the soul, with respect to each thing, through its rejoicing or not rejoicing in it. These I call particular evils, because they are primarily and immediately caused by one particular kind of rejoicing, and are not, save in a secondary and mediate sense, caused by another. The evil of spiritual lukewarmness, for example, is caused directly by any and every kind of joy, and this evil is therefore common to all these six kinds; but fornication is a particular evil, which is the direct result only of joy in the good things of nature of which we are speaking.

The spiritual and bodily evils, then, which directly and effectively come to the soul when it sets its rejoicing on the good things of nature are reduced to six principal evils. The first is vainglory, presumption, pride and disesteem of our neighbor; for a man cannot cast eyes of esteem on one thing without taking them from the rest. From this follows, at the least, a real disesteem for everything else; for naturally, by setting our esteem on one thing, we withdraw our heart from all things else and set it upon the thing esteemed; and from this real contempt it is very easy to fall into an intentional and voluntary contempt for all these other things, in particular or in general, not only in the heart, but also in speech, when we say that such a thing or such a person is not like such another.

The second evil is the moving of the senses to complacency and sensual delight and luxury. The third evil comes from falling into adulation and vain praise, wherein is deception and vanity, as Isaiah says in these words: "My people, he that praises thee deceives thee" [Isaias 3:12]. And the reason is that, although we sometimes speak the truth when we praise grace and beauty, yet it will be a marvel if there is not some evil enwrapped therein or if the person praised is not plunged into vain complacency and rejoicing, or his imperfect intentions and affections are not directed thereto. The fourth evil is of a general kind: it is a serious blunting of the reason and the spiritual sense, such as is effected by rejoicing in temporal good things. In one way indeed it is much worse. For as the good things of nature are more closely connected with man than are temporal good things, the joy which they give leaves an impression and effect and grace upon the senses more readily and more effectively, and deadens them more completely. And thus reason and judgment are not free; but are clouded with that affection of joy which is very closely connected with them; and from this arises the fifth evil, which is distraction of the mind by created things. And hence arise and follow lukewarmness and weakness of spirit, which is the sixth evil, and is likewise of a general kind; this is apt to reach such a pitch that a man may find the things of God very tedious and troublesome, until at last he comes to abhor them. In this rejoicing purity of spirit, at least, is invariably lost first of all. For if any spirituality is discerned, it will be of such a gross and sensual kind that it is hardly spiritual or interior or recollected at all, since it will consist rather in pleasure of sense than in strength of spirit. Since, then, the spirituality of the soul is of so low and weak a character at that time as not to quench the habit of this rejoicing (for this habit alone suffices to destroy pure spirituality, even when the soul is not consenting to the acts of rejoicing), the soul must be living, so to say, in the weakness of sense rather than in the strength of the spirit. Otherwise, it will be seen in the perfection and fortitude which the soul will have when the occasion demands it. Although I deny not that many virtues may exist together with

251

serious imperfections, no pure or delectable inward spirituality can exist while these joys are not quenched; for the flesh reigns within, warring against the spirit, and, although the spirit may be unconscious of the evil, yet at the least it causes it hidden distraction.

Returning now to speak of that second evil, which contains innumerable evils within itself, it is impossible to describe with the pen or to express in words the lengths to which it can go, neither is this unknown or hidden, nor the extent of the misery that arises from the setting of our rejoicing on natural beauty and graces. For every day we hear of numerous deaths, the loss by many of their honor, the commission of many insults, the dissipation of much wealth, numerous cases of emulation and strife, of adultery, rape and fornication, and of the fall of many holy men, comparable in number to that third part of the stars of Heaven which was swept down by the tail of the serpent on earth [Revelation 12:4]. All these disasters come from that cause. The fine gold has lost its brilliance and lustre and is become mire; and the notable and noble men of Sion, who were clothed in finest gold, are counted as earthen pitchers, that are broken and have become potsherds [Lamentations 4:1-2]. How far does the poison of this evil not penetrate?

And who drinks not, either much or little, from this golden chalice of the Babylonian woman of the Apocalypse? [Revelation 17:4]. She seated herself on that great beast, that had seven heads and ten crowns, signifying that there is scarce any man, whether high or low, saint or sinner, who comes not to drink of her wine, to some extent enslaving his heart thereby, for, as is said of her in that place, all the kings of the earth have become drunken with the wine of her prostitution. And she seizes upon all estates of men, even upon the highest and noblest estate—the service of the sanctuary and the Divine priesthood—setting her abominable cup, as Daniel says, in the holy place [Daniel 9:27], and leaving scarcely a single strong man without making him to drink, either little or much, from the wine of this chalice, which is vain rejoicing. For this reason it is said that all the kings of the earth have become drunken with this wine, for very few will be found, however holy they may have been, that have not been to some extent stupefied and bewildered by this draught of the joy and pleasure of natural graces and beauty.

This phrase "they have become drunken" should be noted. For, however little a man may drink of the wine of this rejoicing, it at once takes hold upon the heart, and stupefies it and works the evil of darkening the reason, as does wine to those who have been corrupted by it. So that, if some antidote be not at once taken against this poison, whereby it may be quickly expelled, the life of the soul is endangered. Spiritual weakness will increase, bringing it down to such great evil that it will be like Samson, when his eyes were put out and the hair of his first strength was cut off, and like Samson it will see itself grinding in the mills, a captive among its enemies [Judges 16]; and afterwards, peradventure, it will die the second death among its enemies, even as did he, since the drinking of this rejoicing will produce spiritually in them all those evils that were produced in him physically, and does in fact produce them in many persons to this day. Let his enemies come and say to him afterwards, to his great confusion: Art thou he that broke the knotted cords, that tore asunder the lions, slew the thousand Philistines, broke down the gates and freed himself from all his enemies?

Let us conclude, then by giving the instruction necessary to counteract this poison. And let it be this: As soon as thy heart feels moved by this vain joy in the good things of nature, let it remember how vain a thing it is to rejoice in aught save the service of God, how perilous and how pernicious. Let it consider how great an evil it was for the angels to rejoice and take pleasure in their natural endowments and beauty, since it was this that plunged them into the depths of shame. Let them think, too, how many evils come to men daily through this same vanity, and let them therefore resolve in good time to employ the remedy which the poet counsels to those who begin to grow affectioned to such things. "Make haste now," he says, "to use the remedy at the beginning; for when evil things have had time to grow in the heart, remedy and medicine come late." Look not upon the wine, as the Wise Man says, when its color is red and when it shines in the glass; it enters pleasantly and bites like a viper and sheds abroad poison like a basilisk [Proverbs 23:31-32].

CHAPTER XXIII

Many are the benefits which come to the soul through the withdrawal of its heart from this rejoicing; for, besides preparing itself for the love of God and the other virtues, it makes a direct way for its own humility, and for a general charity toward its neighbors. For, as it is not led by the apparent good things of nature, which are deceitful, into affection for anyone, the soul remains free and able to love them all rationally and spiritually, as God wills them to be loved. Here it must be understood that none deserves to be loved, save for the virtue that is in him. And, when we love in this way, it is very pleasing to the will of God, and this love also brings great liberty; and if there be attachment in it, there is greater attachment to God. For, in that case, the more this love grows, the more grows our love toward God; and, the more grows our love toward God, the greater becomes our love for our neighbor. For, when love is grounded in God, the reason for all love is one and the same and the cause of all love is one and the same also.

Another excellent benefit results to the soul from its renunciation of this kind of rejoicing, which is that it fulfills and keeps the counsel of Our Savior which He gives us through St. Matthew. Let him that will follow Me, He says, deny himself [Matthew 16:24]. This the soul could in no wise do if it were to set its rejoicing upon the good things of nature; for he that attaches any importance to himself neither denies himself nor follows Christ.

There is another great benefit in the renunciation of this kind of rejoicing, which is that it produces great tranquillity in the soul, empties it of distractions and brings recollection to the senses, especially to the eyes. For the soul that desires not to rejoice in these things desires neither to look at them nor to attach the other senses to them, lest it should be attracted or entangled by them. Neither will it spend time or thought upon them, being like the prudent serpent, which stops its ears that it may not hear the charmers lest they make some impression upon it [Psalms 57:5]. For, by guarding its doors, which are the senses, the soul guards itself safely and increases its tranquillity and purity.

There is another benefit of no less importance to those that have become proficient in the mortification of this kind of rejoicing, which is that evil things and the knowledge of them neither make an impression upon them nor stain them as they do those to whom they still give delight. Wherefore the renunciation and mortification of this rejoicing result in spiritual cleanness of soul and body; that is, of spirit and sense; and the soul comes to have an angelical conformity with God, and becomes, both in spirit and in body, a worthy temple of the Holy Spirit. This cannot come to pass if the heart rejoices in natural graces and good things. For this reason it is not necessary to have consent to any evil thing, or to have remembrance of such; for that rejoicing suffices to stain the soul and the senses with impurity by means of the knowledge of evil; for, as the Wise Man says, the Holy Spirit will remove Himself from thoughts that are without understanding—that is, without the higher reason that has respect to God [Wisdom 1:5].

Another benefit of a general kind follows, which is that, besides freeing ourselves from the evils and dangers aforementioned, we are delivered also from countless vanities, and from many other evils, both spiritual and temporal; and especially from falling into the small esteem in which are held all those that are seen to glory or rejoice in the said natural gifts, whether in their own or in those of others. And thus these souls are held and esteemed as wise and prudent, as indeed are all those who take no account of these things, but only of that which pleases God.

From these said benefits follows the last, which is a generosity of the soul, as necessary to the service of God as is liberty of spirit, whereby temptations are easily vanquished and trials faithfully endured, and whereby, too, the virtues grow and become prosperous.

ST. FRANCIS
DE SALES
(1567—1622)

WHEN Frances de Sionas, wife of Francis, Count of Sales, gave birth to her first son, she was hardly more than a child. Her son Francis, born prematurely, was as beautiful as she was, but frail, so that the mother hovered over the infant, nursed him into robust health, and provided him, too, as soon as she could, with the nourishments of religion. She took great pride in this small, graceful, intelligent boy and would have preferred keeping him home, under the tutelage of her chaplains, to foster his religious development. But her husband, high in the councils of the Duke of Savoy, wanted his son prepared for an important political office. So, at six, young Francis went to the neighboring schools at Rocheville and later at Annecy. By the time he was eleven, the boy had already shown he was more attracted to his mother's inclinations, for he begged for and received his father's permission to accept the tonsure. But the old Count de Sales still saw his son as a chief counsellor to the Duke of Savoy.

At thirteen, young Francis was sent to the Jesuit College of Clermont in Paris. For six years he studied Latin, Greek, philosophy, and theology with notable success. To please his father he also acquired the arts of the courtier. He learned how to ride, dance, fence—and how to make courtly bows and small talk appropriate to people of rank. That he was still aware of his tonsure, however, appeared in his consistent piety. He made the spiritual exercises according to the principles of St. Ignatius, prayed with perseverance, and sought out conversations with learned, holy men, particularly the Capuchin friar, Angelus Loyeuse, who had once been a duke and marshal of France. Francis began to wear a hair shirt under his fashionable clothes; later he made a vow of perpetual chastity. He suffered, too, from a prolonged attack of scruples, so that he grew ill and came to the edge of despair. Distraught, he finally rushed to his favorite church of St. Stephen, where he cast himself upon the mercy of the Blessed Mother and experienced a complete restoration of the spirit of tranquillity that he retained throughout his life.

In 1554 his father sent him to the University of Padua to study law. There he lived by a spiritual rule he had drawn up for himself. In addition to his legal studies, he read St. Thomas's *Summa* and St. Robert Bellarmine's *Controversies*. At Padua, too, he almost died—twice. On one occasion a broil of students attacked him in the streets. Francis called into play his skill with the sword and routed them all. On another he fell ill of the plague and was thought to be at the point of death. His friend and tutor, Deage, mournfully asked his instructions about the funeral. Francis suggested cheerfully that his body be given to medical students for dissection. "In that way," he said, "it will be of some advantage when dead, having been of none while alive." But he recovered and shortly after won his doctorate in law.

As was customary in his times, Francis made one of the usual pilgrimages to Rome after completing his studies, to search his soul and nourish his faith at the heart of the church's activity. Among others, he met St. Philip Neri while he was there. St. Philip was then performing his miracles of charity in his rooms above San Girolamo's. Francis was taken by the kindness and generosity of the man and forever afterward was influenced by Philip's teachings.

By this time Francis had decided on his vocation for the priesthood, but he wished to accomplish this design with a minimum of irritation to his proud and loving father. The old Count had already planned his son's life. He had furnished Francis' apartments with a splendid library, procured for him the counsellorship to the parliament at Chambéry, the capital of Savoy, and had picked out a well-born wife for him.

Francis put him off gently, and finally prevailed on his cousin, Louis de Sales, a canon of Geneva, to act as advocate before his father. Sadly, the old Count gave in. Francis was then made the provost of the See of Geneva and, soon after, deacon and priest.

Francis began his clerical career in Savoy under distinctly unfavorable conditions. The Calvinists were in control of Geneva itself and of much of the surrounding area, so that the bishop was forced to reside at Annecy. When the Duke of Savoy reconquered the region, he had found only a handful of Catholics left. He wrote to the bishop asking for preachers. So dangerous was the task that no one but Francis and his cousin would attempt it. Yet within four years, during which the two young priests were in constant danger of assassination, they won back thousands of lapsed Catholics. Francis, particularly, had discovered the secret of successful preaching: lucid exposition, meekness, patience, and an all-encompassing charity. To the amazement of that quarrelsome time, Francis made four visits to Theodore Beza, the successor to Calvin and patriarch of the Calvinist sect in its stronghold at Geneva. The old man, after some initial gruffness, entered into conversation with the young priest. This was perhaps the first example of a Catholic-Protestant dialogue.

As coadjutor and then Bishop of Geneva, Francis continued his missionary activities not only among the heretics but also among the poor and humble of his own diocese. A most sympathetic confessor and director of souls and a preacher of rare simplicity, he was soon in demand all over France. Henry IV and his Queen, Marie de Medici, were so entranced by his writings that they sent a copy of his *Introduction to a Devout Life*, richly bound and embossed with jewels, to James I of England, devoutly hoping to convert their royal cousin. The Cardinal of Paris sought him for a coadjutor and successor. Milan wanted him too. But Francis kept saying that his diocese was like a poor wife and he could not leave it. Nor would he abandon as orphans the religious communities, particularly the nuns of the Visitation, a group he had founded together with St. Jane Frances de Chantal. All through his life St. Francis had to reject the supplications of good souls who thought they knew better than he did what God wanted him to do. But he continued to follow his own clear conscience.

Francis became a writer almost by accident. His first important work, *The Introduction to a Devout Life,* began as a series of letters to Philothea, the fictitious name of a lady who, like many others, had begged him to tell her how she might live a perfect Christian life amid the trials of the world. He had no thought of publishing it until he heard that a group of priests intended to do so if he did not. *The Introduction* differs from conventional spiritual reading, if not in its ultimate purpose, then in its style, tone, and emphasis. St. Francis, for all his efforts to deprecate his ability as a writer, was a superb stylist in the late Renaissance tradition. He wrote with urbanity, wit, and charm, nor did he hesitate to use metaphors, particularly those derived from the garden. His attitude toward the reader was friendly, indeed personal, so that the reader felt that the letter was directed to himself rather than to an anonymous person in a church, or to some Christian soul who vaguely resembled a monk in the desert. Moreover, St. Francis adapted his spiritual counsels to the situation of the reader. He gently ridiculed the attempts of housewives to run their homes like convents, and of nuns to assume the pieties proper to ladies of fashion. His stress was always on the disposition of the will rather than on the performance of set external acts. Constantly aware of his own maxim, "Truth is always charitable; bitter zeal does more harm than good"—he never criticized without applying the balm of consolation and encouragement.

A second and finer work is his *Treatise on the Love of God,* which has great theological importance. Here St. Francis called upon his extensive learning as well as his long pastoral experience, not to argue and refute, but to explain to his readers the centrality of love in the Divine scheme. Although this book is more formal and systematic than his popular *Introduction,* it is at the same time more eloquent and more persuasive.

ST. FRANCIS DE SALES

Declared a Doctor of the Church and the patron of Christian journalists, St. Francis has exercised a great influence on many subsequent Christian writers.

COUNSELS
FOR MARRIED PERSONS

Marriage is a great Sacrament, "but I speak in Christ and in the Church" [Ephesians 5:32]; it is "honorable in all" [Hebrews 13:4] persons, and in every way—that is to say, in all its parts; to all persons, for even virgins should honor it with humility; in all persons, for it is equally holy in the poor and in the rich; in every day, for its origin, its end, its uses, its form and its matter are holy. It is the nursery of Christianity, which fills the earth with true believers; to fill up the number of the elect in Heaven; so that the preservation of the well-being of marriage is extremely important to the commonwealth, for marriage is its root and the source of all its streams.

Would to God that his well-beloved Son were invited to all marriages, as he was to that of Cana. The wine of consolations and blessings would then never be wanting, for, if there be ordinarily but little of such wine, and that only in the beginning, it is because Adonis is invited there in place of our Lord, and Venus in place of our Lady. He that would have fair and speckled lambs, like Jacob, must, like him, present beautiful rods of diverse colors to the sheep when they come together to mate; and they that wish for a happy issue to marriage should, at their weddings, represent to themselves the holiness and dignity of this Sacrament; but instead of that, there are a thousand disorders in entertainments, feasts and words; it is not, therefore, surprising if the results of such marriages be disorderly.

Especially do I exhort married persons to that mutual love which is so much recommended to them by the Holy Spirit in the Scriptures. O you that are married, it is nothing to say:

Love one another with a mutual love, for pairs of turtle-doves do that; nor to say: Love one another with a human love, for pagans have done that well enough; but I say to you, with the great Apostle [Ephesians 5:25]: "Husbands, love your wives, as Christ also loved the Church;" wives, love your husbands as the Church loves her Savior. It was God who brought Eve to our first father, Adam, and gave her to him for his wife: it is also God, my friends, who with his invisible hand has tied the knot of the sacred bond of your marriage, and who has given you one to the other; why do you not love one another with a love that is altogether holy, sacred and divine?

The first effect of this love is the indissoluble union of your hearts. If we glue together two pieces of fir, provided that the glue be good, the union of the two pieces will be so strong that it would be much easier to break the pieces in other parts than in the part where they were joined together; but God joins the husband to the wife with his own blood: and therefore this union is so strong that the soul ought rather to be separated from the body of the one and of the other, than the husband from the wife. Now this is not to be understood so much of the body as of the heart, of the affection and of the love.

The second effect of this love should be the inviolable fidelity of the one to the other. Of old, seals were engraved upon rings which were worn on the fingers, as Scripture itself testifies; this, then, is the explanation of the marriage ceremony: the Church, by the hand of the priest, blesses a ring, and by giving it first to the man testifies that she closes up and puts a seal upon his heart by this Sacrament, so that neither the name nor the love of any other woman may ever enter into it, so long as she lives, who has been given to him in marriage; then the bridegroom puts the ring upon the finger of the bride, that she likewise may know that her heart must never entertain any affection for another man so long as he lives upon the earth, whom our Lord has just given to her.

The third fruit of marriage is the procreation and rightful upbringing of children. It is a great honor to you, O married, that God, wishing to multiply souls who may bless and praise him for all eternity, makes you co-operators with himself in so worthy a work, by the procreation of the bodies, into which he infuses the souls, like drops from heaven, creating them, as he does, when he infuses them into the bodies.

Preserve, then, O husbands, a tender, constant and cordial love towards your wives; for the woman was drawn from that side of the first man which was nearest to his heart, to the end that she might be loved by him cordially and tenderly. The weaknesses and infirmities, whether bodily or spiritual, of your wives, ought not to provoke you to any sort of disdain, but rather to a sweet and loving compassion, for God has created them such, so that, since they are dependent upon you, you may receive more honor and respect thereby, and may have them as companions in such sort that you may be nevertheless their heads and superiors in authority. And you, O wives, love tenderly and affectionately, but with a love that is full of esteem and reverence, the husbands whom God has given you; for truly God created them of a more vigorous and predominant sex, and willed that the woman should depend upon the man, "bone of *his* bones," and "flesh of *his* flesh" [Genesis 2:23], and that she should be fashioned from one of his ribs, drawn from under his arms, to show that she must be under the hand and guidance of the husband; and all Holy Scripture enjoins on you this subjection, which nevertheless the same Scripture renders easy to you, not only wishing you to submit to it with love, but ordering your husbands to exercise their authority with great love, tenderness and sweetness: "Husbands," says St. Peter, "treat your wives with consideration, giving honor to them as to the weaker vessel" [Ephesians 3:7].

But while I exhort you to foster more and more this mutual love which you owe one to another, take care that it be not changed into any sort of jealousy; for it often happens that, as worms breed in the ripest and most delicate fruit, so jealousy is born in the warmest and most devoted love of married persons, the substance of which, however, it spoils and corrupts, for little by little it begets disputes, dissensions and separations. Of a truth, jealousy never appears, where the friendship is mutually founded upon true virtue; and therefore it is an indubitable mark of a love that is in some sort sensual and gross, and which is set up in a heart wherein it has found a virtue that is imperfect, inconstant and prone to suspicion. It is therefore an empty vaunt of friendship to wish to exalt it by jealousy, for jealousy is in truth a mark of the size and grossness of a friendship, but not of its goodness, purity and perfection; since the perfection of friendship presupposes that we are certain of the virtue of the person whom we love, whereas jealousy presupposes that we are uncertain.

O husbands, if you wish your wives to be faithful, give them a lesson by your example. "What claim have you," says St. Gregory Nazianzen, "to exact chastity from your wives if you yourselves live unchastely? How can you demand of them what you do not give them?" Do you wish them to be chaste? Be chaste yourselves, and, as St. Paul [Thessalonians 4:4] says, "let everyone know how to possess his vessel in sanctification." But if, on the contrary, you yourselves teach them to be unfaithful, it is not surprising that you should be dishonored by their infidelity. And you, O wives, whose honor is inseparably bound up with chastity and modesty, guard your glory jealously, and suffer no kind of wantonness to tarnish the spotlessness of your reputation. Fear attacks of any kind, however small they may be; never allow anyone to trifle with you. Whosoever praises your beauty and your charm should be held in suspicion by you; for whosoever praises wares which he cannot buy, is ordinarily much tempted to steal them. But if to praise of yourself anyone add dispraise of your husband, he insults you grossly; for it is clear that he not only wishes to ruin you, but already considers you half ruined, since a bargain is half concluded with the second merchant when one is dissatisfied with the first. Ladies, both in ancient and modern times, have been accustomed to wear many pearls in their ears, for the pleasure, according to Pliny, of hearing the little sounds which they make when they touch one another. But for my part, knowing that the great friend of God, Isaac, sent ear-rings to the chaste Rebecca as the first pledges of his love, I think that this mystical ornament signifies that the first thing which a husband should possess in a wife, and which the wife ought faithfully to keep for him, is her ear, so that no speech nor sound may enter it but the sweet and pleasant sound of chaste and modest words, which are the orient pearls of the Gospel; for we must ever remember that poison enters souls through the ear, just as it enters bodies through the mouth.

Love and fidelity, when united, always beget intimacy and confidence; and therefore holy men and women have made much use of mutual caresses in marriage—caresses that are truly loving, but chaste; tender, but sincere. So Isaac and Rebecca, the most chaste married couple of ancient times, were seen through a window caressing one another in such a way that, although there was nothing immodest in it, Abimelech knew well that they could not be other than husband and wife. The great St. Louis, who was as rigorous towards his own flesh as he was tender in his love of his wife, was almost blamed for being lavish in such caresses, although in truth he rather deserved praise for knowing how to lay aside his martial and courageous spirit, and give these little demonstrations of affection; for although these little demonstrations of pure and frank affection do not bind hearts together, yet they bring them close together, and serve as a pleasant aid to mutual intercourse.

St. Monica, when pregnant with the great St. Augustine, dedicated him often to the Christian religion and to the service of God's glory, as he himself testifies, saying that he had already tasted "the salt of God in the womb of his mother." This is a great example for Christian wives to offer to God the fruit of their wombs, even before it is born; for God who accepts the offerings of a humble and willing heart, usually furthers the good desires of mothers at such a time: witness Samuel, St. Thomas Aquinas, St. Andrew of Fiesole and many others. The mother of St. Bernard, worthy mother of such a son, used to take her children in her arms as soon as they were born and offer them to God, and thereafter she loved them reverently, as holy things entrusted to her by

God; which turned out so happily that in the end all seven became very holy.

But when children come into the world and begin to have the use of reason, fathers and mothers should be very careful to instill into their hearts the fear of God. The good Queen Blanche was most careful to do this in the case of her son, the King St. Louis, for she used oftentimes to say to him: "My dear child, I would much rather see you die before my eyes than see you commit one single mortal sin"; which remained so engraven in the soul of this holy son that, as he himself used to relate, never a day of his life passed in which he did not remember it, endeavoring, as much as he was able, to carry out faithfully this divine teaching. Indeed, races and generations are called, in our speech, houses, and the Hebrews even call the begetting of children the building-up of a house: for it is in this sense that it is said that God "built houses" [Exodus 1:21] for the midwives of Egypt. Now this is to show that, to build a good house, is not to fill it with many worldly possessions, but to bring up the children well in the fear of God and in virtue; wherein no pains nor labor should be spared, because children are the "crown" [Proverbs 17:6] of the father and mother.

Thus did St. Monica combat the evil inclinations of St. Augustine with so much fervor and constancy that, having followed him by sea and by land, she made him more happily the child of her tears by the conversion of his soul, than he had been the child of her blood by the generation of his body.

St. Paul allots to wives "the care of the house" [Titus 2:5]; and therefore many hold this well-grounded opinion that their devotion is more profitable to the family than that of their husbands, who, not coming so much into contact with the members of the household, cannot in consequence so readily influence them to the practice of virtue. For this reason, Solomon, in his Proverbs, makes the happiness of the whole house depend upon the care and industry of the "strong woman" [Chap. 31] whom he describes.

It is said in Genesis [Chap. 25:21] that Isaac, "seeing his

wife Rebecca barren, besought the Lord for her," or, according to the Hebrew, "besought the Lord opposite to her," because the one prayed on one side of the oratory, and the other on the other; and so the prayer of the husband made in this manner was heard. The closest and most fruitful union between husband and wife is that which is effected in holy devotion, to which they ought to encourage one another in a spirit of emulation. There are certain fruits, like the quince, which, by reason of the tartness of their juice, are scarcely palatable except in the form of preserve; there are others, which, by reason of their tenderness and delicacy, will not keep, unless they be preserved in like manner, such as cherries and apricots. So wives ought to wish their husbands to be steeped in the sugar of devotion, for a man without devotion is a severe, harsh and rough creature; and husbands ought to wish their wives to be devout, for without devotion, a woman is very frail, and disposed to waver or become tarnished in virtue. St. Paul has said that "the unbelieving husband is sanctified by the believing wife, and the unbelieving wife by the believing husband" [Corinthians 7:14] because in this strait bond of marriage, the one may easily draw the other to virtue. But what a great blessing it is when a believing husband and a believing wife sanctify one another in the true fear of the Lord.

For the rest, the mutual support of one another ought to be so great, that both should never be angry together and at the same time, so that there may never be dissension and strife between them. The honey-bees cannot stay in a place where there are echoes and resoundings and reverberations of voices; nor, indeed, can the Holy Spirit abide in a house wherein are strife, and the resoundings and reverberations of wrangling and altercation.

St. Gregory Nazianzen testifies that in his time married persons used to keep the anniversary of their marriage as a festival day. I should certainly approve if this custom were introduced now, provided that such a festival day be not kept by indulging in worldly and sensual recreations, but that husbands and wives, having confessed and communicated on that day, recommend to God more fervently than usual the course of their marriage, renewing their good resolutions to sanctify it more and more by mutual love and fidelity, and refreshing themselves in our Lord for the support of the burdens of their state of life.

OF THE HONORABLENESS OF THE MARRIAGE BED

"The marriage bed" must be "undefiled" [Hebrews 13:4], as the Apostle says—that is to say, exempt from immodesty and other defilements. Thus was marriage first instituted in the earthly paradise where, until the time of the fall, there was no disorder of concupiscence in it, nor anything dishonorable.

There is a certain resemblance between the pleasures of the flesh and those of eating, for both of them relate to the flesh, although the former, by reason of their brutish vehemence, are alone called carnal. I will therefore explain what I cannot say of the former by what I shall say of the latter.

1. Eating is ordained for the preservation of life: now, just as eating merely to nourish and preserve life is a thing that is good, holy and commanded, so what is requisite in marriage for the procreation of children and the multiplication of persons is a thing that is good and very holy, for it is the principal end of marriage.

2. To eat, not for the preservation of life, but in order to preserve that mutual intercourse and condescension which we owe one to another, is a very just and right thing: and in the same way, the mutual and legitimate satisfaction of husband and wife is called by St. Peter, a debt [I Corinthians 7:3], but a debt so binding that he will not allow one of the parties to abstain from rendering it without the free and voluntary consent of the other, not even for the sake of exercises of devotion [I Corinthians 7:5], which led me to say the word which I said on this subject in the chapter on Holy Communion [St. Francis is referring here to writing not included in this volume]; how much less, then, may either

party excuse himself from rendering the debt to the other from fanciful pretensions to virtue, or from anger and scorn!

3. As those who eat from the duty of mutual intercourse should eat freely and not as it were by constraint, and, moreover, should try to show some appetite, so the marriage debt should always be rendered faithfully, freely, and just as if it were with the hope of begetting children, even though for some reason there may be no such hope.

4. To eat, not for the two former reasons, but merely to satisfy the appetite, is permissible, but not praiseworthy; for the mere pleasure of the sensual appetite cannot be an end sufficient in itself to make an action praiseworthy; it is enough if it is permissible.

5. To eat, not from mere appetite, but to excess and immoderately, is more or less blameworthy, according as the excess is great or small.

6. Now excess in eating consists not only in eating too much, but also in the way and manner of eating. It is a remarkable thing, dear Philothea, that honey, which is so proper and wholesome a food for bees, may nevertheless be so harmful to them that sometimes it makes them ill, as when they eat too much of it in springtime; for it gives them the flux, and sometimes causes them to die irremediably, as when they become covered with honey all over the head and forepart of their body.

Of a truth, nuptial intercourse which is so holy, so just, so commendable, so useful to the commonwealth, is nevertheless in some cases dangerous to those who make use of it: for sometimes it makes their souls very sick with venial sin, as happens by simple excess; and sometimes it causes them to die of mortal sin, as happens when the order established for the procreation of children is violated and perverted; in which case, such sins are always mortal, and they are more or less detestable, according as one departs more or less from this order. For inasmuch as the procreation of children is the first and principal end of marriage, it is never lawful to depart from the order established for this purpose, though for some accidental cause conception may not be possible, as happens when barrenness or pregnancy prevents procreation and generation; for in such cases the bodily intercourse does not cease to be capable of being just and holy, provided that the laws of generation be preserved, for no circumstances ever make it lawful to transgress the law which the principal end of marriage has imposed. Of a truth, the shameful and execrable act committed by Onan in his marriage was detestable in the sight of God, as the holy text says in the thirty-eighth chapter of Genesis; and although certain heretics of our age, a hundred times more to be blamed than the Cynics, of whom St. Jerome speaks when commenting on the Epistle to the Ephesians, have tried to prove that it was the perverse intention of this wicked man which displeased God, the Scripture nevertheless speaks quite otherwise, and asserts emphatically that the *thing* itself which he did was *detestable* and abominable in the sight of God.

7. It is a true mark of a beggarly, mean, abject and base spirit to think of the dishes and of eating before the time of the repast, and more so still, when afterwards one is taken up with the pleasure which one has had in the meal, dwelling upon it in words and thoughts, and allowing one's mind to wallow in the remembrance of the pleasure enjoyed in swallowing down the mouthfuls; as do those who before dinner have their mind fastened on the spit, and after dinner on the dishes; persons fit to be scullions, who, as St. Paul says [I Philippians 3:19], make *a god* of their *belly*. Persons of honor do not think of the table until they sit down to it, and afterwards they wash their hands and mouth, in order to lose both the taste and the smell of what they have eaten. The elephant is only a huge animal, but he is the most worthy beast that lives on the earth, and the most intelligent. I will give you an instance of his excellence; he never changes his mate and tenderly loves the one of his choice, with whom nevertheless he mates but every third year, and then for five days only and so secretly that he has never been seen to do so; but he is seen again on the sixth day, on which, before doing anything else, he goes straight to some river, wherein

he bathes his whole body, for he has no wish to return to the herd until he has purified himself. Are not these excellent and modest traits in such a beast, by which he invites married persons not to allow their affections to remain attached to the pleasures of sense which they have experienced in accordance with their state of life, but, when these are past, to wash their heart and affection of them, and to purify themselves of them as soon as possible, that afterwards they may perform other actions which are more spiritual and lofty?

In this counsel consists the perfect practice of the excellent doctrine which St. Paul gives to the Corinthians [I Corinthians 7:29]: "The time is short; it remaineth that they who have wives be as if they had none." For, according to St. Gregory, he "has a wife as if he had none," who takes bodily consolations with her in such a way that he is not thereby diverted from spiritual aims; and, what is said of the husband is understood reciprocally of the wife. "Let those that use this world be as if they used it not," says the same Apostle [I Corinthians 7:31]. Let all, then, use the world, each one according to his calling, but in such a way that, by not setting his affection upon it, he may be as free and ready to serve God as if he made no use of it at all. "It is man's great ill," says St. Augustine, "to wish to enjoy those things which he should only use, and to wish to use those things which he should only enjoy." We must enjoy spiritual things, and only use corporal things, for when our use of the latter is changed into mere enjoyment, our rational soul is also changed into one that is brutish and bestial.

I think I have said all that I wished to say, and have made clear, without saying it, that which I did not wish to say.

ST. JANE FRANCES
DE CHANTAL
(1572—1641)

ANYONE might have envied the good fortune of the Baroness de Chantal during the early years of her married life. She had come from an aristocratic family. Her father, Benigne Fremiot, was a president of the Parliament of Burgundy, and her mother, Margaret de Berbisy, was one of the important ladies of the district. Margaret, her sister, married the Count of Effran. Her brother Andrew was an important cleric, destined to become the Archbishop of Bourges. And at twenty, Jane Frances had married the young and distinguished Baron de Chantal, one of Henry IV's most capable officers and head of the noble family of Rabutin. At her husband's estate at Bourbilly she presided with great dignity.

Unlike many of the nobility, the Chantals were greatly devoted to each other and to their son and three daughters. Both of them were good Christians, generous not only with their children but also with their dependents and the poor of the district. Jane Frances was the chief almsgiver, since her husband was frequently absent in the service of the king. The prosperity of their life together was unstained by the frivolity and self-indulgence that are often associated with aristocracy. But suddenly and without warning misfortune fell.

When the Baron came home from his duties in 1601 to a house full of guests, he was prepared for an interval of conversation, entertainment, and recreation. One day a guest, who was a good friend, suggested they go hunting together. They rode into the woods with the gamekeeper and his

271

assistants. Waiting at his hunting station, the guest saw a movement in a bush and fired hastily. He shot the Baron in the thigh. For nine days the young nobleman fought off death while his friend kept murmuring his regrets and repeating that he had mistaken the Baron for a deer. Jane Frances stood by her husband's side praying ardently for his recovery. The good man dictated his last requests. He pardoned all who had offended him, particularly the friend who shot him, and commanded that under no circumstances should he be punished or prosecuted. To his wife he expressed his complete resignation. Finally, after receiving the Sacraments, he died in Jane Frances' arms.

During the year of mourning after her husband's death, the young widow was numb with sorrow. Yet she found immense consolation after she offered up her sufferings to God. She decided to live as a holy widow and vowed herself to perpetual chastity. She prayed, too, for a director of her soul and was rewarded with a vision of a man whose face and features resembled St. Francis de Sales. She did not meet the saint, however, until 1604, when she was staying at her father's house in Dijon. That year Francis was preaching the Lenten sermons at the cathedral and was a frequent visitor at her father's house. She identified him immediately as her destined spiritual director. On his part, the Bishop of Annecy was convinced that Jane Frances was to be the vehicle of many graces. Soon he became her adviser who taught her how to live in the presence of Christ while performing all her obligations to her family.

At that period she used to rise at five in the morning and meditate for one hour. Then she awakened her children and together they attended Mass. The interval before the midday dinner was spent supervising her large household. After dinner she studied scriptures for a half hour before resuming her regular work. In the evening before supper she instructed her own and other children in the catechism. After supper there was more reading, evening prayers *en famille,* and an early retirement to her room where she prayed far into the night. Work and prayer flowed together as streams into one river, so that they never interfered with each other. "Madame," the servants said, "is always praying, but she never troubles anybody." Yet this serene and holy life was not wholly satisfactory to Jane Frances' growing spirit of self-denial. She told St. Francis de Sales that she wished to renounce the world entirely.

The Bishop tested the strength and rightness of her vocation. What would she do with her children? Her eldest daughter soon married. The two youngest she would take with her. Her son, now fifteen, would remain with her father. St. Francis agreed that this exceptional woman should be accepted into the new Congregation of the Visitation. In 1610 she went to Annecy to found the first convent of that order. Her son, her father, and even her crusty old father-in-law wept to see her go.

Eventually one of her daughters died and another married, as did her son. He later died fighting the Huguenots in 1627. He left a young wife with a child, Marie de Rabutin-Chantal, who was to become the famous Madame de Sévigné.

Jane Frances' career as foundress of the Visitation was, in a sense, a counterpart to that of St. Francis de Sales. His spirit, at once austere yet joyous, permeated her own spiritual thinking. Like him, she insisted upon the minute observance of ordinary duties: spending time profitably, exercising constant small acts of charity, above all, concentrating on the love of God. Characteristically she wrote to him that, "The whole world would die of love for so amiable a God if I could make it feel the sweetness which a soul tastes in loving him." On another occasion she wrote, "Abandon yourself, renounce yourself, then you will find an incomparable sweetness in God's service." This constitutes the secret of her philosophy. With beautiful simplicity she reflects St. Francis' rule of self-denial. Should one look for crosses? Rather, take those that come in everyday life. "Desire nothing, refuse nothing."

Toward the end of her life, Jane Frances was, to her intense embarrassment, already received as a saint. She saw eighty-six houses of her congregation established during her lifetime. After her death, no less a person than St. Vincent de Paul, her confessor during her residence in Paris, testified that he saw her soul, like a ball of fire, fly upward to join a larger ball of fire, the soul of St. Francis de Sales, and both together join the immense bright fire that represented the Divine Essence.

INSTRUCTION XXII

Given in 1633, on these words:
Nothing Can Profit the Soul Without
Love and Without Obedience

My most dear Daughters, you must put this maxim deep down in your minds, that nothing can profit the religious soul without submission to obedience. Love indeed is what gives value to our works, but obedience is the proof how much our works are worth, for they are of worth only so far as they are done with charity and obedience.

I assure you, my dear Daughters, that even though you had the gift of tears to such a degree as to wear yourselves away in weeping for your neighbors' sins; though you had the gift of prophecy; though you were ravished in ecstasy and saw angels; though you were always recollected and united to God; if you are not obedient and simple, all that I have just said is but a deceit of your enemy, and your love is but an illusion; for our Savior has said: "Not every one that saith to Me, Lord, Lord," this is, who prays often, "shall enter into the kingdom of heaven; but he that doth the will of My Father." See how this good Savior has placed the mark of true love in obedience; "If you love Me, keep My commandments: by that I shall know that you love Me." And in another place, He shows that blessedness is given because of obedience: Blessed shall you be, says He, when you shall have done all that I have taught you, and shall have fulfilled all these least commandments. My dear Daughters, all these things are truths of Scripture; recompense is given in proportion to love, and obedience is the proof of true love. Now, I greatly desire that you should love supremely this practice of obeying in all things, submitting in all, and do nothing without obedience, obedience stamped with the love of your Spouse.

I would not have you think that you must do great things to show our Lord that you love Him; no, my Daughters, great things are good when God presents them; but, let us offer our little things to His goodness with great love and great submissiveness, and the recompense will be in proportion to these two things: love and submissiveness.

Our Lord, in no place of Scripture, says: My son, give Me thy head, thine arms, thy life, but only: "My child, give Me thy heart;" whoso has a man's heart, has the whole man. The heart is the seat of love; when I shall have thy heart, I will set My love upon it; and even I will make My love dwell therein, and then all the rest will follow as a consequence.

I have always much esteemed what St. Ignatius said to a brother who was sweeping carelessly: "For whom are you doing that, brother?" he said to him. "For God, Father." "Oh! brother," replied the Saint, "you are not doing it for God, you are doing it for man, for God is so great a Lord that it is unexcusable to offer Him a thing done so carelessly." Remark, how this great Saint wishes that everything, even to the least actions, should be done not only by obedience, but also with fervent love. If you were bidden only to sweep a room, fail not to accept this with love, and to do it with good will, care, and fervor; and think not that it will be without recompense because it is small, for listen to what our Savior says: "Whosoever shall give a cup of cold water in My name, he shall not lose his reward." Oh! how great is God's goodness! What is more at our command than water? This signifies to us that however little the thing may be which we are commanded, from the moment we do it in the name of our Lord, that is to say for His love and to please Him, He gives us a degree of grace in this life and assigns us a degree of glory in the other; and, thereby, He shows us the incomparable depth of His mercy, the inconceivable height of His riches and bountifulness, which gives things so precious for things so slight. What think you thereof, my Daughters? Is not a single degree of grace worth more than all the world? a single degree of glory, more than we can tell? Saint Paul says that these celestial things are above all that man can think. We must not work for the recompense, but for the love of our Lord, purely and simply; nevertheless, we must from time to time consider what is here said and bless our Lord for it.

Keep well in mind this first point, walk all your life with these two feet: love and obedience, whether to the Rules, the customs, or the ordinances of your Superiors or Mistresses; and be well assured that what you do without this intention of obeying and pleasing God, cannot profit you anything for eternity, as was declared to those who said: "We have cast out devils in Thy name," to whom our Lord answered: "Depart from Me, ye workers of iniquity, I know you not." I will not, however, say that you are to constrain your mind to say at every step: I do this for God; but you must, besides the general offering in the morning, make it virtual and actual in the principal things.

The second thing I desire to see you practicing is the love of your neighbor. Cultivate these three things: the disposition to love and honor him, promptitude in serving him and helping him in his need, and that gentle bearing with him which makes you careful never to take umbrage at his faults nor to conceive disesteem for him on their account. Be very careful about this, my Daughters, and believe that we are all frail. Your Sister stumbles now, gently bear with her and pray for her; that is nothing, that is the offspring of this wretched life wherein each in turn commits some faults: my Sister now, and I soon; and thus never open your heart to the depreciation of your neighbor; but love him constantly and perfectly with cordial affection. Our Lord never said: "Love your neighbors who are perfect or those who never commit faults," for well our good Savior knew that few mortals are perfect, and that none are exempt from some faults; therefore He said indifferently: "Love one another as I have loved you."

I desire thirdly, Daughters, that you give yourselves heartily to practice this teaching: "Ask for nothing, refuse nothing;" having obtained of our Savior the grace of the religious vocation, "ask for nothing, refuse nothing" of all which is found therein: but keep your heart in a holy abnegation of everything here below. The soul that is truly indifferent asks not only her own perfection, but, with meek and constant fidelity, she employs the occasions which our Lord presents to her for His service and leaves to Him the care of the rest. When we have inconveniences, we must lay them simply before the Superior or the Novice Mistress, and then "ask for nothing and refuse nothing."

When we have any proud thoughts, we must treat them severely and say: What! Little earthworm, poor wretch, thou are but a little heap of dirt and thou wouldest lift up thy head? I will put my foot on thee; either break or come down and learn humility.

ST. JOHN EUDES
(1601—1680)

EVERY saint is extraordinary, at least in the sense that he achieves by his co-operation with grace the character that God willed him to achieve. Hence, even the most obscure saints stand out, as if ringed in light, from the murk of the commonplace. This does not mean that they live extraordinary lives in the sense that they all counsel kings and popes or start great new movements. Many simply re-form the lives of individuals in the most ordinary ways—by administering the sacraments, by preaching, by a consistent but never spectacular charity. John Eudes was such a saint.

John was born in Ri, Normandy, in 1601, the son of Isaac Eudes, a small farmer reputed to possess expert knowledge of the medicinal value of herbs, and Martha Corbin. In his quiet corner of France, he knew only at second hand that his native land had been torn by religious wars ever since the Huguenot Revolt of 1562. But he undoubtedly heard, at the Jesuit College at Caen, which he attended from 1615 to 1621, of the devastating effects of these wars. For years the ordinary people had been neglected; many parishes were in ruins. He heard too that a new generation of priests and prelates, such as St. Vincent de Paul and Cardinal de Bérulle, now regarded France—only recently the best-instructed land of Christendom —as a missionary country.

John felt an overwhelming attraction to join the missionaries. Although his parents had arranged a good marriage for him, he persisted in his wish to become a priest. At that time, Cardinal Pierre de Bérulle, together with St. Francis de Sales, was a champion of religious reform. He had just established in Paris a Congregation of the Oratory, fashioned on the model of St. Philip Neri's congregation in Rome. The chief aim of Oratorians was the sanctification of the clergy. Their zeal, devotion, and intelligence were like magnets to young John. In 1623 he joined the congregation. Fortunate in his teacher, the inspiring Père Condren who was, according to St. Jane Frances de Chantal "capable of instructing angels," John made such rapid progress that he was permitted to preach before ordination to the priesthood. After he was ordained in 1625, he retired to Aubervilliers for a year of study, meditation, and prayer. Now he was ready for the missions.

Another missionary, the plague, anticipated him. All over Europe, and particularly in his native Normandy, the black sickness devastated towns and countrysides already short of priests. John asked his superior, de Bérulle, for permission to attend the victims of the plague. With the Abbé Lament, he spent three years in the stricken areas, caring for the sick, administering the sacraments to the dying, burying the dead. When the plague abated, he returned to his original plan to join the mission.

At that time a mission was a new activity sponsored by St. Vincent de Paul and his Priests of the Mission. It consisted of a course of instruction, a week or more long, in which specially trained priests reviewed the main points of Christian doctrine and attempted to revive the desire to follow the commandments. More often than not the missions stirred up the clergy as well as the congregations, so that through France there was a marked rebirth of Christian life. John Eudes was among the outstanding mission priests.

His great success was no easy accomplishment. True, he worked with great care to make his sermons lucid, short, and meaningful. But he added to these efforts nights of prayer, fasting, and other penances. He did not have to say to his large audiences: Do as I say, not as I do. As a result, he profoundly stirred even the most hard-hearted. Among his many converts were hundreds of women who were driven to prostitution in the chaos of war, plague, and famine. In 1636 they were so numerous that he founded a house for them at Caen and placed it under the charge of nuns. Out of this foundation grew the Institute of the Good Shepherd, now spread to many parts of the world.

ST. JOHN EUDES

The older he became, the more John Eudes believed that the heart of religious revival was a body of devoted, intelligent priests. With other reformers, he paid close attention to the development of the new seminaries, where the vocations of candidates for the priesthood were more carefully tested, and where a more elaborate and careful program of studies was enforced. He saw, too, the necessity of specially trained priest-teachers. In 1643 he assembled a group of secular priests at Caen. Thus began the Eudists, officially the Congregation of Jesus and Mary, who devoted themselves to seminary teaching. But John Eudes did not abandon his popular preaching. He gave missions to Louis XIV and his court at Versailles and to the people of Paris in the parish church at St. Sulpice. Moreover, he wrote continuously: letters, sermons, instructions for missionaries, treatises on his favorite devotions to the Sacred Hearts of Jesus and of Mary.

Contemporary accounts tell us that St. John was a warm-hearted preacher who frequently aroused his audience to great enthusiasm. Because his particular devotion to the sacred humanity of Christ was opposed by powerful Jansenistic elements, later condemned by the church, John Eudes was often regarded as an emotional preacher. But in his preaching, religious feeling was always subordinated to a strenuous logic. As the selections below indicate, his characteristic approach was by way of the intelligence.

ON OUR OBLIGATIONS
TO GOD AS CHRISTIANS

First Point: Our Obligations
As Children of God, Brothers,
and Co-heirs of Christ

To be a Christian is to be a child of God, sharing one and the same Father with Jesus Christ His Only Son. "He gave them power to be made the sons of God" [John 1:12]. "I ascend to my Father and to your Father," says our Savior [John 20:17]. "Behold what manner of Charity the Father hath bestowed upon us, that we should be called, and should be the sons of God," says St. John [I John 3:1]. By creation, God is our creator, our origin, our efficient cause, our king, our sovereign; and we are His creatures, His handiwork, His subjects and His servants. By our regeneration and the new birth given us in baptism, in which we receive new being and a new and divine life, God becomes Our Father, and we His children, so that we can and must say: "Our Father who art in Heaven."

The consequence of this divine adoption are as follows:

1. By the new birth of baptism we emanated from the bosom of the Father, so we shall always remain there and be borne continually in His bosom. Otherwise, if He ceased to bear us for a single moment, we would lose the new being and life we received in baptism. He also says "Hearken unto me, O house of Jacob, all the remnant of the house of Israel, who are carried by my bowels, are borne up by my womb" [Isaias 46:3].

2. We are brothers of Jesus Christ, of His royal and divine race, sharers in His heritage. Whence it follows that the Christian, the new man and the new creature who is born only of God, knows no other genealogy than that of Jesus Christ, no other Father but God: "And call none your father upon earth" [Matthew 23:9]. "Wherefore henceforth, we know no man according to the flesh" [II Corinthians 5:16], says St. Paul. "That which is born of the Spirit, is spirit," says our Lord [John 3:6].

3. We are co-heirs with Jesus Christ, and heirs of God. O marvels! O dignity! O nobility! O greatness of the Christian! "Behold what manner of charity the Father hath bestowed upon us, that we should be called, and should be the sons of God" [I John 3:1]. What a tremendous favor of God to have made us Christians! How deeply we are indebted to His goodness! How miserable is the wretched creature who denies God

for his Father and wishes to be a child of the devil! This is
what those do who commit mortal sin. To them our Lord says:
"You are of your father the devil, and the desires of your
father you will do" [John 8:44]. Let us humble ourselves at
sight of our sins. Let us renounce Satan and give ourselves to
God, firmly resolving to live henceforth as true children of
God, not to degenerate from the nobility of our birth, not to
sully our race, and not to dishonor our Father. The wise son
is the glory of his father; he who does not act wisely is the
ignominy of his father.

Second Point:
Our Obligations As Members
of Jesus Christ

A Christian is a member of Jesus Christ. "Know you not that
your bodies are the members of Christ?" [I Corinthians 6:15].
Our alliance and union with Jesus Christ is consequently much
more noble, more intimate and perfect than the members of
a human and natural body with their head. Hence it follows
that we belong to Jesus Christ as members to their head; that
we are dependent upon Him and under His direction as members are upon their head; that we are one with Him as members are one with their head.

We must not be amazed when He assures us that His
Father loves us as He loved Him: "Thou hast loved them, as
thou hast also loved me" [John 17:23]; that He will write His
name upon us: "I will write upon him the name of my God"
[Apocalypse 3:12]; that we will share one abode with Him,
namely, His Father's bosom: "Where I am, there also shall my
minister be" [John 12:26]; and He will let us sit with Him
upon His throne [Apocalypse 3:21]. What goodness; God is
not content to call us His friends, His brothers, His children;
He wishes us to be His members.

Let us love and bless Him and consider that this membership obliges us to live the life of our Head, to perpetuate His
life upon earth, and to continue all the virtues He practiced.

How far removed we are from that holy life! How horribly guilty is he who commits a mortal sin! He dismembers Jesus Christ; he tears one of His members from Him to make it a member of Satan. Let us give ourselves to Jesus Christ as His members, and profess to live His life henceforth. It would be an outrage to see a member live any other life than that of its head. Wherefore, St. Gregory of Nyssa says: "Christianity is the profession of the life of Christ" *(Ad Harmonium, De professione Christiana).*

Third Point:
Our Obligations as Temples
of the Holy Ghost

A Christian is a temple of the Holy Ghost. "Know you not," says St. Paul, "that your members are the temple of the Holy Ghost?" [I Corinthians 6:19]. Being children of God and one with the Son of God as members with their Head, it necessarily follows that we must be animated by the same spirit. St. Paul says: "And because you are sons, God hath sent the Spirit of his Son into your hearts" [Galatians 4:6]; and "if any man have not the Spirit of Christ, he is none of His" [Romans 8:9]. Hence the Holy Spirit has been given us to be the Spirit of our spirit, the Heart of our heart and the Soul of our soul, to be always with us and within us, not only as if dwelling in His temple, but actually as part of the mystical body of Jesus Christ, which should be animated by His Spirit, for the members and every part of the body should be animated by the spirit of their Head.

This being so, who can tell or even imagine the excellence of the Christian religion, the dignity of a Christian who is a child of God, a member of Jesus Christ and animated by His Spirit? How great is our obligation to God, what should be the sanctity of our life; and how guilty he is who commits mortal sin? For he drives the Holy Ghost from His temple to give entrance to the evil spirit; he crucifies Jesus Christ in himself, stifling His indwelling spirit to establish His enemy, Satan, in his soul.

All these truths are essentially solid and infallible. Let us consider them attentively, weigh them carefully and engrave them deeply upon our hearts, to excite ourselves to bless and love God because of our infinite obligations to Him for having made us Christians. We must resolve to detest our ingratitude and our past sins, and henceforth to lead a life worthy of the perfection of the Father whose children we are, and of the purity of the Spirit whose body we share.

Ejaculatory prayer:

"Our Father Who art in Heaven, Thy Will be done on earth as it is in Heaven." *Pater noster qui es in coelis, fiat voluntas tua sicut in coelo et in terra.*

ON THE CHOICE
OF A STATE OF LIFE

First Point:
Conformity to the
Holy Will of God in the Choice
of Your State of Life

You are not permitted to choose any state of life but the one God has designed for you from all eternity. You must not take up any work except that to which He is pleased to call you. You are not your own, but His, by an infinity of rights: by the claim of creation, preservation, redemption, justification, His complete sovereignty over all creatures, and by as many claims as there were thoughts entertained, words spoken, actions performed, sufferings endured, and drops of blood shed by the Son of God, to redeem you from the slavery of the devil and of sin.

Therefore, it is His divine right to dispose of you, of your life and works, for you belong to Him infinitely more than a subject to his king, a slave to his master, a house to its purchaser, or a child to his father. Hence, renounce yourself, affirm that you desire not only to be His and to serve Him, but to serve Him in the way that will be most pleasing to Him, and in the state to which He deigns to call you. Ask Him to make known His holy will on this point, and resolve to dispose yourself as best you can to know and follow His providential plan.

Second Point:
Means of Knowing the Will of God

You have seven things to do in order to dispose yourself to learn the divine will concerning your vocation.

The first is to humble yourself profoundly, acknowledging that you are infinitely unworthy to serve God in any state or condition whatever. Being involved in darkness, you cannot of yourself know God's will on this point, and you do not deserve that He should communicate His divine light to you.

The second step is to purify your soul from all sin and affection for sin, by means of sincere repentance and an extraordinary confession, to remove everything that might prove an obstacle to the heavenly light and graces you require for this decision.

The third step is to declare to God that you desire to be absolutely His, to serve Him with all your heart, for love of Him, in the kind of life to which He deigns to call you.

Fourthly, you must attain complete neutrality towards the professions in which you might please God, and rid yourself of all sorts of designs and aspirations, placing your ideas, tastes, desires and inclinations at the feet of our Lord, that He may clothe you with His own, fully resigning your liberty that He may dispose of you as He pleases, placing your heart in His hands like soft wax or like a blank page, for Him to engrave or write on it the message of His adorable will.

Fifthly, you must pray earnestly, with greatest confidence, that by His infinite mercy, He may place you in the state He has deigned to choose for you from all eternity, although you are infinitely unworthy of it; and that He may give you the light and grace you need to embrace this state and to serve Him faithfully therein.

Sixthly, you should fortify your prayers with mortification, alms, or other works of mercy, corporal or spiritual.

The seventh and last step is to implore the help of the Blessed Virgin, of St. Joseph, of your guardian angel and of all the other angels and saints, that they may obtain for you the grace to know and follow what God asks of you.

These are the seven things you have to do to dispose yourself to know your vocation. Ask Almighty God to give you the grace to follow them; and, on your part, endeavor to dispose yourself with the aid of His holy grace.

Third Point:
Signs Whereby You May Know
the Will of God

If after following the preceding steps, and entering into the dispositions indicated, you feel an inclination to a particular kind of life, you must not immediately follow this desire. First, you must examine it thoroughly, for fear of following the attractions of your own will, or of self-love, or of the evil spirit, in place of the inspirations of the Spirit of God. In order not to be deceived, consider carefully: one, whether the state to which you feel drawn is one in which you can readily serve God and work out your salvation; two, whether God has given you the necessary physical and mental qualities and the requisite conditions to enter that state; three, whether your desire is stable and permanent; four, whether your motive is pure and disinterested, having no other intention but to honor God and accomplish His most holy will; five, whether your desire is approved and confirmed by the advice of God's earthly representatives, capable of directing you in a matter of such importance.

These are the five marks of a true vocation from God. If they are to be found in your desire for any state, there is nothing left but for you to resolve firmly to embrace it, to seek the means leading to this end, to ask God to give you all the graces necessary to attain it, to serve and honor Him in it in accordance with His omnipotent designs, and to invoke the intercession of the Blessed Virgin, of the angels and saints.

Ejaculatory prayer:

"Make the way known to me, wherein I should walk: for I have lifted up my soul to thee." *Notam fac mihi viam in qua ambulem, quia ad te levavi animam meam* [Psalms 142:8].

ST. ALPHONSUS
LIGUORI
(1696—1787)

WHEN Pius IX declared St. Alphonsus Liguori a Doctor of the Church in 1871, the reputation of the great founder of the Redemptorists had already spread throughout the Christian world. Clerical students in the now-numerous seminaries studied his *Moral Theology* to prepare themselves for hearing confessions. Theologians shaped their theses in the light of his doctrine of probabilism—the view that one is permitted to follow "a solidly probable opinion in favor of liberty" to resolve a doubt when the law is not clear. Countless Christians in the pews had read his devotional manuals on prayer and on the glories of Mary. But there was a time when St. Alphonsus had been almost completely neglected. In his old age, when he was all but blind and deaf, he was forced to sign a revision of his rule to accommodate the civil authorities. Pope Pius VI, who later declared him Venerable, placed the Redemptorists under his own immediate jurisdiction. Alphonsus, the founder, was virtually expelled from his own community. How all this happened is a heart-breaking and heart-warming story intimately linked with the befuddled society of Eighteenth-Century Naples.

Alphonsus Maria Anthony John Liguori was born in Marianella, a suburb of Naples, the first of seven children. His father, Don José de Liguori, was a naval officer, presumably of Spanish blood, as was his mother. The family retained the *hidalgo* character of the Spanish ascendancy in Naples, and Alphonsus was very properly educated at home by private tutors. There he studied, as befitted a gentleman, the liberal arts, languages, music, manners, and riding and fencing. He never learned to shoot well because of his bad eyesight. This small, precocious boy did so well in his studies that he entered the University of Naples at an age most youths graduate from grammar school. He was only sixteen, four years younger than the statutory age, when he received his doctorate in law in 1713. Two years later he was admitted to the bar.

The diminutive lawyer seemed to be a child masquerading in his father's clothes as he pleaded cases in the Neapolitan courts. But he gradually gained great respect because, year after year, he won many cases by the force of his logic and his thorough knowledge of the law. By the time he was twenty-one he was at the top of his profession. Yet even he must have been overwhelmed by the honor of becoming one of counsel in a lawsuit with the Grand Duke of Tuscany involving an immense sum of money. With his usual care he assembled and studied the documents. At the first day of trial he delivered a brilliant opening speech, setting forth the evidence he would present and the points of law he would raise. He sat down, confident of winning. A clerk handed him the principal document upon which he had founded his case. Although the young lawyer had examined it many times before, he scrutinized it once more. Suddenly, in consternation, he realized that he had misread the document. But why? Not stupidity, but the passion of the advocate, compounded by vanity and greed, had almost blinded him to justice. He rose from his seat and begged the court's permission to admit his error and to concede the case.

Blazing with embarrassment, he rushed out of the court. For three days he was inconsolable. Disgusted with himself, he was even more disgusted with a profession that tempted him, at every turn, not to serve the truth but to suborn it. For two months he stormed with inner debate. One day, in a church dedicated to the redemption of captives, he heard an inner voice counselling him to leave the world. Soon this counsel coincided with the wish to become a priest of the Oratory. But Don José de Liguori, for all his piety, would not hear of it. For two months they argued back and forth. Finally Alphonsus agreed to live at home, and the father consented to his becoming a priest.

ST. ALPHONSUS LIGUORI

After his ordination in 1726, Alphonsus associated himself with a group of priests dedicated to conducting missions among the beggars of Naples, the so-called Lazzaroni. Shortly afterwards he met Father Thomas Falcoia, an active apostle of reform, who in 1730 became Bishop of Castellamare. His diocese in the mountains was as poor in religion as it was in wealth. Would Alphonsus organize some missionary priests for work among the peasants? He would. In 1732 there was formed the Congregation of the Most Holy Savior, later known as the Congregation of the Most Holy Redeemer.

The new congregation was destined to suffer a most unhappy infancy. At one time Alphonsus seemed to have lost all his friends, including the Bishop of Castellamare, Sister Maria Celeste, a nun who had encouraged him and whom he had helped, and all but two of his own followers. Later, when the order was prospering, he ran into trouble with the government. Charles IV, King of Naples and Sicily, chose to follow the policies of the enlightenment in its opposition to religion. Bernardo Tanucci, the King's chief minister, refused to recognize the Redemptorists, but he allowed them to exist only under the constant threat of suppression. Then, although he pleaded the specifications of his rule forbidding the acceptance of honors, Alphonsus was commanded by the Pope to become Bishop of Sant' Agata de Goti, a destitute diocese of 30,000 people. For thirteen years Alphonsus struggled to raise the level of a countryside riddled by ignorance and scandal. In a short time, St. Agatha of the Goths became one of the better dioceses in Italy. Alphonsus not only restored order and discipline; he also assured their continuance by improving the local seminary. He instituted a course in moral theology that presented the age-old teaching of the church in the precise formulations of the law.

When Alphonsus was permitted to resign from his see in 1775, he was almost eighty years old, worn out by service and sickness. He had earned a peaceful and honorable retirement. Instead he was asked to take on the greatest suffering of his life. His congregation almost disintegrated. He himself lived in a haze of physical pain and spiritual agony. But just six years after his death in 1787, Naples, now governed in the name of Ferdinand I by the Queen Mother Maria Carolina, recognized his order and its original rule. In 1796 Pius VI declared him Venerable. Henceforth his name lived on in glory.

THE WAY OF SALVATION
AND OF PERFECTION

CHAPTER 5

1. All holiness consists in loving God. The love of God is that infinite treasure in which we gain the friendship of God [Wisdom 7:14]. God is ready to give this treasure of his holy love, but he wills that we earnestly desire it. He that faintly desires any good thing takes little trouble to gain it. On the other hand, St. Laurence Justinian said that an earnest desire lightens all toil, and gives us strength. And thus, he who little desires to advance in divine love, instead of becoming more ardent in the way of perfection, ever becomes more and more lukewarm; and thus is ever in imminent peril of falling headlong down some precipice. And, on the other hand, whoever aspires with fervent desire after perfection, and strengthens himself daily to advance in its path, little by little, with time will attain it. St. Teresa said, "God never gives many favors, except to those who earnestly desire his love." And again, "God leaves no good desire without its reward." And therefore the saint advises every one not to suffer his desires to slacken, because, trusting in God, and strengthening ourselves little by little, we shall reach that point which all the saints have reached.

It is a deceit of the devil, according to the opinion of the saint, which makes us think that it is a mark of pride to desire to become saints. It would be pride and presumption, if we trusted in our own works or intentions; but if we hope for all from God, He will give us that strength which we have not.

Let us, then, desire, with a very great desire, to attain to a lofty height of divine love; and let us say, with courage, "I can do all things through Him that strengtheneth me" [Philippians 4:13]. And if we do not find that we possess this great desire, at least let us ask it urgently of Jesus Christ, that He may give it to us.

2. We will now pass on to the second means—resolution. Good desires must be accompanied by a determined spirit to strengthen ourselves in the attainment of the desired blessing. Many desire perfection, but take no right means to gain it; they want to live in a desert, to accomplish great works of penance and prayer, to endure martyrdom; but such desires are nothing better than mere fancies, which, instead of benefiting them, do them great harm. "These are the desires which slay the slothful man" [Proverbs 21:25]. Such a person feeding himself upon these fruitless desires, pays no heed to the cure of his defects, the mortification of his appetites, and patience in suffering contempt and crosses. He would do great things, but such as are incompatible with his present condition, and therefore his imperfections increase; in every time of adversity he is agitated, every infirmity makes him impatient; and thus he lives imperfect, and imperfect he dies.

If, then, we truly desire to become saints, let us resolve—

1. To avoid every venial sin, however slight.

2. To detach ourselves from every earthly desire.

3. Let us not cease our accustomed exercises of prayer and mortification, however great may be the weariness and dryness we feel in them.

4. Let us meditate daily on the Passion of Jesus Christ, which inflames with divine love every heart that meditates upon it.

5. Let us resign ourselves in peace to the will of God in all things that trouble us, as Father Balthazar Alvarez said, "He that in troubles resigns himself to the divine will, runs to God as swift as by a post."

6. Let us continually beg of God the gift of His holy love.

Resolution, resolution, said St. Teresa: "The devil has no dread of irresolute souls." On the contrary, he who resolves to give himself truly to God will overcome even what seemed impossible. A resolved will conquers everything. Let us study to redeem the time that is lost; the time that remains, let us give it all to God. All time that is not devoted to God is lost. Do we not fear lest God should abandon us to our lukewarmness, which may lead us to utter ruin? Let us take courage, and live from this day forth upon the holy maxim, "We must please God even to death." Souls thus resolute are assisted by the Lord to fly in the way of perfection.

He that would belong wholly to God must resolve—

1. Not to commit even the slightest venial sin.

2. To give himself to God without reserve, and therefore to neglect nothing which may be pleasing to God, always with the approbation of his director.

3. Out of all good things, to choose that which is most pleasing to God.

4. Not to wait for the morrow, but whatever can be done to-day, to do it.

5. To pray daily to God, that he may increase in His love. With love everything can be done; without love, nothing. To gain everything, we must give everything. Jesus has given Himself wholly to us, that we may be wholly His.

O miserable being that I am! O Thou God of my soul! for so many years I have lived upon earth, and what progress have I made in Thy love? My progress has been in my faults, in self-love, in sins, And shall I live this life even unto death? No; Jesus, my Savior, help me; I would no longer be so ungrateful as I have been till now. I would truly love Thee, and would leave all to please Thee. Give me Thy hand, O Jesus! Thou who hast poured forth all Thy blood, that Thou mightest see me Thine. Such I would be, with Thy grace. Even till death, aid me, and strip me of everything which may hinder me from belonging wholly to Thee, who hast so much loved me. Grant it me through Thy merits; from Thee I hope it. And I hope it also from thee, O my Mother Mary. With thy prayers, which can obtain everything from God, obtain for me the grace of belonging wholly to Him.

CHAPTER 6

There are two kinds of sciences upon earth,—one heavenly, the other worldly. The heavenly is that which leads us to please God, and makes us great in heaven. The worldly is that which moves us to please ourselves, and to become great in the world. But this worldly science is folly and madness in the sight of God. "The wisdom of the world is foolishness with God" [I Corinthians 3:19]. It is folly, for it makes fools of those who cultivate it; it makes them fools, and like the brutes, for it teaches them to gratify their carnal appetites like the beasts. St. John Chrysostom wrote, "We call him a man who preserves complete the image of a man; and what is the image of a man?—to be rational." Hence it is that if a brute were ever to act according to reason, we should say that such a brute acted like a man; so we say that a man who acts upon sensual appetites and contrary to reason acts like a brute.

But to return to the human and natural knowledge of earthly things, what do men know of all things which they have studied? What are we but so many blind moles, who, besides the truths which we know by faith, know only by means of our senses, or by conjecture; so that everything is uncertain and fallible. What writers on such subjects, however applauded by many, have escaped the criticism of others? But the evil is that the knowledge of the world puffs us up [I Corinthians 8:1], and makes us proud and prone to despise others—a pernicious fault, for, as St. James says, "God resists the proud, and gives grace to the humble" [James 4:6].

"Oh that they would be wise and understand, and know the latter end" [Deuteronomy 32:29]! Oh, if men would act by reason and the divine law, and thus would learn to provide, not so much for a temporal existence, which speedily ends, as for eternity, they would assuredly not occupy themselves in the attainment of any knowledge, except such as aids them in obtaining eternal happiness and avoiding eternal pains.

St. John Chrysostom advises us to walk among the tombs of the dead, in order to learn the knowledge of salvation. Oh, what a school of truth are the sepulchres for learning the vanity of the world! "Let us go to the tombs: there," said the saint, "there I see nothing but corruption, bones, and worms." From all these skeletons which I see, I cannot tell which belonged to the ignorant and which to the learned; I only see that with death all the glories of the world were finished for them. What remained to a Cicero, a Demosthenes, an Ulpian? "They have slept their sleep, and have found nothing in their hands" [Psalms 75:6].

Blessed is he who has received from God the science of the saints [Wisdom 10:10]. The science of the saints is to know the love of God. How many in the world are well versed in literature, in mathematics, in foreign and ancient languages! But what will all this profit them, if they know not the love of God? Blessed is he, said St. Augustine, who knows God, even if he knows nothing else. He that knows God and loves Him, though he be ignorant of what others know, is more learned than the learned who know not how to love God.

"Let the unlearned arise, and seize upon heaven!" cried the same Augustine. How learned were St. Francis of Assisi, St. Pascal, St. John of God! ignorant in worldly knowledge, but well skilled in that which is divine. "Thou hast hidden these things from the wise and prudent, and hast revealed them to babes" [Matthew 11:25]. By the wise, we are here to understand the worldly wise, who labor for the possessions and glories of the world, and think little of eternal joys. And by babes we are to understand simple souls (like those of children), who know little of worldly wisdom, but devote all their care to pleasing God.

Let us not, then, envy those who know many things; let us only envy those who know how to love Jesus Christ; and let us imitate St. Paul, who said that he desired to know nothing but Jesus Christ, and Him crucified. Happy are we if we attain to the knowledge of the love which Jesus crucified had for us, and from this book of love attain to the love of Him. O Thou who art my true and perfect lover, where shall I find one who has so loved me as Thou hast! During my life that is past, I have lost my time in attaining the knowledge of many things which have profited my soul nothing, and I have thought nothing of knowing how to love Thee. I see that my life has been lost. I perceive that Thou callest me to Thy holy love; behold, I leave all; from this day forth, my one thought shall be to please Thee, my highest good. I give myself wholly to Thee; accept me; give me help to be faithful to Thee; I desire to be no longer my own, but all, all Thine. O mother of God! do thou also help me with thy prayers.

CHAPTER 7

Prayer is not only useful, but necessary for salvation; and therefore God, who desires that we should be saved, has enjoined it as a precept, "Seek, and it shall be given you" [Matthew 7:7]. It was an error of Wickliff, condemned by the Council of Constance, to say that prayer was a subject of divine counsel to us, and not of command. "It is necessary,"—not, it is advisable or fitting,—"always to pray" [Luke 18:1]. Wherefore Doctors of the Church always say that he cannot be held innocent of grievous sin who neglects to recommend himself to God, at least once in a month, and at all times when he finds himself assaulted by severe temptation.

The reason of this necessity of recommending ourselves often to God arises from our inability to do any good work, or to entertain any good thoughts, of ourselves: "Without Me ye can do nothing" [John 15:5]. "We are not sufficient of ourselves to think anything of ourselves" [II Corinthians 3:5]. Therefore, St. Philip Neri said that he despaired of himself. On the other hand, St. Augustine wrote that God desires to bestow His graces, but only on those who beg them. And, especially, said the saint, God only gives the grace of perseverance to those who seek it.

It is a fact that the devil never ceases to go about to devour us, and therefore we need ever to defend ourselves by prayer. "Continual prayer is necessary for man," said St. Thomas. And Jesus Christ first taught us, "We must always pray, and not faint" [Luke 18:1]. Otherwise, how can we resist the perpetual temptations of the world and the devil? It was the error of

Jansenius, condemned by the Church, that the observance of certain precepts was impossible, and that sometimes grace itself fails to render it possible to us. God is faithful, said St. Paul, who does not suffer us to be tempted above our strength [I Corinthians 10:13]. Yet He desires that, when we are tried, we should have recourse to Him for help to resist. St. Augustine wrote: "The law is given, that grace may be sought; grace is given, that the law may be fulfilled." Granting that the law cannot be obeyed by us without grace, God has yet given us the law, in order that we may seek the grace to fulfill it; and, therefore, He gives the grace that we may fulfill it. All this was well expressed by the Council of Trent, in these words: "God does not command things that are impossible, but, in commanding us, He counsels thee both to do what thou canst, and seek for aid for what thou canst not do, and He helps thee that thou mayst be able to do it."

Thus, the Lord is ever ready to give us His help, in order that we may not be overcome by temptation; but He only gives this help to those who fly to Him in the time of trial, and especially in temptations against chastity, as the Wise Man wrote: "Because I knew that thus only could I preserve continence, if God should grant it, therefore I went to the Lord and besought him" [Wisdom 8:21]. Let us rest assured that we can never overcome our carnal appetites, if God does not give us help, and this help we cannot have without prayer; but if we pray, we shall assuredly have power to resist the devil in everything, and the strength of God, who strengthens us; as St. Paul says, "I can do all things, through God who strengthens me" [Philippians 4:13].

It is also most useful to us, in order to obtain the divine grace, that we should have recourse to the intercession of the saints, who have great power with God, especially for the benefit of those who have a particular devotion to them. And this is not a mere devotion dependent upon our private fancy, but it is a duty, as St. Thomas writes, that the divine law requires that we mortals should receive the aid which is necessary for our salvation, through the prayers of the saints. Especially this aid comes through the intercession of Mary, whose prayers are of more value than those of all the saints; so much so, indeed, as St. Bernard says, that it is through her intercession that we have access to Jesus Christ our Mediator and Savior. "Through thee we have access to the Son, O thou giver of grace, and Mother of our salvation! that through thee He may receive us, who through thee was given for us." This, indeed, I have sufficiently proved in my book called "The Glories of Mary;" and, so in my work "On Prayer," I have brought forward the opinion of many saints, especially St. Bernard, and many theologians, as, for example, Father di Alessandro and Father Contenson, that through Mary we receive all the graces which we receive from God. Hence, also, St. Bernard says, "Let us seek for grace, and let us seek it through Mary; for he that seeks finds, and cannot be deceived." The same was said by St. Peter Damian, St. Bonaventure, St. Bernardine of Sienna, St. Antoninus, and others.

Let us then pray, and pray with confidence, says the Apostle. Let us go boldly to the throne of grace, that we may obtain mercy and find grace to help us in time of need [Hebrews 4:16]. Jesus Christ now sits on the throne of grace to comfort all who fly to Him, and says, "Seek and it shall be given to you." On the day of judgment He will also sit upon His throne, but it will be a throne of judgment; what madness, then, it is in those who, having it in their power to be delivered from their miseries by going to Jesus, now that He sits on His throne of grace, wait till He becomes their judge, and will not avail themselves of His mercy. Now He says to us that whatever we ask of Him, if we have confidence, He will give us all. And what more can one friend do to another to show his love than say, "Seek what thou wilt, and I will give it thee" [Mark 11:24]. St. James adds more, and says, "If any man need wisdom, let him ask it of God, who gives to all men liberally, and reproaches not, and it shall be given him" [James 1:5]. By "wisdom" is here meant the knowledge of the salvation of the soul; to have this wisdom, we must seek of God the graces necessary to bring us to salvation. And will God give them? Most assuredly He will give them, and in still greater abundance than we ask them. Let us observe also the words,

"He does not reproach us." If the sinner repents of his sins, and asks salvation from God, God does not that which men do, who reproach the ungrateful with their ingratitude, and deny them what they ask; but He gives it to them willingly, and even more than they beg for. If, then, we would be saved, we must have our lips ever opened to pray, and say, "My God, help me; my God, have mercy; Mary, have mercy." When we cease to pray, we are lost. Let us pray for ourselves: let us pray for sinners, for this is most pleasing to God. Let us pray also daily for holy souls in purgatory; those holy prisoners are most grateful to all who pray for them. Whensoever we pray, let us seek grace of God through the merits of Jesus Christ, for He Himself assures us that whatever we ask in His name, He will give it to us [John 16:23].

O my God! this is the grace which, above all others, I ask through the merits of Jesus Christ: grant that throughout my life, and especially in time of temptation, I may recommend myself to Thee, and hope for Thy help through the love of Jesus and Mary. O holy Virgin! obtain for me this grace on which depends my salvation.

CHAPTER 8

Mental prayer is, in the first place, necessary, in order that we may have light to go on the journey to eternity. Eternal truths are spiritual things that are not seen with the eyes of the body, but only by the reflection of the mind. He that does not meditate, does not see them; and thus he advances with difficulty along the way of salvation. And, further, he [who] does not meditate, does not know his own failings, and thus, says St. Bernard, he does not detest them; so, also, he does not see the perils of his state, and therefore does not think of avoiding them. But when we meditate, our failings and perils quickly present themselves; and when we see them we seek to remedy them. St. Bernard said that meditation regulates our affections, directs our actions, and corrects our defects.

In the second place, without meditation we have no strength for resisting temptations and practicing virtues. St.

Teresa said that when a man leaves off meditation, the devil has no need of carrying him to hell, for he throws himself into it. And the reason is, that without meditation there is no prayer. God has every willingness to give us his graces; but St. Gregory said that before giving them he desires to be asked, and that he is, as it were, compelled to give them though our prayers. But without prayer we shall have no strength to resist our enemies, and thus shall not obtain perseverance in what is good. Palafox, in his note upon the tenth letter of St. Teresa, wrote thus: "How will the Lord give us perseverance if we do not ask for it? and how shall we ask it without meditation?" While he who practices meditation is like a tree planted by the water-side [Psalms 1:3].

And, further, meditation is the happy furnace in which souls are inflamed with divine love; "in my meditation a fire shall flame out" [Psalms 38:4]. St. Catherine of Bologna said, "Meditation is the bond which binds the soul to God; the king brought me into the wine-cellar, he fixed his love upon me." This wine-cellar is meditation, in which the soul becomes so inebriated with divine love that it loses, as it were, its sense for the things of the world; it sees only that which pleases its beloved; it speaks only of the beloved; it would only hear of the beloved; every other discourse wearies and troubles it. In meditation, the soul, retiring to converse alone with God, rests upon itself: "He shall sit solitary and hold his peace; because he hath taken it upon himself" [Lamentations 3:28]. When the soul sits,—that is, shuts itself up in meditation to consider how worthy is God of love, and how great is the love he bears to it,— it thus tastes of God, and fills itself with holy thoughts, and detaches itself from earthly affections, and conceives great desires for becoming holy, and finally resolves to give itself wholly to God. And where but in meditation have the saints made their most generous resolutions, which have lifted them up to the highest point of perfection?

Let us hear what St. John of the Cross said, speaking of mental prayer: "Here we open our heart, here we learn sweet doctrine, and make ourselves wholly to belong to God, reserving nothing, and espousing ourselves to Him." And St. Aloysius Gonzaga said that no one will ever attain a high degree of perfection who is not much given to meditation. Let us, then, earnestly apply ourselves to it, and not leave it for any weariness that we may experience; this weariness which we endure for God will be abundantly recompensed by Him.

Pardon me, O my God, my slothfulness; what treasures of grace have I lost in so often neglecting to meditate! For the future give me grace to be faithful through life in conversing with Thee, with whom I hope to converse forever in heaven. I do not ask Thee to delight me here with Thy consolations; I do not deserve it; it is enough that Thou dost suffer me to approach Thy feet to recommend to Thee my poor soul, which is thus miserable because it has separated itself from Thee. Here, O my crucified Jesus! the sole memory of Thy Passion shall keep me detached from earth, and united with Thee. O holy Virgin Mary! aid me with thy prayers.

CHAPTER 9

In order to practice mental prayer, or meditation, well, and to make it truly profitable to the soul, we must well ascertain the ends for which we attempt it. First, we must meditate in order to unite ourselves more completely to God. It is not so much good thoughts in the intelligence, as good acts of the will, or holy desires, that unite us to God; and such are the acts that we perform in meditation, acts of humility, confidence, self-sacrifice, resignation, and especially of love and of repentance for our sins. Acts of love, says St. Teresa, are those that keep the soul inflamed with holy love.

Secondly, we must meditate in order to obtain from God, by prayer, the graces that are necessary in order to enable us to advance in the way of salvation, to avoid sin, and to take the means that will lead us to perfection. The best fruit, then, that comes from meditation is the exercise of prayer. Almighty God, ordinarily speaking, does not give grace to any but those who pray. St. Gregory writes, "God desires to be entreated, He desires to be constrained, He desires to be, as it were, conquered by importunity." Observe his words, "to be conquered by importunity." At times, in order to obtain graces of special value, it is not enough simply to pray; we must pray urgently, and, as it were, compel God, by our prayers, to give them. It is true that at all times the Lord is ready to hear us; but at the time of meditation, when we are most truly in converse with God, He is most bountiful in giving us His aid.

Above all, we must apply to meditation, in order to obtain perseverance and the holy love of God. Final perseverance is not a single grace, but a chain of graces, to which must correspond the chain of our prayers; if we cease to pray, God will cease to give us His help, and we shall perish. He who does not practice meditation will find the greatest difficulty in persevering in grace till death. Palafox, in his notes on St. Teresa's letters, writes thus: "How will the Lord give us perseverance, if we do not ask it? And how shall we ask for it without meditation? Without meditation there is no communion with God."

Thus must we be urgent with prayers to obtain from God His holy love. St. Francis de Sales said that all virtues come in union with holy love. "All good things came to me together with her" [Wisdom 7:2]. Let our prayer for perseverance and love, therefore, be continual; and, in order to pray with greater confidence, let us ever bear in mind the promise made us by Jesus Christ, that whatever we seek from God through the merits of His Son, He will give it us [John 16:23]. Let us, then, pray, and pray always, if we would that God should make us abound in every blessing. Let us pray for ourselves, and, if we have zeal for the glory of God, let us pray also for others. It is a thing most pleasing to God to be entreated for unbelievers and heretics, and all sinners. "Let the people confess to Thee, O God! let all the people confess to Thee" [Psalms 66:6]. Let us say, O Lord! make them know Thee, make them love Thee. We read in the lives of St. Teresa and St. Mary Magdalen of Pazzi how God inspired these holy women to pray for sinners. And to prayer for sinners let us also add prayers for the holy souls in purgatory.

Thirdly: we must apply ourselves to meditation, not for the sake of spiritual consolations, but chiefly in order to learn what is the will of God concerning us. "Speak, Lord," said Samuel to God, "for Thy servant heareth" [Kings 3:9]. Lord, make me to know what Thou wilt, that I may do it. Some persons continue meditation as long as consolations continue; but when these cease, they leave off meditation. It is true that God is accustomed to comfort His beloved souls at the time of meditation, and to give them some foretaste of the delights He prepares in heaven for those who love Him. These are things which the lovers of the world do not comprehend; they who have no taste except for earthly delights despise those that are celestial. Oh, if they were wise, how surely would they leave their pleasures to shut themselves in their closets, to speak alone with God! Meditation is nothing more than a converse between the soul and God; the soul pours forth to Him its affections, its desires, its fears, its requests, and God speaks to the heart, causing it to know His goodness, and the love which He bears it, and what it must do to please Him. "I will lead her into solitude, and speak to her heart" [Osea 2:14].

But these delights are not constant, and, for the most part, holy souls experience much dryness of spirit in meditation. "With dryness and temptations," says St. Teresa, "the Lord makes proof of those who love Him." And she adds, "Even if this dryness lasts through life, let not the soul leave off meditation; the time will come when all will be well rewarded." The time of dryness is the time for gaining the greatest rewards; and when we find ourselves apparently without fervor, without good desires, and, as it were, unable to do a good act, let us humble ourselves, and resign ourselves, for this very meditation will be more fruitful than others. It is enough then to say, if we can say nothing more, "O Lord! help me, have mercy on me, abandon me not!" Let us also have recourse to our comforter, the most holy Mary. Happy he who does not leave off meditation in the hour of desolation. God will make him abound in graces; and therefore let him say:

"O my God, how can I expect to be comforted by Thee! I, who, until this hour, have deserved to be in hell, forever separated from Thee, and deprived of the power of loving Thee any more! I do not therefore grieve, O my God! that Thou deprivest me of Thy consolations; I do not deserve them; I do not pretend to them. It is enough for me to know that Thou wilt never repel a soul that loves Thee. Deprive me not of the power of loving Thee, and then do with me what Thou wilt. If thou wilt that I continue thus afflicted and desolate even till death, and through all eternity, I am content; it is enough that I can say with truth, 'O my God, I love Thee, I love Thee!' Mary, Mother of God, have pity on me!"

OF WHAT, WHEN, AND HOW WE SHOULD CONVERSE WITH GOD.

PART 1

Never, then, forget His sweet presence, as do the greater part of men. Speak to Him as often as you can; for He does not grow weary of this nor disdain it, as do the lords of the earth. If you love Him, you will not be at a loss what to say to Him. Tell Him all that occurs to you about yourself and your affairs, as you would tell it to a dear friend. Look not upon Him as a haughty sovereign, who will only converse with the great, and on great matters. He, our God, delights to abase Himself to converse with us, loves to have us communicate to Him our smallest, our most daily concerns. He loves you as much, and has as much care for you, as if He had none others to think of but yourself. He is as entirely devoted to your interests as though the only end of His providence were to succor you, of His almighty power to aid you, of His mercy and goodness to take pity on you, to do you good, and gain by the delicate touches of His kindness your confidence and love. Manifest, then, to Him freely all your state of mind, and pray to Him to guide you to accomplish perfectly His holy will. And let all your desires and plans be simply bent to discover His good pleasure, and do what is agreeable to His divine heart: "Commit thy way to the Lord [Psalms 36:5]: and desire of Him to direct thy ways, and that all thy counsels may abide in Him" [Tobias 4:20].

Say not, But where is the need of disclosing to God all my wants, if He already sees and knows them better than I? True, He knows them; but God makes as if He knew not the necessities about which you do not speak to Him, and for which you seek not his aid. Our Savior knew well that Lazarus was dead, and yet He made as if He knew it not, until the Magdalene had told Him of it, and then He comforted her by raising her brother to life again [John 11:1].

PART 2

When, therefore, you are afflicted with any sickness, temptation, persecution, or other trouble, go at once and beseech Him, that His hand may help you. It is enough for you to present the affliction before Him; to come in and say, "Behold, O Lord, for I am in distress" [Lamentations 1:20]. He will not fail to comfort you, or at least to give you strength to suffer that grief with patience; and it will turn out a greater good to you than if He had altogether freed you from it. Tell Him all the thoughts of fear or of sadness that torment you; and say to Him, My God, in Thee are all my hopes; I offer to Thee this affliction, and resign myself to Thy will; but do Thou take pity on me,—either deliver me out of it, or give me strength to bear it. And he will truly keep with you that promise made in the Gospel to all those who are in trouble, to console and comfort them as often as they have recourse to Him: "Come to Me, all you that labor and are burdened, and I will refresh you" [Matthew 11:28].

He will not be displeased that in your desolations you should go to your friends to find some relief; but He wills you chiefly to have recourse to Himself. At all events, therefore, after you have applied to creatures, and they have been unable to comfort your heart, have recourse to your Creator, and say to Him, Lord, men have only words for me; "my friends are full of words" [Job 16:21]; they cannot comfort me, nor do I any more desire to be comforted by them; Thou art all my hope, all my love. From Thee only will I receive comfort; and let my comfort be, on this occasion, to do what pleaseth Thee. Behold me ready to endure this grief through my whole life, through all eternity, if such be Thy good pleasure. Only do Thou help me.

Fear not that He will be offended if you sometimes gently complain, and say to Him, "Why, O Lord, hast Thou retired afar off?" [Psalms 9:1]. Thou knowest, Lord, that I love Thee, and desire nothing but Thy love; in pity help me, and forsake me not. And when the desolation lasts long, and troubles you exceedingly, unite your voice to that of Jesus in agony and dying on the cross, and beseech His mercy, saying, "My God, my God, why hast Thou forsaken me?" [Matthew 27:46]. But let the effect of this be to humble you yet more at the thought that he deserves no consolations who has offended God; and yet more to enliven your confidence, knowing that God does all things, and permits all, for your good: "All things work together unto good" [Romans 8:28]. Say with great courage, even when you feel most troubled and disconsolate: "The Lord is my light and my salvation; whom shall I fear" [Psalms 26:1]? Lord, it is Thine to enlighten me, it is Thine to save me; in Thee do I trust: "In Thee, O Lord, have I hoped; let me never be confounded" [Psalms 30:2]. And thus keep yourself in peace, knowing there never was any one who placed his hopes in God and was lost: "No one hath hoped in the Lord, and hath been confounded" [Ecclesiasticus 2:11]. Consider, your God loves you more than you can love yourself; what do you fear? David comforted himself, saying, "The Lord is careful for me" [Psalms 39:18]. Say to Him, therefore, Lord, into Thy arms I cast myself; I desire to have no thought but of loving and pleasing Thee; behold me ready to do what Thou requirest of me.

Thou dost not only will my good, Thou art careful for it; unto Thee, then, do I leave the care of my salvation. In Thee do I rest, and will rest for evermore, since Thou willest that in Thee I should place all my hopes: "In peace, in the self-same, I will sleep and I will rest; for Thou, O Lord, singularly hast settled me in hope" [Psalms 4:9].

"Think of the Lord in goodness" [Wisdom 1:1]. In these words the Wise Man exhorts us to have more confidence in the divine mercy than dread of the divine justice; since God is immeasurably more inclined to bestow favors than to punish; as St. James says, "Mercy exalteth itself above judgment" [James 2:13]. Whence the Apostle St. Peter tells us that in all fears, whether about our interests for time or for eternity, we should commit ourselves altogether to the goodness of our God, who keeps the greatest care of our safety: "Casting all your care upon Him, for He hath care of you" [I Peter 5:7]. Oh, what a beautiful meaning does this lend to the title which David gives to the Lord, when he says that our God is the God who makes it his care to save: "Our God is the God of salvation" [Psalms 67:21]; which signifies, as Bellarmine explains it, that the office peculiar to the Lord is, not to condemn, but to save all. For while He threatens with His displeasure those who disregard Him, He promises, on the other hand, His assured mercies to those who fear Him; as the divine Mother said in her Canticle, "And His mercy is to them that fear Him." I set before you, devout soul, all these passages of Scripture, that when the thought disquiets you, Am I to be saved or not? Am I predestined or not? You may take courage, and understand from the promises He makes you what desire God has to save you, if only you are resolved to serve Him and to love Him as He demands at your hands.

PART 3

Further, when you receive pleasant news, do not act like those unfaithful, thankless souls who have recourse to God in time of trouble, but in time of prosperity forget and forsake Him. Be as faithful to Him as you would be to a friend who loves you and rejoices in your good; go at once and tell Him of your gladness, and praise Him and give Him thanks, acknowledging it all as a gift from His hands; and rejoice in that happiness because it comes to you of His good pleasure. Rejoice, therefore, and comfort yourself in Him alone: "I will rejoice in the Lord [Habakkuk 3:18]; and I will joy in God my Jesus" [Psalms 12:6]. Say to him, My Jesus, I bless, and will ever bless Thee, for granting me so many favors, when I deserved at Thy hands not favors, but chastisements for the affronts I have given Thee. Say to Him, with the sacred Spouse, "All fruits, the new and the old, my Beloved, I have kept for Thee" [Canticle of Canticles 7:13]. Lord, I give Thee thanks; I keep in memory all Thy bounties, past and present, to render Thee praise and glory for them forever and ever.

But if you love your God, you ought to rejoice more in His blessedness than in your own. He who loves a friend very much sometimes takes more delight in that friend's good than if it had been his own. Comfort yourself, then, in the knowledge that your God is infinitely blessed. Often say to Him, My beloved Lord, I rejoice more in Thy blessedness than in any good of mine; yes, for I love Thee more than I love myself.

PART 4

Another mark of confidence highly pleasing to your most loving God is this: that when you have committed any fault, you be not ashamed to go at once to His feet and seek His pardon. Consider that God is so greatly inclined to pardon sinners that He laments their perdition, when they depart far from Him and live as dead to His grace. Therefore does He lovingly call them, saying, "Why will you die, O house of Israel? Return ye, and live" [Ezekiel 18:31]. He promises to receive the soul that has forsaken Him, so soon as she returns to His arms: "Turn ye to me, . . . and I will turn to you" [Zacharias 1:3]. Oh, if sinners did but know with what tender mercy the Lord stands waiting to forgive them! "The Lord waiteth, that He may have mercy on you" [Isaias 30:18]. Oh, did they but know the desire He has, not to chastise, but to see them converted, that He may embrace them, that He may press them to His heart! He declares: "As I live, saith the Lord God, I desire not the death of the wicked, but that the wicked turn from his way and live" [Ezekiel 33:2]. He even says: "And then come and accuse Me, saith the Lord: if your sins be as scarlet, they shall be made as white as snow" [Isaias 1:18]. As though He had said, Sinners, repent of having offended Me, and then come unto Me: if I do not pardon you, "accuse Me;" upbraid Me, and treat Me as one unfaithful. But no, I will not be wanting to My promise. If you will come, know this: that though your consciences are dyed deep as crimson by your sins, I will make them by My grace as white as snow. In a word, He has declared that when a soul repents of having offended Him, He forgets all its sins: "I will not remember all his iniquities" [Ezekiel 18:22].

As soon, then, as you fall into any fault, raise your eyes to God, make an act of love, and with humble confession of your fault, hope assuredly for His pardon, and say to Him, "Lord, behold he whom Thou lovest is sick" [John 11:3]; that heart which Thou dost love is sick, is full of sores: "heal my soul; for I have sinned against Thee" [Psalms 40:5]. Thou seekest after penitent sinners; behold, here is one at Thy feet, who has come in search of Thee. The evil is done already; what have I now to do? Thou wilt not have me lose courage: after this my sin Thou dost still love me, and I too love Thee. Yes, my God, I love Thee with all my heart; I repent of the displeasure I have given Thee; I purpose never to do so any more. Thou, who art that God, "merciful and gracious, patient and of much compassion" [Psalms 85:5], forgive me; make me to hear what Thou didst say to Magdalene, "Thy sins are forgiven thee" [Luke 7:32]; and give me strength to be faithful unto Thee for the time to come.

That thou mayest not lose courage at such a moment, cast a glance at Jesus on the cross; offer His merits to the Eternal Father; and thus hope certainly for pardon, since He "spared not even His own Son" [Romans 8:32]. Say to Him with confidence, "Look on the face of Thy Christ" [Psalms 83:10]. My God, behold Thy Son, dead for my sake; and for the love of that Son forgive me. Attend greatly, devout soul, to the instruction commonly given by masters of the spiritual life, after your unfaithful conduct, at once to have recourse to God, though you have repeated it a hundred times in a day; and after your falls, and the recourse you have had to the Lord (as has been just said), at once to be in peace. Otherwise, while you remain cast down and disturbed at the fault you have committed, your converse with God will be small; your trust in him will fail; your desire to love him grow cold; and you will be little able to go forward in the way of the Lord. On the other hand, by having immediate recourse to God to ask His forgiveness, and to promise Him amendment, your very faults will serve to advance you further in the divine love. Between friends who sincerely love each other it often happens that when one has displeased the other, and then humbles himself and asks pardon, their friendship thereby becomes stronger than ever. Do you likewise; see to it that your very faults serve to bind you yet closer in love to your God.

PART 5

In any kind of doubtfulness also, either on your own account or that of others, never leave acting towards your God with a confidence like to that of faithful friends, who consult together on every matter. So do you take counsel with Himself, and beseech Him to enlighten you that you may decide on what will be most pleasing to Him: "Put those words in my mouth, and strengthen the resolution in my heart" [Judith 9:18]. Lord, tell me what Thou wouldst have me to do or to answer; and thus will I. "Speak, Lord; for Thy servant heareth" [Kings 3:10].

PART 6

Use towards Him also the freedom of recommending not only your own needs, but also those of others. How agreeable will it be to your God that sometimes you forget even your own interests to speak to Him of the advancement of His glory, of the miseries of others, especially those who groan in affliction, of those souls, His spouses, who in purgatory sigh after the vision of Himself, and of poor sinners who are living destitute of His grace! For these especially say to Him: Lord, Thou who art so amiable, and worthy of an infinite love, how dost Thou, then, endure to see such a number of souls in the world, on whom Thou hast bestowed so many favors, and who yet will not know Thee, will not love Thee, nay, even offend and despise Thee? Ah! my God, object of all love, make Thyself to be known, make Thyself to be beloved. "Hallowed be Thy name, Thy kingdom come;" may Thy name be adored and beloved by all; may Thy love reign in all hearts. Ah, let me not depart without granting me some grace for those unfaithful souls for whom I pray.

PART 7

It is said that in purgatory those souls who in this life have had but little longing for heaven are punished with a particular suffering, called the pain of languor; and with reason, because to long but little for heaven is to set small value on the great good of the eternal kingdom which our Redeemer has purchased for us by His death. Forget not, therefore, devout soul, frequently to sigh after heaven: say to your God that it seems to you an endless time for you to come and see Him, and to love Him face to face. Long ardently to depart out of this banishment, this scene of sinning, and danger of losing His grace, that you may arrive in that land of love where you may love Him with all your powers. Say to Him again and again, Lord, so long as I live on this earth, I am always in danger of forsaking Thee and losing Thy love. When will it be that I quit this life, wherein I am ever offending Thee, and come to love Thee with all my soul, and unite myself to Thee, with no danger of losing Thee any more? St. Teresa was ever sighing in this way, and used to rejoice when she heard the clock strike, because another hour of life, and of the danger of losing God, was past and gone. For she so greatly desired death in order to see God, that she was dying with the desire to die; and hence she composed that loving canticle of hers, "I die, because I do not die."

GOD ANSWERS THE SOUL THAT SPEAKS TO HIM.

In a word, if you desire to delight the loving heart of your God, be careful to speak to Him as often as you are able, and with the fullest confidence that He will not disdain to answer and speak with you in return. He does not, indeed, make Himself heard in any voice that reaches your ears, but in a voice that your heart can well perceive, when you withdraw from converse with creatures, to occupy yourself in conversing with your God alone: "I will lead her into the wilderness, and I will speak to her heart" [See 2:14]. He will then speak to you by such inspirations, such interior lights, such manifestations of His goodness, such sweet touches in your heart, such tokens of forgiveness, such experience of peace, such hopes of heaven, such rejoicings within you, such sweetness of His grace, such loving and close embraces,—in a word, such voices of love,—as are well understood by those souls whom He loves, and who seek for nothing but Himself alone.

ST. JEAN MARIE VIANNEY:

THE CURÉ D'ARS

(1786—1859)

IF one looks for an example of how sanctity is the work of God, Who shapes human clay in His own image and fires it with His own spirit, one can find it in St. John Vianney, the patron of parish priests. For here is a man with few natural endowments, born into a poor family, at a time most unpropitious for the fostering of religious vocations. Everything was against him, save God.

Jean Marie was born on a farm at Dardilly, near Lyons, to Matthieu and Marie Vianney on May 8, 1786. He was only three when the French Revolution exploded. During the impressionable period of childhood, he received no religious instruction except from his parents, who, loyal Christians that they were, refused to attend services in the parish church as the priest had sworn allegiance to the state religion. In fact, Jean Marie heard Mass rarely and then in out-of-the-way barns and hayricks. Two evicted nuns surreptitiously prepared him for his first Communion, which he received in 1799 at Ecully, in a house close-shuttered against the prying of the police. During this period of persecution, he developed into a sturdy farm boy, pious and given to preaching make-believe sermons, but without formal education.

After Napoleon overthrew the Revolutionary regime, he signed a concordat with the Pope that re-established the Catholic religion in France in 1802. Jean Marie, then sixteen years old, began to think seriously about becoming a priest. But it was not until 1805 that his father agreed to release him from the farm. Then he went, not to a seminary, but to a kind of preparatory class conducted by the Abbé Balley, the pastor at Ecully.

Jean Marie was the oldest and stupidest boy in the class. He had trouble with his French, let alone with Latin. Moreover, his memory seemed to be pathologically weak. He made a pilgrimage to a shrine dedicated to St. John Francis Regis to pray for stronger wits. Only the sympathy of the Abbé, himself a saintly person, prevented his discouragement.

In 1809 Napoleon conscripted the men from Dardilly for his ill-fated invasion of Spain. Jean Marie, then twenty-three, pleaded exemption on the grounds of being a clerical student. But, since he was not officially accepted by a seminary, he was stuffed into a uniform, handed a musket, drilled, and sent off to the Pyrenees. His agony of spirit may well be imagined. How could he, who thought it a sin to strike a beast in anger, kill fellow Christians who were resisting a foreign tyrant? While he was ill and confined to barracks his regiment received marching orders. Jean Marie was ordered to follow as soon as he could. A few days later he straggled after the column, but lost his way in the Pyrenees, and stumbled into a town whose people were hostile to Napoleon. There he stayed as a welcome guest for two years. Technically a deserter (once he was almost captured by one of Napoleon's patrols), he did not go home until the amnesty of 1811.

Then twenty-five, and no further advanced in his studies than a freshman in high school, he once more sat at the feet of his friend, the Curé of Ecully, in an attempt to prepare himself for the beloved vocation. In 1812 he entered the Minor Seminary at Verrières where he was the two-hundredth man in a class of two hundred. His career at the Major Seminary of St. Irénée in Lyons was, if possible, even less successful. Eventually, again through the good offices of the Abbé Balley, he was ordained and returned to his tutor for further instruction and service as an assistant. He remained at Ecully for three years until the death of Balley. What could they do with him now?

The least desirable benefice in the diocese was in the

village of Ars. The broken-down church was not even a church, but a chapel attached to the Chateau of the Marquis D'Ars. The parish was not even a parish but a village of two hundred souls long estranged from religion. The vicar general said to Jean Marie when he gave him his assignment: "There's not much love of God in this village. Your job will be to instill it."

That is just what he did—by his presence, by his preaching, by his penances. Jean Marie was always before his flock. He arose early in the morning, after a brief sleep, to say his Mass. Immediately after Mass he went to his confessional where, as time went on, he found hundreds of penitents not only from his own village but from all over France. At noon he stood up while he dined on cold potatoes and a little milk. Then he returned to his confessional where he remained until midnight, except for brief intervals of visiting the sick, teaching catechism, and other parochial duties.

The Curé D'Ars' sermons were no literary masterpieces, although at first he wrote them out and carefully committed them to memory, but they plowed a straight furrow through the weeds and nettles of his parishioners. He preached on the sins that affected them, not on sin in general. In that farming community the chief evils were: indifference to attendance at Mass, for farmers felt exempt from church when the weather was good for haying; late dancing on Saturday nights, for the dancers were too tired to get up for Mass; drinking, for this took place at the hours when they should be working or praying. Jean Marie was a rigorist in his ideas and in his preaching, at least until he brought Ars up to the level of a more-than-decent Christian village and modified his theological views after reading St. Alphonsus Liguori.

Penance was the third and the most potent weapon of the Curé D'Ars' apostolate. Late in life, special excursion trains and horse buses brought thousands to hear him speak or to have him hear their confessions; his advice was sought by the peasantry, by harassed pastors, even by bishops and archbishops. One priest came to him to complain about the religious apathy in his parish. The Curé D'Ars looked at him, and without realizing it, recalled his own solutions to such a situation as he told the young man, "You've preached? You've prayed? Have you fasted? Have you scourged yourself? Have you slept on bare boards? As long as you haven't done that, you have no right to complain."

The Abbé Vianney endured, too, the scorn of some of his fellow priests, who felt that he was too lenient with his penitents. This charge was far from true, for the Curé D'Ars had the special gift of reading souls; he was a strict, but merciful, confessor. Others complained that he was too ignorant of theology to guide anyone. This, too, was unfounded, and the defense lies in the thousands of reconciled sinners and in the thousands of lives that were elevated from a not-so-golden mediocrity to the heights of charity. According to reputable authorities, Jean Marie also suffered direct attacks from the devil. And it has been asserted that for twenty years his brief period of sleep was interrupted by hideous sounds, spoken taunts, and physical seizures, even by the burning of his furniture.

In physical appearance the Curé D'Ars was short, bright-eyed, and white-haired. His portraits show a startling resemblance to Voltaire, but in contrast to the brilliant skepticism of the writer-philosopher, Jean Marie exhibited the simplicity of his eternal wisdom.

ON ENVY,
A PUBLIC PLAGUE

As you know, my dear brethren, we are bound as fellow creatures to have human sympathy and feelings for one another. Yet one envious person would like, if he possibly could, to destroy everything good and profitable belonging to his neighbor. You know, too, that as Christians we must have boundless charity for our fellow men. But the envious person is far removed indeed from such virtues. He would be happy to see his fellow man ruin himself. Every mark of God's generosity toward his neighbor is like a knife thrust that pierces his heart and causes him to die in secret. Since we are all members of the same Body of which Jesus Christ is the Head, we should so strive that unity, charity, love, and zeal can be seen in one and all. To make us all happy, we should rejoice, as St. Paul tells, in the happiness of our fellow men and mourn with those who have cares or troubles. But, very far from experiencing such feelings, the envious are forever uttering scandals and calumnies against their neighbors. It appears to them that in this way they can do something to assuage and sweeten their vexation.

But, unfortunately, we have not said all that can be said about envy. This is the deadly vice which hurls kings and emperors from their thrones. Why do you think, my dear brethren, that among these kings, these emperors, these men who occupy the first places in the world of men, some are driven out of their places of privilege, some are poisoned, others are stabbed? It is simply because someone wants to rule in their place. It is not the food, nor the drink, nor the habitations that the authors of such crimes want. Not at all. They are consumed with envy.

Take another example. Here is a merchant who wants to have all the business for himself and to leave nothing at all for anyone else. If someone leaves his store to go elsewhere, he will do his best to say all the evil he can, either about the rival businessman himself or else about the quality of what he sells. He will take all possible means to ruin his rival's reputation, saying that the other's goods are not of the same quality as his own or that the other man gives short weight. You will notice, too, that an envious man like this has a diabolical trick to add to all this: "It would not do," he will tell you, "for you to say this to anyone else; it might do harm and that would upset me very much. I am only telling you because I would not like to see you being cheated."

A workman may discover that someone else is now going to work in a house where previously he was always employed. This angers him greatly, and he will do everything in his power to run down this "interloper" so that he will not be employed there after all.

Look at the father of a family and see how angry he becomes if his next-door neighbor prospers more than he or if the neighbor's land produces more. Look at a mother: she would like it if people spoke well of no children except hers. If anyone praises the children of some other family to her and does not say something good of hers, she will reply, "They are not perfect," and she will become quite upset. How foolish you are, poor mother! The praise given to others will take nothing from your children.

Just look at the jealousy of a husband in respect of his wife or of a wife in respect of her husband. Notice how they inquire into everything the other does and says, how they observe everyone to whom the other speaks, every house into which the other enters. If one notices the other speaking to someone, there will be accusations of all sorts of wrongdoing, even though the whole episode may have been completely innocent.

This is surely a cursed sin which puts a barrier between brothers and sisters, too. The very moment that a father or a mother gives more to one member of the family than the others, you will see the birth of this jealous hatred against the parent or against the favored brother or sister—a hatred which may last for years, and sometimes even for a lifetime. There are children who keep a watchful eye upon their parents just to insure that they will not give any sort of gift or privilege to one member of the family. If this should occur in spite of them, there is nothing bad enough that they will not say.

We can see that this sin makes its first appearance among children. You will notice the petty jealousies they will feel against one another if they observe any preferences on the part of the parents. A young man would like to be the only one considered to have intelligence, or learning, or a good character. A girl would like to be the only one who is loved, the only one well dressed, the only one sought after; if others are more popular than she, you will see her fretting and upsetting herself, even weeping, perhaps, instead of thanking God for being neglected by creatures so that she may be attached to Him alone. What a blind passion envy is, my dear brethren! Who could hope to understand it?

Unfortunately, this vice can be noted even among those in whom it should never be encountered—that is to say, among those who profess to practice their religion. They will take note of how many times such a person remains to go to Confession or of how So-and-So kneels or sits when she is saying her prayers. They will talk of these things and criticize the people concerned, for they think that such prayers or good works are done only so that they may be seen, or in other words, that they are purely an affectation. You may tire yourself out telling them that their neighbor's actions concern him alone. They are irritated and offended if the conduct of others is thought to be superior to their own.

You will see this even among the poor. If some kindly person gives a little bit extra to one of them, they will make sure to speak ill of him to their benefactor in the hope of preventing him from benefiting on any further occasion. Dear Lord, what a detestable vice this is! It attacks all that is good, spiritual as well as temporal.

We have already said that this vice indicates a mean and petty spirit. That is so true that no one will admit to feeling envy, or at least no one wants to believe that he has been attacked by it. People will employ a hundred and one devices to conceal their envy from others. If someone speaks well of another in our presence, we keep silence: we are upset and annoyed. If we must say something, we do so in the coldest and most unenthusiastic fashion. No, my dear children, there is not a particle of charity in the envious heart. St. Paul has told us that we must rejoice in the good which befalls our neighbor. Joy, my dear brethren, is what Christian charity should inspire in us for one another. But the sentiments of the envious are vastly different.

I do not believe that there is a more ugly and dangerous sin than envy because it is hidden and is often covered by the attractive mantle of virtue or of friendship. Let us go further and compare it to a lion which we thought was muzzled, to a serpent covered by a handful of leaves which will bite us without our noticing it. Envy is a public plague which spares no one.

We are leading ourselves to Hell without realizing it.

But how are we then to cure ourselves of this vice if we do not think we are guilty of it? I am quite certain that of the thousands of envious souls honestly examining their consciences, there would not be one ready to believe himself belonging to that company. It is the least recognized of sins. Some people are so profoundly ignorant that they do not recognize a quarter of their ordinary sins. And since the sin of envy is more difficult to know, it is not surprising that so few confess it and correct it. Because they are not guilty of the big public sins committed by coarse and brutalized people, they think that the sins of envy are only little defects in charity, when, in fact, for the most part, these are serious and deadly sins which they are harboring and tending in their hearts, often without fully recognizing them.

"But," you may be thinking in your own minds, "if I really recognized them, I would do my best to correct them."

If you want to be able to recognize them, my dear brethren, you must ask the Holy Ghost for His light. He alone will give you this grace. No one could, with impunity, point out these sins to you; you would not wish to agree nor to accept them; you would always find something which would convince you that you had made no mistake in thinking and acting in the way you did. Do you know yet what will help to make you know the state of your soul and to uncover this evil sin hidden in the secret recesses of your heart? It is humility. Just as pride will hide it from you, so will humility reveal it to you.

ST. THERESE
OF LISIEUX:
THE LITTLE FLOWER
(1873–1892)

O N Sunday, November 20, 1887, ninety-seven
pilgrims from the diocese of Bayeux knelt at the eight o'clock
Mass in the Pope's private chapel at St. Peter's in Rome. The
venerable Leo XIII was soon to receive them in a special
audience at the Vatican.

The most excited pilgrim of all was fifteen-year-old Marie
Françoise Thérèse Martin. As she followed her father, Louis
Martin and her sister Céline into the majestic reception hall,
her heart raced with fear. She had resolved to ask the Pope
to allow her to enter the convent one year before the time
the regulations permitted. She saw the diminutive figure of
Leo XIII seated on a dais surrounded by dignitaries. Father
Révérony, the vicar general of Bayeux and the leader of
the pilgrimage, bowed and offered the homage of the diocese
on the occasion of the fiftieth anniversary of Leo XIII's
ordination to the priesthood. He then presented His Holiness
with a lace rochet and begged permission to introduce the
pilgrims. One by one each pilgrim climbed the steps of the
dais, knelt, kissed the Pope's slipper and his hand, received
his blessing and, at the signal from the noble guards standing
on either side of the throne, rose and made way for the next
pilgrim. Soon it would be Thérèse's turn. She fingered her
pilgrim's sash of white silk with blue stripes and a medal with
Leo's image. Then her father stepped forward. In introducing
him, Father Révérony mentioned to the Pope that two of
M. Martin's older daughters were Carmelite nuns. As the

Pope was bestowing a special blessing on M. Martin, Father Révérony glanced at Thérèse.

"Remember," the priest said, addressing himself to the whole pilgrimage but keeping his eyes fixed on her, "no one must speak to the Holy Father." He had heard of Thérèse's intention.

"My heart beat wildly, as if it would break," Thérèse explained later, "and I looked for counsel to Céline who whispered: 'Speak.' The next moment I was on my knees before the Pope. . . ."

The seventy-seven-year-old Pontiff gazed down on the beautiful girl, whose oval face was framed in long golden hair, but whose eyes were blinded with tears. She spoke in a rush.

"Holy Father, I have a great favor to ask of you."

The Pope, slender and frail, no bigger than herself, immediately bent down so that his head almost touched hers. His piercing black eyes seemed to be reading her soul.

"Holy Father, in honor of your Jubilee, allow me to enter Carmel at the age of fifteen."

Father Révérony flushed with displeasure.

"Holy Father," he interrupted, "this is a child who desires to become a Carmelite, and the superiors of Carmel are looking into the matter."

The Pope kept scrutinizing the tear-stained face.

"Well, my child," he said deliberately, looking deeply into her eyes, "do whatever the superiors may decide."

Thérèse began to speak again. She wanted to communicate her certainty to him, to tell him of her miraculous cure by the Blessed Virgin when she was ten years old; of how God answered her prayers for the murderer Pranzini, who died penitent; of the insistent divine call that she could no more stop than she could her own breath; of her long talks with Pauline and Marie, her sisters, who were now in the Carmelite convent home in Lisieux. Her hands were resting on the Holy Father's knees.

"Holy Father," she said, "if only you were to say 'Yes,' everyone else would be willing."

"Well, child! Well, you will enter if it be God's will."

Thérèse showed no signs of moving. The noble guards took her by the arms and lifted her to her feet. She was still trying to talk. The Pope put his hand gently on her lips and then raised it and blessed her. His eyes followed her as she went weeping from the room.

We do not know what Pope Leo thought about the little drama, in which he had so gracefully and kindly played his role of prudence. Perhaps he felt that it was just another display of adolescent religiosity. More likely, since he was skilled in judging sanctity, he was just as impressed as the vicar general of Bayeux who, a few days after, agreed with M. Martin that Thérèse's vocation was truly extraordinary.

Extraordinary it was, and would continue to be. For this beautiful child, born on January 2, 1873, in Alençon in Normandy, had from her earliest years been enveloped in radiance that the Martins, all of them uncommonly holy, could only ascribe to the special providence of God. She had, as she later confessed, "refused nothing to the good God" since she was three. When her mother died in 1877, she had accompanied her family to Lisieux where the five girls, Pauline, Marie, Céline, Léonie, and herself, the youngest, could be looked after by their maternal aunt, Madame Guérin. She went to the Benedictine convent school where she excelled in her studies. When Pauline and then Marie entered the Carmelite convent, Thérèse wanted to follow suit. The little house at Lisieux was a small monastery, with a white-haired father as abbot; thus, long before she entered the convent, Thérèse was a postulant by desire. When she finally obtained the permission to enter Carmel at fifteen, and, on the day of her clothing, she begged God to grant her a request—"Martyrdom either of the heart, or of the body, or rather give me both!"

Thérèse's career in Carmel lasted from 1888 to 1897. Yet in those nine years she lived an infinite number of lives. She abided by the severe penitential rules of her order and accommodated herself to the inevitable spiritual trials of one dedicated to martyrdom. Little would be known of her interior life were it not for the good sense of her sister, who as Mother Agnes of Jesus, was elected prioress in 1893. She, who knew every corner of her sister's soul, directed Thérèse, or Sister Teresa of the Child Jesus, the name she took on entering the order, to write the story of her childhood. Later, Thérèse was ordered to bring the story up to date. This *Autobiography*, together with 238 known letters, provide the revelation of a soul that may be ranked with those of St. Augustine, St. Teresa, and St. John of the Cross.

It is difficult to characterize the spirituality of the Little Flower. Many sophisticated readers have been repelled by her sentimental language and her fondness for ardent repetition. She is a scandal to these sophisticates, indeed to any who cannot read rapturous love letters without thinking that some canon of good taste is being offended. Yet for others, her childlike simplicity, her concrete sense of human brotherhood, her ability to relate all joy and all pain to the sufferings of Christ, her passionate desire not only to save sinners, but to make everyone love Christ as she loved Him, all make her writings persuasive and endearing. Her "little way" was a complete abandonment to the will of God. Her prayer was less word than action.

Once a sister asked her, "What do you say to Jesus?"

"I say nothing," she answered. "I just love Him."

If asked how should one pray she might have answered in these words contained in her own writing:

"Complicated prayers are not for simple souls. . . . I do as a child would who cannot read—I just say what I want to say to God, quite simply, and He never fails to understand. For me, prayer is an uplifting of the heart, a glance towards Heaven, a cry of gratitude and of love in times of sorrow as well as of joy. It is something noble, something supernatural, which expands the soul and unites it to God."

During the last two years of her life Thérèse suffered excruciatingly from tuberculosis and other illnesses. As she lay dying she said, "I feel that my mission is now to begin—my mission to bring others to love the good God as I love Him and to give to souls my little way of trust and self-surrender."

St. Teresa died in 1897 after having suffered severely. Her *Autobiography* appeared the following year, and almost immediately she became the favorite saint of thousands. So numerous were the miracles of grace and physical cures attributed to her intercession that she was declared venerable, beatified, and finally canonized only twenty-seven years after her death. She is patroness of France, patroness of the missions, and one of the chief glories of the contemporary church.

THE NEW COMMANDMENT
ST. THERESE,
THE LITTLE FLOWER OF JESUS

Among the numberless graces I have received this year, not the least is a deeper insight into the precept of charity. I had never before fathomed the words of Our Lord: "The second commandment is like to the first: Thou shalt love thy neighbor as thyself" [Matthew 22:39]. I had labored above all to love God, and it was in loving Him that I discovered the hidden meaning of these other words: "Not every one that saith to me: Lord, Lord! shall enter into the Kingdom of Heaven, but he that doth the will of My Father" [cf. John 13:34]. This will Our Lord revealed to me through the words of His *new Commandment* addressed to His Apostles at the Last Supper, when He told them *"to love one another as He had loved them"* [cf. Matthew 7:21]. I set myself to find out how He had loved His Apostles, and I saw that it was not for their natural qualities, seeing they were but ignorant men, whose minds dwelt chiefly on earthly things. Yet He calls them His friends, His brethren; He desires to see them near Him in the Kingdom of His Father; and to open this Kingdom to them He wills to die on the cross, saying: "Greater love than this no man hath, that a man lay down his life for his friends" [John 15:23].

As I meditated on these words, I understood how imperfect was the love I bore my Sisters in religion, and that I did not love them as Our Lord does. Now I know that true charity consists in bearing all my neighbor's defects, in not being surprised at mistakes, but in being edified at the smallest virtues.

Above all else I have learned that charity must not remain shut up in the heart, for "No man lighteth a candle and putteth it in a hidden place, nor under a bushel; but upon a candlestick, that they who come in may see the light" [Luke 11:33]. This candle, it seems to me, Mother, represents that charity which enlightens and gladdens, not only those who are dearest to us, but likewise *all those who are of the household*.

In the Old Law, when God told His people to love their neighbor as themselves, He had not yet come down upon earth; and knowing full well man's strong love of self, He could not ask anything greater. But when Our Lord gave His Apostles a new Commandment—*"His own Commandment"* [John 15:12]—He not only required of us to love our neighbor as ourselves, but would have us love even as He does, and as He will do until the end of time.

O my Jesus! Thou dost never ask what is impossible; Thou knowest better than I how frail and imperfect I am; Thou knowest that I shall never love my Sisters as Thou hast loved them, unless Thou lovest them Thyself within me, my dearest Master. It is because Thou dost desire to grant me this grace, that Thou hast given a new Commandment, and dearly do I cherish it, since it proves to me that it is Thy Will *to love in me* all those Thou dost bid me love.

When I show charity towards others I know that it is Jesus who is acting within me, and the more closely I am united to Him, the more dearly I love my Sisters. Should I wish to increase this love, and should the devil bring before me the defects of a Sister, I hasten to look for her virtues and good motives. I call to mind that though I may have seen her fall once, she may have gained many victories over herself which in her humility she conceals, and also that what appears to be a fault may well, owing to the good intention that prompted it, be an act of virtue. I have all the less difficulty in persuading myself that this is so, because of my own experience.

One day, during recreation, the portress came to ask for a

Sister to help her in some particular task which she mentioned. Now I had the eager desire of a child to do this very thing, and as it happened, the choice fell upon me. I began immediately to fold up our needlework, slowly enough, however, to allow my neighbor to fold hers before me, for I knew it would please her to take my place. Noticing how deliberate I was the portress said laughingly: "Ah! I thought you would not add this pearl to your crown, you were too slow." And all the community were left under the impression that I had acted according to nature.

I cannot tell you what profit I derived from this incident, and how indulgent it has made me towards others. It still keeps in check any feeling of vanity when I receive praise, for I reflect that since my small acts of virtue can be mistaken for imperfections, why should not an imperfection be mistaken for virtue? And I repeat with St. Paul: "To me it is a very small thing to be judged by you, or by man's day. But neither do I judge myself. He that judgeth me is the Lord" [I Corinthians 5:3, 4]. Since, therefore, the Lord is my Judge, I will try always to think leniently of others, that He may judge me leniently—or not at all, since He says: "Judge not and ye shall not be judged" [Luke 6:37].

Returning to the Holy Gospels where Our Lord explains to me clearly in what His new Commandment consists, I read in St. Matthew: "*You have heard that it hath been said, Thou shalt love thy neighbor, and hate thy enemy: but I say unto you, Love your enemies and pray for them that persecute you*" [Matthew 5:43, 44].

There are, of course, no enemies in Carmel; but, after all, we have our natural likes and dislikes. We may feel drawn towards one Sister and may be tempted to go a long way round to avoid meeting another. Well, Our Lord tells me that this last is the Sister I must love and pray for, even though her manners might lead me to believe that she does not care for me. "If you love them that love you, what thanks are to you? For sinners also love those that love them" [Luke 6:32]. Nor is it enough to love; we must prove our love. We take a natural delight in pleasing friends, but that is not charity; even sinners do the same.

Elsewhere Our Lord teaches me: "Give to everyone that asketh thee; and of him that taketh away thy goods, ask them not again" [Luke 6:30]. To give to everyone who asks is less pleasant than to give spontaneously and of one's own accord. Again, if a thing be asked in a courteous way consent is easy, but if, unhappily, tactless words have been used, there is an inward rebellion unless we are perfect in charity. We discover no end of excuses for refusing, and it is only after having made clear to the guilty Sister how rude was her behavior, that we grant *as a favor* what she requires, or render a slight service which takes perhaps, one-half of the time we have lost in setting forth the difficulties and our own imaginary rights.

If it be difficult to give to anyone who asks, it is still more difficult to let what belongs to us be taken without asking to have it back. I say this is difficult, but I should rather say that it seems so, for *"The yoke of the Lord is sweet and His burden light"* [Matthew 11:30]. And when we submit to that yoke we at once feel its sweetness.

I said just now that Jesus does not wish me to reclaim what belongs to me. This ought to appear quite natural, since in reality I own nothing, and ought to rejoice when an occasion brings home to me the poverty to which I am solemnly vowed. Formerly I used to think myself detached from everything, but since Our Lord's words have become clear, I see how imperfect I am. When starting to paint, for instance, if I happen to find the brushes in confusion, if a ruler or penknife be missing, I am sorely tempted to lose patience, and have strongly to resist the impulse to demand, and sharply demand, the articles required.

I may, of course, ask for them, and if I do so humbly I am not disobeying Our Lord's command. On the contrary, I am like the poor who hold out their hands for the necessaries of life and who if refused are not surprised, because no one owes them anything. To soar above all natural sentiment brings the deepest peace, nor is there any joy equal to that which is felt by the truly poor in spirit. Sometimes they ask with detachment for what is really needful: not only are they refused, but an attempt is made to deprive them of what they already possess. Yet they follow the Master's advice: "If any man take away thy coat, let go thy cloak also unto him" [Matthew 5:40].

It seems to me that to give up one's cloak is to renounce every right, and look upon oneself as the servant, the slave of all. Divested of a cloak, however, it is easier to walk or run, so that Master adds: "And whosoever will force thee one mile, go with him other two" [Matthew 5:41]. Hence it is not enough for me to give to the one who asks, I ought to anticipate thy wish; I should show myself honored by the request for service, and if anything set apart for my use be taken away I should appear glad to be rid of it.

I cannot always, indeed, carry out to the letter the words of the Gospel, for occasions arise when I am compelled to refuse a request. Yet, when charity has taken deep root in the soul, it shows itself outwardly, and there is always a way of refusing so graciously what one cannot give, that the refusal affords as much pleasure as the gift itself. It is true that people are more ready to beg from those who are most ready to give; still, on the pretext that I shall be forced to refuse, I ought not to avoid an importunate Sister, since the Divine Master has said: "From him that would borrow of thee turn not away" [Matthew 5:42]. Neither should I be kind for the sake of being considered so, nor in the hope that the Sister will return the service, for once again it is written: "If you lend to them of whom you hope to receive, what thanks are to you? For sinners also lend to sinners for to receive as much. But you, do good and lend, hoping for nothing thereby, and your reward shall be great" [Luke 6:34, 35].

Along this path it is but the first step that costs—even on earth the reward will be great. To end without hope of return may seem hard; one would rather give outright, for a thing once given is no longer ours. When a Sister comes to you and says: "I have our Mother's leave to borrow your help for a few hours, and you may rest assured that later on I will do as much for you," we may be practically certain that the time so lent will never be repaid, and therefore feel sorely tempted to say: "I will *give* what you ask!" The remark would gratify self-love, it being more generous to give than to lend, and in addition, it would let the Sister feel how little reliance you put in her promise.

The divine precepts do assuredly run counter to our natural inclinations, and without the help of grace it would be impossible to understand them, far less put them in practice.

I fear, dear Mother, that I have expressed myself more confusedly than usual, and I cannot think what you will find to interest you in these rambling pages. However, I am not writing a literary work, and if I have wearied you by this discourse on charity you will at least find in it a proof of your child's good will. I have to confess that I am far from living up to the lights I have received, yet the mere desire of doing so brings me peace. If I happen to stumble in the matter of charity, I rise again immediately, and for some months past I have not even had to struggle. With our Father, St. John of the Cross, I have been able to say: "My house is entirely at peace," and that peace I attribute to a certain victory which I gained over myself. Ever since then, the hosts of Heaven have hastened to my aid, not wishing me to be wounded after my valiant fight on the occasion I am about to describe.

Formerly, a holy nun of our community was a constant source of annoyance to me: the devil must have had something to do with the trial, for undoubtedly it was he who made me see so many disagreeable points in her. Unwilling to yield to my natural antipathy, I remembered that charity ought not merely to exist in the heart but also to show itself in deeds; so I endeavored to treat this Sister as I should my most cherished friend. Whenever I met her I prayed for her, at the same time offering to God her virtues and her merits. I knew this would delight Our Lord exceedingly, for there is no artist who is not gratified when his works are praised, and the Divine Artist of souls is therefore well pleased when we do not stop at the exterior, but penetrate to the inner sanctuary He has chosen for His abode and admire its beauty.

I did not rest satisfied with praying earnestly for the Sister who gave me such occasions for self-mastery, but I tried also to render her as many services as I could; and when tempted to make a disagreeable answer, I made haste to smile and change the subject of conversation. The *Imitation* says: "It is more profitable to leave to everyone his way of thinking than to give way to contentious discourses"; [Imit. Ch. 44:1] and sometimes when the temptation was particularly violent, if I could slip away without her suspecting my inward struggle, I would run like a deserter from the battlefield. The outcome of all this was that she said to me one day, with a beaming countenance: "Tell me, Soeur Thérèse, what it is that attracts you to me so strongly? I never meet you without being welcomed with your most gracious smile?" Ah! what attracted me was Jesus hidden in the depths of her soul, Jesus who makes sweet even that which is most bitter.

I spoke just now, Mother, of my last resource for escaping defeat—namely . . . flight. It was scarcely an honorable method, I confess, but whenever I had recourse to it during my novitiate, it was always successful. Here is a striking example which I think will amuse you.

For several days you had been ill with bronchitis and we were all very anxious. One morning in discharge of my office of sacristan I entered your infirmary, very gently, to put back the keys of the Communion grating. Though I took care not to show it, I was inwardly rejoicing at the opportunity of seeing you. One of the Sisters, however, feared I should wake you, and discreetly wished to take the keys from me. I told her, with all possible politeness, that I was as anxious as she that there should be no noise, adding that it was my duty to return them. I see now it would have been more perfect to yield, but I did not think so then and consequently tried to enter the room.

What she feared came to pass—the noise we made awoke you, and the blame was cast upon me. The Sister made a lengthy discourse, the point of which was that I was the guilty person. I was burning to defend myself when happily it occurred to me that if I began to do so, I should certainly lose my peace of mind, and that as I had not sufficient virtue to keep silence when accused, my only chance of safety lay in flight. No sooner thought than done, and I fled. . . . But my heart beat so violently, that I could not go far and had to sit down on the stairs to taste in peace and quiet the fruits of my victory. This is without doubt an odd kind of courage, yet I think it better not to expose oneself in the face of certain defeat.

When I think over my novitiate days I see clearly how far removed I was from perfection; some things there are that make me laugh. How good God has been to have trained my soul and lent it wings! All the nets of the hunter can no longer frighten me, for "A net is set in vain before the eyes of them that have wings" [Proverbs 1:17].

It may be that at some future day my present state will appear to me full of defects, but nothing now surprises me. Nor does my utter helplessness distress me; I even glory in it, and expect each day to reveal some fresh imperfection. Indeed these lights on my own nothingness do me more good than lights on matters of faith. Remembering that "Charity covereth a multitude of sins" [Proverbs 10:12], I draw from the rich mine which Our Savior has opened up to us in the Gospels; I search the depths of His adorable words, and I cry out with the Psalmist: "I have run in the way of Thy commandments since Thou hast enlarged my heart" [Psalm 118:32]. And charity alone can widen my heart. O Jesus! ever since its sweet flame consumes me, I run with delight in the way of Thy *new Commandment*, and I desire so to run, until that glorious day when with Thy retinue of virgins I shall follow Thee through Thy boundless realm, singing Thy new canticle—the Canticle of Love.

God in His infinite goodness has given me, dear Mother, a clear insight into the deep mysteries of Charity. If only I could express what I know, you would hear a heavenly music; but alas! I can only stammer like a child, and if the words of Jesus were not my support, I should be tempted to beg leave to hold my peace.

When the Divine Master tells me to give to anyone who asks of me, and to allow what is mine to be taken without asking for it back, it seems to me that He speaks not only of the things of earth but also of the goods of Heaven. Neither the one nor the other are really mine; I renounced the first by the vow of poverty and the others are gifts which are simply lent. If God withdraw them, I have no right to complain. But our own ideas, the fruit of our own mind and heart, we regard as a sacred and personal treasury upon which none may lay hands. For instance, if I communicate to a Sister some light given me in prayer and she afterwards reveals it as though it were her own, it would seem she is appropriating what is mine. Or if during recreation someone makes a witty remark, which her neighbor repeats to the community without acknowledging whence it came, its originator will look on this as a sort of theft. At the time, she preserves an unwilling silence, but on the first opportunity she will insinuate delicately that her thoughts have been borrowed.

Had I not experienced all these human weaknesses, Mother, I could not so well explain them. I should have preferred to believe myself the only one who endured such petty temptations, had you not bidden me listen to the novices' difficulties and give them suitable advice. In the discharge of this duty I have learnt much, and above all I have found myself forced to practice what I preached. I can say with all truth that now, by God's grace, I am no more attached to the gifts of the intellect than I am to material things. Should any thought of mine please my Sisters, I find it quite easy to let them regard it as their own. It belongs to the Holy Ghost, not to me, for St. Paul assures us that "without the Spirit of Love we cannot call God our Father" [cf. Romans 8:15], and is not the same Holy Spirit free to use me as a channel to convey a good thought to a soul, without my daring to look on that thought as my private property?

Besides, while I am far from depreciating beautiful thoughts which bring us nearer to God, I have long been of opinion that we must guard against overestimating their worth. Even the highest inspirations are of no value without good works. Others may derive profit from these lights, provided they be duly grateful to Our Lord for allowing them to share in the abundance of one of His more privileged souls; but should that privileged soul take pride in her spiritual wealth and imitate the Pharisee, she becomes like a person dying of starvation before a well-spread table, while her guests enjoy the richest fare, and cast envious glances, perhaps, at the possessor of so many treasures.

How true it is that God alone can sound the heart! How short-sighted are His creatures! When they find a soul whose lights surpass their own, they conclude that the Divine Master loves them less. Yet when did He lose the right to make use of one of His children to provide others with the nourishment they need? That right was not lost in the days of Pharaoh, for God said unto him: "And therefore have I raised thee, that I may show My power in thee, and My name may be spoken of throughout all the earth" [Exodus 9:16]. Centuries have passed since these words were spoken by the Most High, but His ways have remained unchanged—He has even chosen human agents to accomplish His work among souls.